DEADLY

THE TRUE STORY OF THE
MILE HIGH BANK MASSACRE

HEIST

STEVEN B. EPSTEIN

STEVEN B. EPSTEIN

DEADLY

THE TRUE STORY OF THE
MILE HIGH BANK MASSACRE

HEIST

BLACK LYON PUBLISHING, LLC

DEADLY HEIST

The True Story of the Mile High Bank Massacre

Copyright © 2025 by Steven B. Epstein

This is a work of non-fiction. In Black Lyon True Crime titles, direct quotes are either from recorded interviews, interviews with individuals by local media at the time or the recollection of the individuals during interviews with the author of what was said at the time. When possible, those interviewed reviewed their recollected quotes for accuracy. (Please see Author's Note for more information specific to this title.)

Our books may be ordered through your local bookstore or by visiting the publisher:

www.BlackLyonPublishing.com

Black Lyon Publishing, LLC
PO Box 567
Baker City, OR 97814

ISBN: 979-8-9865124-9-5
Library of Congress Control Number: 2024949375

Published and printed in the United States of America.

PRAISE FOR THIS BOOK

"With a clear, crisp writing style, Steve Epstein has managed to capture something often lost in the retelling of a true crime: the deep human toll. It's not just the four bank employees who lost their lives that day, but the ones who survived, left with lasting trauma and guilt. *Deadly Heist* is a compelling read, and also a vivid reminder of the intense human efforts so vital to bringing those accused of heinous crimes to justice."
—Erin Moriarty, *CBS News* and *48 Hours* correspondent and host of podcast *My Life of Crime with Erin Moriarty*

"An engrossing story brilliantly told. This is a thorough behind-the-scenes breakdown of a horrific murder case, followed by the meticulous investigation seeking justice for victims and their families. This book made me nostalgic for my days as a homicide prosecutor and simultaneously inspired me as a true crime author. I can enthusiastically recommend!"
—Matt Murphy, Orange County, California homicide prosecutor (1993-2020), ABC legal analyst, and bestselling author of *The Book of Murder*

"*Deadly Heist* is a fast-paced, extraordinary read, not only for true crime enthusiasts, but for anyone who loves a tight, well-told story, filled with suspense. Steve Epstein has carefully researched what is arguably Colorado's crime of the century. His background as an attorney helps him bring the characters to life and sheds new light on this incredible true story. Epstein's insight and access to the legal proceedings provide a rare behind-the-scenes look at what happens during a high-profile investigation and murder trial. It's a book you'll continue to think about long after you put it down."
—Ron Peterson, Jr., bestselling true crime author of *Under the Trestle, Chasing the Squirrel, Eyes of a Monster,* and *In the Wind*

MORE PRAISE FOR THIS BOOK

"Steve Epstein does a masterful job weaving together the story of this shocking murder-robbery that had me on the edge of my seat until the last page ... I was particularly riveted to his crisp retelling of the back-and-forth action in the courtroom. The book was thoroughly researched and well-written—a real page-turner true crime aficionados will savor."
—Alexandra Shapiro, defense attorney for Sean "Diddy" Combs, Sam Bankman-Fried, and other high-profile defendants, and author of crime novel *Presumed Guilty*

"Steve Epstein takes you on a riveting ride from the massacre at the bank, to the sprawling investigation that followed, and the battle royale inside the courtroom ... I couldn't put it down. This book is a must for any true crime fan, and for anyone who wants a rare, behind-the-scenes tour of the roller coaster that is the criminal justice system. Top-notch!"
—Dave Aronberg, State Attorney, Palm Beach County, FL (2013-2024), host of *Court Authorities* YouTube channel

"*Deadly Heist* takes you inside a fascinating criminal tragedy. This saga unfolds after four unarmed bank guards were murdered in a robbery with all the hallmarks of an inside job. The telling of the arrest and trial of James King evokes the tension in a high-profile criminal case—between giving a suspect the benefit of reasonable doubt or convicting them on compelling circumstantial evidence. The writing is crisp and informative, a must-read for true crime and crime procedural readers."
—McCracken Poston Jr, bestselling author of *Zenith Man: Death, Love, and Redemption in a Georgia Courtroom*

"...Undoubtedly the most violent and puzzling bank robbery of the many encountered during my 30 years with the FBI ... Extremely complete, well written, well researched, easy to read, very interesting, and above all very important; it also provides lessons to be learned for law enforcement, prosecutors, defense attorneys, banks, and the general public."
—Bob Pence, Special Agent in Charge, FBI Denver Field Office (1986-1992), and author of *My Non-Political FBI: From Hoover to a Violent America*

For my amazing wife, Alétia, whose love,
encouragement, and smile make me
the luckiest man on Earth.

AUTHOR'S NOTE

This is a work of nonfiction based on numerous sources of information, including interviews of key participants, trial footage, investigative reports, court records, TV news, newspaper, and magazine accounts, and other books on this subject.

Because the events described occurred more than 30 years ago—several participants now deceased or unwilling/unable to share their recollections—in some instances it wasn't possible to render dialogue as actually spoken or internal monologues as characters considered their circumstances.

For scenes in which I considered dialogue helpful to advance the narrative where no source material existed to ensure complete accuracy, I've reconstructed the conversations to approximate the speakers' words. I've also taken the liberty of suggesting the inner voices of several characters to convey what may have been going through their minds at important junctures of the story. Apart from those instances of creative license, I have verified to the best of my ability every quotation and factual detail contained in the pages that follow.

FOREWORD

As a reporter and correspondent who has devoted more than 35 years to covering the news, some stories stand out for a lifetime, seared in my brain, despite the nonstop whirlwind of news-gathering and years that followed.

I've been on-site, mic in hand, reporting on earth-shattering events including plane crashes, terror attacks, Kobe Bryant's fatal helicopter crash, the Miracle on the Hudson, and the mass shooting at Virginia Tech. All of them left indelible marks on the local communities involved—and far beyond.

The pages that follow tell a story that is every bit as gripping and memorable as any I've covered, details of which I can recall in vibrant color to this day even though it has been over 30 years since I was swimming up their stream, cutting my teeth as a young TV reporter.

I grew up in Littleton, part of metro Denver, crossing the graduation stage at Arapahoe High in 1982. From a young age, I was a news junkie, dreaming of working among the best television journalists at the time.

After earning a broadcast journalism degree from the University of Colorado at Boulder, I landed my first gig at a local station in El Paso, Texas before returning to my hometown of Denver in 1989.

Our community was not immune to crime and violence, but in 1991, it still felt like John Denver's version of Colorado. People migrated to our quiet neighborhoods to escape criminal activity infesting other, mostly larger, cities. On most days, we enjoyed a unique slice of peace and serenity at the foot of the Rockies. That's why what happened that Father's Day was so utterly shocking and horrifying—shaking the Mile High City to its very core.

I was just 27, working my dream job, the late-news reporter at 9NEWS/KUSA-TV—then the ABC station, Channel 9 on the dial—by every objective measure, one of the finest local newsrooms in the country. That meant I usually got to bed around midnight after chasing stories across the region for the ten o'clock newscast.

When my head hit the pillow on Father's Day eve, I had no clue that I—and every local and regional reporter worth their salt—was about to be sucked into a vortex that would hold us captive for an entire year. Mind you, this was an era during which families huddled around their TV sets to devour the local news—the modern internet and smart phones still years away from altering the way we consumed the news.

On Father's Day, I awoke to a typically beautiful summer morning. The sky was bright blue—a hue and richness that is a Colorado trademark—our downtown streets nearly barren as families prepared to congregate at swimming pools, baseball games, and barbecues.

I was single at the time and planned to gather with my own family later in the day—unless my pager went off notifying me of a breaking story.

Just after 10:00 a.m., that's precisely what transpired. As I scrambled to find a phone, sirens screamed through the city streets, squad cars from across every police district racing across town. They ultimately converged at the United Bank of Denver on Seventeenth and Lincoln, an architectural marvel— a skyscraper in the form of a cash register—widely considered the most iconic structure in our skyline.

The suspect was long gone by the time police officers flooded the lobby, the details of what happened sketchy at first. Had someone actually robbed the bank on a Sunday morning? Was anyone even working there at the time? As more information trickled in, we learned not just about the robbery, but also the human carnage a deranged killer had left in his wake. It was among the most brutal, gruesome crimes to have hit our city and state in decades.

For the police department, the DA's Office, and those of us working in the local news, it was the start of an exhausting—yet exhilarating—manhunt, chasing leads and focusing on alleged suspects only to get detoured into dead ends. Had the killer left the city? The state? Or was he about to hit another bank and murder even more innocent victims?

The search for the gunman dominated Colorado news—nearly every front-page headline and every newscast—from sunrise each morning through my shift on the ten o'clock news.

My legendary 9NEWS colleague, Paula Woodward, a tenacious and intrepid reporter, worked her sources within the Denver PD, breaking new twists and turns in the investigation. Meanwhile, I worked the streets, knocking on doors and looking for any nugget, any clue into what had actually occurred at the bank—and why. The pressure to break some unique angle to the story—which I felt not only from my bosses and competing media outlets, but also internalized—was as intense as for any story I've covered throughout my career.

Along with other beat reporters, I pounded the pavement for 18 solid days as the frightened populace hung on our every word—printed and broadcast. Though we were like a fraternity, we were also fiercely competitive, hoping to land any scoop to help our station or newspaper be the first to break whatever blockbuster news was sure to come.

But when the most consequential moment finally arrived, I—along with every other reporter covering the fast-breaking story—was sound asleep.

At 5:00 a.m. on Thursday, July 4, the 9NEWS assignment desk rousted me from bed with the jaw-dropping news none of us had been there to cover: a retired Denver cop, James W. King, had been hauled off to jail for murdering four unarmed security guards and making off with nearly $200,000 from the bank.

Was he actually the sociopath responsible for one of the most despicable crimes in Colorado history? What on earth could possibly have motivated him to turn the gun he'd used to protect our community on his fellow citizens? Or had the authorities nabbed the wrong man?

From that moment, the race was on. Within the hour, I was on the air from the newsroom, reporting what our law-enforcement sources would tell us—which was actually very little. But as a native Coloradan, it felt like our citizens could finally breathe a collective sigh of relief.

Later that same day, I was standing outside the King family residence in nearby Golden—the modest bungalow where the ex-cop lived with his wife and youngest of three sons—as FBI agents paraded boxes of evidence out his front door. Had they found the stolen loot? The murder weapon?

Before long, our onsite reporting shifted from the crime scene and accused killer's home to the courtroom, where some of the most colorful characters in Denver legal history did battle in what many Denverites of my generation consider Colorado's trial of the century. One of the very first to be broadcast, gavel to gavel, on Court TV. The courtroom proceedings produced even more twists and turns before 12 of our citizens were entrusted with one of the weightiest decisions of their lives—the defendant's life hanging in the balance.

Deadly Heist captures all this, and much more. From the terrifying moments inside the bank to the mesmerizing legal battle, Steve Epstein gives us a front-row seat to the action. As I relived this story through his propulsive narrative, chills ran down my spine. It is a masterful retelling, replete with heart-pounding moments and surprises, chock full of suspense. All with brand-new insights Steve was able to add thanks to his impeccable research, meticulous attention to detail, and analytical prowess as a trial lawyer himself.

Above all else, Steve makes sure we don't forget what this tragedy, and this case, was really all about: four flesh-and-blood human beings snatched from those who loved them—robbed of their lives on Father's Day—fully worthy of the tireless efforts by investigators, detectives, prosecutors, defense lawyers, a judge, and jury to ensure that justice was ultimately done.

By the time you turn the last page, you'll get to make up

your own mind as to whether that lofty ideal was actually achieved.

Tom Costello
Senior Correspondent, NBC News
Washington, D.C.
February 2025

PART ONE

UNSPEAKABLE CRIME

1

42 MINUTES

Denver, Colorado
Father's Day, June 16, 1991

Like a mighty glass-and-concrete fortress, the 52-story tower at the corner of Lincoln Street and Seventeenth Avenue stretched into the pitch-black sky, its lights twinkling at the center of Denver's skyline. Upon its completion in 1983, locals had branded the massive structure the Cash Register Building, because its uppermost floors curve together to resemble the shape of an antique cash register. Its distinctive design was symbolic, as the skyscraper and two smaller buildings across the street were home to the United Bank of Denver, the city's largest bank.

As they did every weekend morning at 12:30 a.m., Bill Mc-Cullom and Phil Mankoff descended the elevator to the underground concourse level beneath the three-building complex. The uniformed security guards zig-zagged their way through a byzantine maze of hallways, using their access cards to enter the "mantrap" — a vestibule-like security chamber with an outer and inner door — leading into the guard monitor room. They were buzzed through the inner door by the departing guards, who exited through the same mantrap. McCullom and Mankoff each clocked in, grabbed a massive set of keys and two-way radio, and claimed a red swivel chair beside a U-shaped console of TV monitors.

Though Bill McCullom was eight years younger than his 41-year-old partner, his nine months on the job made him one of the bank's most experienced weekend guards. The muscular African American bachelor worked 12-hour shifts each Saturday and Sunday to supplement his income from the insurance company where he worked during the week. He'd taken the $5.42/hour part-time position as a last resort, to fend off a slew of delinquency notices stemming from his student-loan debt.

Phil Mankoff's financial predicament was considerably more dire. His debts had spiraled out of control during sustained periods of unemployment before he finally landed a decent-paying job in state government. With four kids to support—two sons from a prior marriage and two stepdaughters with his current wife—Mankoff had little choice but to declare bankruptcy. Despite his college degree, he toiled 65 hours a week just to make ends meet, having been on the job at United Bank less than three months.

After taking turns making their assigned rounds, the bearded guards passed the time as best they could, each minute of their graveyard shift crawling along at a snail's pace. They chatted about topics far and wide as their eyes flitted across the monitors—each screen carrying a black-and-white feed from security cameras arrayed throughout the complex. Mankoff shared with McCullom details of his Father's Day plans with his wife and stepkids later that afternoon. Their banter meandered to the topic of Major League Baseball's announcement just six days earlier that an expansion team—later to be named the Colorado Rockies—would soon be playing in the Mile High City.

The pair also discussed the changes occurring at United Bank since its acquisition by Minneapolis-based Norwest Corp., which had been finalized in April. The change most directly affecting them was Norwest's edict that security guards could no longer carry firearms. Yet neither McCullom nor Mankoff felt unsafe working weekend shifts because the bank was closed, downtown Denver a veritable ghost town on Saturday and Sunday mornings. The prospect of the bank being attacked during their shifts seemed as likely as a volcano erupting from a nearby mountain peak.

Though the two usually worked alone until the next shift of guards arrived at 12:30 p.m., every so often they'd be tasked with training a newly hired guard during a "swing shift," which ran from 6:00 a.m. to 6:00 p.m. On June 1, a 21-year-old Metro State College student named Todd Wilson—who'd previously worked in the bank's credit card fraud department—had been hired to train as a weekend guard. It therefore was no surprise when the uniformed Wilson strolled into the monitor room promptly at 6:00 a.m. What was a surprise, however, was that Wilson wasn't alone.

The ultra-tall young man trailing just behind him was adorned in a vertically striped, short-sleeved button-down shirt, dark slacks, and cowboy boots. Wilson introduced him as his best friend, Scott McCarthy, at whose wedding he'd served as best man the prior August. Thanks to the good word he'd put in for his buddy with the guard supervisor, McCarthy had been hired the prior day. The short turnaround hadn't left sufficient time for him to receive the white shirt and gray slacks that comprised the bank's official guard uniform.

"I'll have my uniform by next Saturday," McCarthy assured the more experienced guards, informing them that he'd taken the part-time position as a steppingstone to becoming a police officer. "But they were able to make me this card," he added, holding up a cream-colored, plastic access card bank employees referred to as a "Markey" card. The 21-year-old newlywed could hardly contain his exuberance, ready to hunker down and get to work.

"Come with me," Mankoff said, rising from his seat. "I'll take you on my rounds and show you around."

••••

Another collection of employees at the bank on Sunday mornings were "armored tellers," who worked in the cash vault, just down the hallway from the guard monitor room. Unlike the weekend guards, the tellers didn't work on Saturdays, having the luxury of sleeping to a reasonable hour before arriving for their 7:00 a.m. Sunday shift. On this particular morning, six tellers reported for duty, four women and two men.

The group was managed by David Barranco, a 24-year-old with aspirations of becoming a bank executive. Though he'd grown up in Tucson—graduating from the University of Arizona—he was lured to Denver's snow-capped mountains by his passion for skiing. Employed at the bank since the previous September, this was only his third Sunday working in the cash vault. At 6'2", the lanky and amiable Barranco proved a good team leader, quickly earning his coworkers' respect.

Every Sunday between 7:30 and 8:30 a.m., armored cars from Loomis and Wells Fargo would deliver, on average, approximately one million dollars in cash. The armored couriers would pull into a parking area behind the Cash Register Building, unload their canvas bags into large carts, and roll them to an elevator that would take them from street level down to the concourse. They would then walk through a corridor and wait to be buzzed into the cash vault directly beneath Lincoln Street. The couriers would slide their bags through a secure window, where the vault manager would log in their deliveries.

The bags would then be divided among the tellers, who were responsible for reconciling the money delivered with what the bank's commercial accounts claimed they were depositing. Each teller was assigned a numbered "station" or "booth"—a cubicle encased in windows extending up to the ceiling. Because the bank wasn't open to the public on Sundays, they were allowed to dress casually, listen to the radio, and chit chat to pass the time. The environment was always casual, the mood light and friendly.

The group was hard at work by 7:30 a.m. Father's Day morning counting cash, food stamps, and segregating checks a "proof department" employee would retrieve later that morning. Their collective goal was to clear their desks by 2:00 p.m. so they could enjoy the remainder of the near-summer afternoon. By the end of their shift, the tens of thousands of bills they'd count that morning would be strapped together in tidy bundles, each containing 100 bills of a single denomination—$1s, $5s, $10s, $20s, $50s, or $100s. Because the main vault and its giant safe were locked up for the weekend, all of the bundles would ultimately be deposited into two smaller safes located in the "Saturday vault."

••••

At 9:10 a.m., while Todd Wilson was making his rounds, the other three guards were seated in the monitor room, riveted to a small television connected to a VCR airing a recorded episode of the CBS courtroom drama "The Trials of Rosie O'Neill," starring Sharon Gless of "Cagney & Lacey" fame. The TV rested on a small table at the opposite end of the room from the U-shaped security console.

At 9:14 a.m., the telephone rang. Phil Mankoff slid his swivel chair over to the console to take the call.

"I'll send a guard upstairs right away, Mr. Bardwell," the others overheard him say.

Bill McCullom peeled his gaze away from the TV. "Who was that?"

"One of the VPs, a Bob Bardwell," Mankoff said. "Says he forgot his Markey card and needs an escort to his office." He dispatched McCullom to take the freight elevator to Lincoln Street to meet the stranded vice president at the loading dock.

Mankoff remained seated by the console. At 9:20 a.m., one of the security monitors caught his eye. A message displayed indicating that an alarm had gone off in Stairwell C—not far from the freight elevator. He got ahold of Wilson on his hand-held radio and asked him to investigate the problem. The father of four then claimed the empty chair next to Scott McCarthy, now barely three hours into his employment.

At 9:24 a.m., the two men had their eyes focused on the TV screen when they heard footsteps approaching from behind—footsteps they had every reason to believe belonged to Bill McCullom or Todd Wilson returning from their assigned tasks.

"Get up!" a menacing voice demanded. As they swiveled their heads to see who was behind them, the unarmed guards realized in an instant their Father's Day had taken an ominous turn. Behind their chairs was a man gripping a .38 Special. He instructed them to march forward into a small room filled with shelves of auxiliary batteries. Reluctantly, Mankoff and McCarthy trudged into the room.

"Down on your knees!" the armed invader ordered. "Hands behind your heads."

Once again, the guards complied. Before they could begin to formulate a plan of what to do next, the gunman opened fire, spraying his entire cylinder of ammo into their heads and torsos. Mankoff fell to the floor first, landing facedown parallel to a shelf of batteries. Blood from his head and back wounds pooled beneath him. When McCarthy fell, his right leg ended up draped over his fellow guard's back, his head face-up beside another row of batteries. Blood poured out of his neck, forming a puddle that quickly filled the corner of the room.

Phillip Lee Mankoff wouldn't get to spend Father's Day with his wife and stepdaughters after all. Scott Raymond McCarthy would never become a police officer—or celebrate his first wedding anniversary—his first day as a bank guard his final day on Earth.

••••

Meanwhile, as hard as Todd Wilson tried to figure out the location of Stairwell C, he found himself spinning in circles, utterly confused. He decided to head back to the monitor room to find a map. When he entered through the inner mantrap door at 9:26 a.m., he was shocked to find nobody there. A mere 15 days into his training, even he knew that the monitor room needed to be manned at all times. He decided to remain until another guard returned and stepped toward the U-shaped console. Wilson had no idea he'd just walked into a murder trap.

The gunman snuck up behind him without making a

sound. Before the 21-year-old college student had the slightest inkling of what was happening—before he could turn his head or utter a single syllable—the monster who'd slaughtered his fellow guards pumped a flurry of bullets into his head and back. Todd Allen Wilson's lifeless body tumbled to the floor like a ragdoll.

• • • •

With the armored couriers gone, the tellers were at their stations processing money, checks, and food stamps, engaged in casual banter as music played in the background. Everything was calm and peaceful. Until it wasn't.

At 9:48 a.m., tellers David Twist and Maria Christian were counting money at a two-person station called the "bank cage," chatting with their boss David Barranco. Out of the corner of his eye, Twist noticed a flash of motion. "Did you see that?" he asked the others.

Barranco shook his head. "See what?"

"Did you see that guy walk by—near the coin unit?"

"Was it a guard?" Barranco asked.

"No," Twist said. "He was wearing a suit."

Barranco finally spotted the man moving down a corridor in the opposite direction. The three employees decided to follow him. But after they'd taken only four or five steps, the well-dressed man spun around to confront them, his right hand pulling out a black revolver and cocking the hammer. Barranco, Twist, and Christian froze in their tracks—Christian instinctively throwing her arms in the air as she trembled in fear.

In that moment, the three were able to make out the intruder's features: he was about 6' tall, Caucasian, and had a thick, well-groomed salt-and-pepper mustache. His head was covered by a dark, narrow-brimmed fedora-style hat. He was wearing reflective sunglasses, a tweed sport coat, dark pants, and black shoes. A band-aid covered a portion of his left cheek.

"Get down on the floor!" the man demanded. "On your stomachs and cover your eyes. *Don't look at me.*" The three obeyed his instructions. For a moment, his footsteps seemed to trail off. Seconds later, however, they were back, as were tellers Kenetha Whisler and Chong Choe. The gunman ordered Whisler and Choe onto the floor beside their coworkers, the five squirming bodies now bunched together as if they were playing a macabre game of Twister.

"Who is the cashier?" the intruder asked, his voice stern.

At first, no one answered, the term "cashier" not registering with any of them. Barranco finally broke the silence. "I'm… I'm the manager," he said meekly, his lips pressed against the floor.

"Get up!" the gunman barked. As Barranco rose to his feet, he tiptoed around the other four tellers—his eyes tricking him into believing all five were present and accounted for. Though he was deathly afraid, he summoned every ounce of courage he possessed, trying his best to protect the others.

"There's a black bag around the corner," the man told Barranco, his gun still pointed at the slender 24-year-old's chest. "Go get it and fill it with money."

About 15 feet away, Barranco spotted a double-handled, black leather satchel on the floor that resembled a doctor's bag. He cautiously approached the satchel, picked it up, and headed over to the bank cage where David Twist and Maria Christian had been processing large denominations of currency.

"No loose money and no bait money," the gunman instructed. "Only strapped money. I want 20s, 50s, and 100s. No ones or fives." As Barranco began filling the bag with strapped bundles, the gunman turned to face the others, who were still lying face-down a few feet away.

"The rest of you, crawl into the mantrap," he ordered. Unsure of what he wanted them to do—because they were still covering their eyes as he'd insisted—no one moved. The man repeated himself, bellowing, "Yes, I want you to crawl on your bellies into that little room." He waved his gun in the direction he wanted them to crawl. "And stay down!" This time, the tellers scurried forward—Army style—into the 5' x 6' security chamber a few feet away, the top half of which was enveloped with bullet-resistant glass. By design, the steel door that latched behind them couldn't be opened from the inside.

Meanwhile, Barranco grabbed every bundle of $20s, $50s, and $100s he could find in the bank cage and piled them into the bag, barely filling its bottom. With the gunman nipping at his heels, he proceeded to the adjacent row of booths where teller Nina McGinty had been working. Until that point, he'd assumed McGinty had been herded into the mantrap with the others. But when he stopped beside her station, he was startled to find her hiding beneath the counter—behind a garbage can—shaking uncontrollably.

"There's no cash here," Barranco told the robber—lying through his teeth—hoping to conceal his coworker's presence. He pointed at the counter opposite her hiding spot that was teeming with scattered slips of paper. "These are just food stamps."

His ploy to divert the gunman's attention worked, as the man's eyes now scanned the room in an attempt to locate more cash. "Where else is money being counted?"

"Over there," Barranco pointed, leading the robber to the neighboring booth Chong Choe had occupied.

"Keep filling it up," the robber demanded, pointing his revolver at the black satchel. After the vault manager deposited the last of the strapped bundles from Choe's booth into the bag, the man asked, "Anywhere else money is being counted?"

"There's one more station," Barranco said. He led the intruder to Kenetha Whisler's station in the far row of booths, where he scooped additional stacks of $20s, $50s, and $100s off the counter and dropped them in the bag. By the time he'd loaded the last bundle, the leather satchel contained $197,080 in loot—some 18,000 pieces of currency—and weighed over 18 pounds. But it was still partially empty. Hundreds of thousands of dollars of unstrapped money were left lying on counters at the tellers' stations.

As he stood behind Barranco—the barrel of his gun aimed at his mid-section—the gunman asked, "What's in the vault?" With his free hand, he pointed to the Saturday vault in the corner of the room, which hadn't yet received the day's deposits.

"All that's back there is paperwork," Barranco said. He

purposely didn't mention the two safes—or the million dollars filling them.

"Then get in the mantrap with the others." The robber snatched the satchel off Whisler's desk and followed Barranco to the edge of the mantrap, closing the door behind him.

"Get down on the floor!" he snarled. "None of you get up for any reason."

Barranco sank to the floor beside his four terrified subordinates, forcefully exhaling every molecule of oxygen in his lungs.

Though it had seemed like an eternity, the group's encounter with the sharply dressed armed robber had lasted all of eight minutes—eight minutes David Barranco, Maria Christian, David Twist, Kenetha Whisler, and Chong Choe would have nightmares about for years to come. And yet, as they sat on the floor praying and consoling one another, none of them had the foggiest clue how close to meeting their maker they'd just come.

2

ESCAPE

Danelle Taylor arrived at the bank shortly after 10:00 a.m., hoping to complete several tasks in an hour's time. In her twelfth year of employment with United Bank, she worked in the investigations unit of the risk and bank security department, which was located on the concourse level—adjacent to the guard monitor room. It wasn't unusual for Taylor to come in on the weekend to get a head start on the upcoming workweek.

When she reached her department's locked rear door—to which she didn't have a key—she pressed the buzzer to get the attention of a security guard, waiting patiently for one of their voices to come over the intercom.

She'd followed this same procedure on Saturdays and Sundays many times before, each time resulting in quick access to her office. Yet for some reason, today was different. Even after buzzing the monitor room several more times, nobody responded. Taylor considered that rather odd, as she knew the monitor room needed to be manned at all times.

Confused and just a little perturbed, she looped around through a hallway to reach her department's front door. Even though it too was supposed to be locked, the door opened right up when she turned the knob. *What the heck is going on?* she wondered as she let herself in. She marched straight to the rear door—where she'd been a moment earlier—and propped it open to avoid being locked out again. She buzzed the monitor room again, trying to reassure herself that everything was okay. But there was still no response. And when she tried calling into the room by phone, no one picked up.

Now pretty sure something was amiss, she called the bank's security manager at his home to alert him to the problem. But when she couldn't get ahold of him, she convinced herself—for the moment at least—that she was probably getting worked up over nothing. She decided to complete her work and let someone else figure out what was going on with the guards.

A short time later, however, a frustrated employee from the proof department wandered into Taylor's office, flummoxed over her inability to get the attention of a guard to let her into the cash vault—her normal practice on Sunday mornings. Her department wouldn't be able to process the checks Loomis and Wells Fargo had delivered, she said, without retrieving them from the tellers in the vault.

Upon hearing her story, Taylor called the monitor room, once again to no avail. Now on a mission, she shoved her work aside and traversed the entire concourse—and a flight of stairs—to reach the main lobby at 1 United Bank Center, the 52-story skyscraper at which the United Bank of Denver was merely one of several tenants. Uniformed guards from a security company hired by the building's owner—unaffiliated with the bank—were seated at a circular desk in the reception area.

"Have you seen any of *our* guards recently?" Taylor asked, her voice tinged with exasperation.

"No," one of them said with a shake of his head. "That's real strange. We haven't seen any of them since 8:30 this morning."

• • • •

While commiserating over the terrifying ordeal they'd all just endured, the five cash vault employees sealed up in the mantrap—where the armed robber had left them—had become desperate to determine whether their coworker, Nina Mc-Ginty, was all right. David Barranco shared with the others that he'd spotted her hiding under the counter when he and the gunman were beside her booth. But he had no idea what had happened to her since.

About ten minutes after he'd been forced at gunpoint to join the others, Barranco rose to a crouched position to peek through the glass window encasing the upper half of the man-trap. There was no sign of the robber—or McGinty. "The coast is clear," he announced, now stretching to his full height. The others cautiously rose to their feet as well, each of them scanning the window-filled vault in search of McGinty.

"Nina!" one of them yelled. "Are you out there?"

"Nina, please let us out of here!" another shouted. Apart from the echo of their own voices, they were greeted by dead silence.

"Do you think she's okay?" one of the tellers asked as her panicked eyes swept across McGinty's station.

"I sure hope so," Barranco said. They took turns banging on the bullet-resistant glass, screaming for their coworker.

"How the hell are we going to get out of here?" one of them asked anxiously. The Monday morning crew wouldn't arrive for nearly 24 hours.

Just when their plight was beginning to seem hopeless, a burst of inspiration seized Kenetha Whisler. She spotted a metal spoon on the ledge, where the glass and drywall joined together. With the others nervously peering over her shoulders, Whisler used the handle of the spoon to try jimmying the lock on the mantrap's rear door. After fiddling with it for nearly 20 minutes, miraculously, the door popped open.

"Let's get the hell out of here!" she squealed. It was now 10:45 a.m.

The group raced down the corridor the armored couriers had used to reach the cash vault and located a fire exit. After climbing multiple flights in the emergency stairwell, they pushed open another door, which fed into the third floor of the parking garage.

The lobby of 1 United Bank Center—where each had entered the bank to begin their shift—was clear across the other side of the garage.

"They've got security guards in there," Barranco said excitedly. "Run!"

The two men and three women sprinted across the pavement, barging through the skyscraper's side entrance, gasping for air as they finally reached the guard desk.

A chill ran down Danelle Taylor's spine as she turned to face the frantic bank employees.

"We've been robbed!" Maria Christian screeched. She was shaking, hunched over as if she might puke. "We were in the vault … when this guy came in with a gun and … and robbed us. He locked us in … in the mantrap and we … we finally escaped."

"Oh my God!" Taylor exclaimed. "I knew something wasn't right. Is everyone okay?"

"One of us is still missing," Barranco chimed in, flapping his arms as he struggled to fill his lungs with oxygen. "Nina McGinty. She was under … under the counter in her booth, hiding when he was robbing us. I have … I have no idea where she is."

Taylor spun back around to the uniformed guards, now beginning to freak out herself. "Call 911!"

● ● ● ●

Nina McGinty was still at her station, crouched behind the garbage can beneath the counter, her heart thumping furiously against her ribcage.

She'd been in the same scrunched position—scared out of her mind—for a solid hour. Every muscle in her body ached.

By this point, she was all alone, though she had no idea if the gunman was lurking around a corner—or whether her coworkers were even still alive.

Eying the telephone resting on the opposite counter, she summoned the courage to abandon her hiding spot and expose herself to danger. But when she dialed into the guard monitor room, there was no response.

Tears streaming down her cheeks, the frazzled bank teller steadied her shaking hand long enough to press three numbers on the keypad: 9-1-1.

3

MAD SCRAMBLE

Patricia Westerkamp couldn't believe her ears. She'd been patrolling Denver's streets since early that morning when a seemingly absurd all-points-bulletin came over her squad car's radio at 10:53 a.m.: "Possible robbery at United Bank of Denver." *Nobody's gonna rob a bank on a Sunday morning,* she scoffed. Her tires squealed as she made an abrupt U-turn and activated her flashing red and blue lights and siren. Minutes later, she was standing in the lobby of 1 United Bank Center, where a uniformed guard confirmed that someone had indeed robbed the bank.

Well, I'll be damned, Westerkamp thought, her Sunday morning suddenly brimming with unanticipated excitement.

Several more patrol officers soon funneled into the building's lobby. Not certain whether the armed robber was still lurking somewhere on the premises, they extended their guns as they weaved their way through the underground concourse—getting lost several times in pursuit of the elusive cash vault. They were eventually joined by Danelle Taylor, who led the officers all the way to the vault's outer mantrap door. It was only upon reaching the door that Taylor realized her Markey card wasn't programmed to allow access into the vault. She left the group to find David Barranco, whom she knew would be able to let them in.

Meanwhile, Nina McGinty was back under the counter,

trembling in fear, still on the line with an emergency dispatcher. The dispatcher told her police officers had arrived and were now just outside the vault. "Do you think you can let them in?" he asked.

"Nooooo!" McGinty shrieked hysterically. "I can't move."

"That's okay, ma'am," the dispatcher said. "They'll get inside to help you soon enough. Hang in there!"

Once Taylor returned with David Barranco and his Markey card, the officers stormed into the vault, weapons drawn, clearing every nook and cranny before approaching McGinty's station—her incessant wailing leading them directly to her. The poor bank teller was shaking ferociously, barely able to speak.

It took the strength of two burly officers to straighten out her crumpled body so she could stand on her own two feet. Yet no matter how much McGinty urged them to, neither would budge an inch—as if she'd just stepped into a tub of drying cement. She had to be carried out of the building and rushed to the hospital.

Denver General Hospital would also be the destination of the next three employees Denver's finest were about to find. But unlike Nina McGinty, they'd be leaving the building in body bags—headed directly to the morgue.

• • • •

As the group of officers accumulating in the cash vault swelled, they were joined by several officials from United Bank, who informed them that four security guards had been assigned to work that morning. Yet none were responding in the monitor room or to attempts to reach them on their radios. Finding the four men quickly became the group's primary mission.

Danelle Taylor grabbed a key ring off the security manager's desk and led a parade of cops to the monitor room's outer mantrap door. They had no reason to suspect that gaining entry would pose any particular difficulty. Yet for the next 30 minutes, the outer mantrap door proved as impenetrable as the doors guarding Fort Knox.

Taylor tried several keys, but none of them made it very far into the keyhole because another key had apparently broken off inside that had never been removed. Though she was able to locate a Markey card programmed to provide access into the monitor room, when she inserted it into the card reader, the heavy steel door still wouldn't budge. As the group was about to learn, an empty Mountain Dew can had been strategically wedged between the inner mantrap door and the door jamb, preventing the door from latching closed. Precisely as the mantrap was designed, the partially open inner door rendered the outer door completely inoperable.

Left with no other way to access the monitor room, the officers had to use carpentry tools to remove the outer door's hinges. Once they'd removed the last hinge, they used a crowbar Taylor found in the maintenance supply closet to pry the door out of its frame. It took several cops to lift it off the floor and set it against the wall.

Their dark-blue uniforms now drenched in sweat, the officers finally entered the mantrap. Though the bullet-proof glass window to their right should have allowed them to glimpse inside, the lights had been turned off. All they could see were the flickering black-and-white screens in the security console.

Fearful the gunman might be hiding in the darkness, the first officer to enter through the inner door proceeded cautiously—body crouched low to the ground, firearm extended. When he located the switch for the lights and flipped them on, his eyes were immediately drawn to the floor between the two sides of the security console. He stared at the gruesome spectacle, gasping in disbelief. "Man down!" he finally hollered, holding his position near Todd Wilson's bloody corpse as additional cops entered the room.

Another officer worked the perimeter, eventually reaching the far corner of the room. He gently nudged the door to the auxiliary battery room, allowing his eyes to drift downward. He winced reflexively the moment the carnage—and the river of blood extending from it—entered his field of view. "Two more down!"

There was no sign whatsoever of the fourth security

guard, who the first responders learned was an African American male named Bill McCullom. When the first wave of police detectives arrived, they didn't hesitate to make the 6', 190-pound bachelor the prime suspect in the slaughter of his fellow guards.

4

MANHUNT

Norm Early could light up a room with his infectious smile and hearty laugh. The tall, broad-shouldered, mustachioed 45-year-old had been a trailblazer his entire life. At American University, he'd not only been a track-and-field superstar—setting records never to be eclipsed—he'd also served as the school's first Black student body president.

After completing law school at the University of Illinois, the Washington, D.C. native migrated to Denver, joining the District Attorney's Office in 1973 and quickly rising to become a chief deputy. When the elected DA stepped aside in 1983, Early persuaded Colorado's governor to appoint him as the county's first Black DA. Despite Denver's relatively small African American population—barely a blip over ten percent—he easily won election in 1984 and re-election in 1988. The affable DA now had his sights set on higher office, seemingly destined to become the Mile High City's first Black mayor.

Early's popularity stemmed largely from his tough-on-crime image. He and his surrogates were quick to tout statistics showcasing Denver's plummeting crime rate during his tenure as DA. In the months preceding the May 21 mayoral election, he'd outraised and outspent his rivals six-to-one, filling his campaign coffers with nearly a million dollars in cash. But when voters cast their ballots on election day, Early fell short of garnering the majority needed to avoid a runoff, capturing just 41% of the vote. Placing second at 30% was City Auditor Wellington Webb, also an African American. A runoff was slated for Tuesday, June 18.

The savage murders at United Bank held the potential to shake up the mayoral race with just two days to go, and Early was savvy enough to recognize that very real possibility. He'd been attending a Sunday afternoon campaign rally in North Denver with actor Yaphet Kotto—often a cop in his TV and movie roles—when he received a call about the massacre. He and Kotto raced downtown to meet with officers and detectives, who by then were swarming all over the bank's three-building complex.

The pair was escorted to the guard monitor room, where Early had to shield his eyes as he took in the morbid display. Sharing his reaction with a TV reporter later that day, he said, "This is one of the most grotesque, horrendous crimes I've seen in this city since I've been here."

In the weeks and months to follow, Norm Early would remain firmly in charge of the efforts to secure justice for the slain guards' families—continuing on in his role as DA. It wasn't his destiny to become Denver's first Black mayor after all, an honor the city's electorate instead bestowed on Wellington Webb, who garnered 57% of the vote in the runoff.

••••

Where was Bill McCullom? Was he the mastermind behind the diabolical plot that unfolded that morning? And if so, what were his plans now? Those were the central questions vexing detectives as paramedics loaded three body bags onto gurneys and wheeled them out of the monitor room. Finding the 33-year-old security guard—as fast as humanly possible—had quickly become the Denver Police Department's number-one priority.

As crime-scene investigators combed through the monitor room, a large battalion of SWAT team members donning bullet-proof vests and full riot gear fanned out across the bank complex. They started on the top floor of each building, progressively working their way downward one floor at a time. Every door was opened and every square foot eyeballed for any sign of McCullom or his potential accomplices.

Meanwhile, a search warrant was hastily prepared to allow officers access to McCullom's basement apartment on Moline Street in Aurora, some eight miles east of the United Bank. The area was well known to law enforcement as a haven for drug dealers and venue for violent gang activity. At this embryonic stage of the investigation, the notion that McCullom had joined with a band of thugs from his neighborhood to pull off the deadly heist seemed as logical as any.

By mid-afternoon, a half dozen cops in tactical gear gathered with FBI agents across the street from McCullom's apartment building to strategize over last-minute details before storming his residence. They were armed to the teeth, enough weaponry and ammo to mow down every resident of the neighborhood.

The officers enlisted the support of the apartment's property manager, who conveniently lived directly across from McCullom's unit. After they knocked on the door several times with no sign of a response, the property manager let them in with his master key. The cops and FBI agents rushed inside, their guns and assault rifles pointed in every direction as they spread out across the one-bedroom apartment. But alas, it was empty, nothing even the slightest bit amiss.

Shocked by the massive display of force, the property manager explained that McCullom was a nice man and a good tenant who always paid his rent on time. He'd been living in the basement apartment for five years, he said, without any trouble at all. Perhaps they'd gotten him mixed up with someone else.

• • • •

United Bank employees referred to the lowest underground floor as the "lower-concourse" or "sub-basement" level. It was situated one floor below the monitor room and cash vault, accessible by either an elevator or stairwell.

Though the lower concourse was now used mainly for storage, years earlier, one of the rooms had relied on a fire-breathing incinerator to burn confidential records on site, a process that had been halted by environmental regulators years earlier. By 1991, the incinerator room was a relic of bank history few employees even knew about. It was located at the end of a hallway, about 70 feet from the nearest elevator. Since the dingy room no longer held any purpose, it was kept locked at all times.

By 5:45 p.m., members of the SWAT team had descended to the lower concourse, grimy and sweaty from many hours of arduous work in their heavy gear. When they finally reached the incinerator room—the last room they needed to search—they used a master key to unlock the door. As the door swung out into the hallway, one of the officers aimed his 12-gauge shotgun into the darkness, using the light at the end of its barrel to gain visibility inside.

When the light illuminated the back-left corner of the room, a well-built, African American male—flat on his back—suddenly came into view. His bearded face was covered in blood. On the floor beneath his head, a partially coagulated pool of blood leeched outward toward the baseboard. Chunky particles of brain matter were spattered on the wall. The man was adorned in the unmistakable white shirt and gray slacks worn by United Bank security guards.

William Rogers McCullom, Jr. was no longer the prime suspect in the murders of Phil Mankoff, Todd Wilson, and Scott McCarthy. Instead, he was the fourth and final victim to be wheeled out of the building in a body bag.

5

LOST SOULS

During his brief time on Earth, Todd Wilson had overcome significant obstacles. He was born with severe nystagmus, a condition causing one's eyes make repetitive, involuntary movements, affecting vision, depth perception, and even balance and coordination. Despite undergoing corrective surgery on his right eye when he was 18 months old, he was classified as legally blind, attending North Dakota's School for the Blind until the third grade. Two years later, he, his parents, two brothers, and sister moved to Englewood, Colorado, just south of Denver.

As he progressed through the public school system, the brown-haired youngster got used to being teased about his lazy right eye, disarming his classmates with his quick wit and kind heart. He kept up with his course work by relying on specialized books containing extra-large print. Though he found sports challenging, Todd mustered the grit to play one season on the Englewood High football team, ultimately swapping out his helmet and pads for a spot in the band, where he played tuba and the bass. When his friends started getting their driver's licenses, he had to settle for being a passenger in their cars, as his disability rendered it impossible for him to drive.

During high school, Todd worked as a dishwasher at the Mission Trujillo restaurant in nearby Littleton. It was there that he met the boy who quickly became his best friend, Scott Mc-Carthy, who washed dishes alongside him. Between the two, Todd was the chatterbox, Scott often preferring to keep his thoughts to himself. Their boss, owner John Trujillo, branded the blond-haired McCarthy "Gabby"—a tongue-in-cheek reference to his reticence—and Todd "Loco Ojo," for his lazy right eye.

Scott, his mom, and two brothers had migrated to Englewood from the marshy coast of northern Washington when he was in middle school. He attended Heritage High, Englewood's crosstown rival. With his tall, slender frame—he'd eventually sprout to 6'4"—athletics came naturally and he excelled on the football team. He and Todd—who'd ultimately reach 6' himself—would often head to the mountains to fish and ride four-wheelers.

Scott fell in love with a girl from Littleton named Jennifer McElhaney—who stood about a foot shorter than him—the pair meeting in 1987 while working for the same Mexican restaurant. After the couple attended the senior prom, however, they headed in opposite directions, Jenny to the University of Wisconsin—spending the 1988-89 school year studying abroad in Peru—and Scott to Fort McClellan in Alabama, where he was stationed in the Army. He became a military police officer, infatuated with the idea of one day becoming a real-live cop.

But much to his dismay, his military service was cut short by a shoulder and back injury after just 18 months. He returned to Englewood, where he resumed his friendship with Todd—and also asked Jenny to marry him. She said, "Yes."

On August 4, 1990—three months after his bride-to-be graduated from college—Scott beamed jubilantly in his ivory tux as he locked his gaze on Jenny gliding down the aisle, her father at her arm. Todd was right there beside him as his best man. After saying his "I dos" and dancing the night away, Scott became a loving, supportive husband. Interviewed in the aftermath of his horrific murder, Jenny's mom described him as "the best son-in-law you could ask for," noting how he treated his new wife "like a princess."

Though he was quite handsome himself—his chocolate-brown hair always neatly parted to the side—as of the fall of 1990, Todd hadn't yet found his soulmate, or a girlfriend for that matter. He'd just begun his sophomore year at Metropolitan State College of Denver, commuting to school and to work by city bus. His goal was to become a certified substance abuse counselor. During high school, he had friends who'd become addicted to drugs and was proud of the work he'd done to help them get clean. He felt a calling to make drug counseling a career.

Todd could sit at his computer for hours, using the device to play video games and for more creative endeavors. He'd churn out colorful and witty e-cards for just about any occasion—Father's Day no exception. To help pay for college, he'd gotten a job as a clerk in the credit card fraud department at United Bank.

When Norwest's acquisition became final that April, he learned the bank's new owner was wiping out his department to consolidate operations and save costs. Todd was told that if he wanted to continue his employment at the bank, he'd need to transition to a position as a security guard. Yet his father was dead-set against the idea—largely because of Todd's poor vision and the danger he believed would be inherent in the job.

"Dad, I gotta make a couple of decisions in my life on my own," Todd had pushed back, deciding to accept the position despite his father's misgivings. He was working just his sixth day as a security guard the morning he was killed. And thanks largely to Todd's incessant badgering of his boss, Scott was there that morning on his very first.

Fittingly, five days after the gruesome murders, the Wilson and McCarthy families gathered together for a joint funeral at Littleton's Holy Trinity Lutheran Church. The air beneath the sanctuary's vaulted ceiling hung heavily, saturated with sorrow and stunned disbelief. Jenny McCarthy—who'd morphed from ecstatic newlywed to grieving widow—shed a river of tears alongside the victims' devastated parents, siblings, friends, and relatives.

Todd Wilson's and Scott McCarthy's polished oak caskets tugged at every set of eyeballs as hundreds of mourners absorbed prayers, scripture readings, Christian hymns, and fond remembrances of the best friends' happiest days. As the service concluded, pallbearers sidled up to the twin coffins, recessing caravan style toward the church entrance. Though Todd's casket was closed, Scott's was left open for mourners to bid a last farewell, his babyface exuding innocence and boundless potential.

Everyone in attendance was left to wonder why two sweet young men who'd never harmed anyone—who'd barely begun their adult lives—had been snatched away in such a brutal fashion. And what type of monster could have committed such an abominable act.

••••

Of the four security guards who'd lost their lives that tragic Father's Day morning, only Phil Mankoff had been born and raised exclusively in Denver—one of four children in a Jewish family of six. Sadly, during his freshman year at North High School, he and his three sisters lost their dad, Harold Mankoff, who was just 59.

Despite that awful setback, Phil remained resilient, staying on track and completing his high school education, then enrolling in college at Western State. It was there he fell in love with a girl named Susan, whom he married in 1971. After graduating with a bachelor's degree in education, he began working in the banking sector, performing data processing and systems analysis.

From 1973 to 1987, Phil rose steadily in seniority and compensation, becoming an operations officer at Colorado National Bank and a vice president at both Columbine National Bank and First Interstate Bancorp. While his career flourished, however, his marriage to Susan withered. They finally divorced in 1985, the same year Phil's mom passed away. Adding insult to injury, Susan took their two young sons and moved hundreds of miles away, making it extremely difficult for Phil to see them.

And then, at the worst possible time, while he was still dealing with the financial strain of the divorce, he was laid off from his job. He went from being a senior bank executive to standing in the unemployment line. Left with no other choice—and $143,000 in unpaid debts—he declared bankruptcy. Though his sisters knew all about his divorce and the difficulties he was having seeing his kids, Phil was too proud to make them aware of his financial struggles—much less his bankruptcy filing—even though his brother-in-law, a successful orthodontist, could have extended him a financial lifeline.

Despite his financial turmoil, Phil's last years on Earth were his happiest. He fell head-over-heels in love with a woman named Ann, who had two beautiful daughters of her own, both a good bit older than his boys. When they tied the knot in 1989, he moved into Ann's townhome in Aurora. As his relationship with his sons grew more distant—despite his heartfelt efforts—the loving bond he was able to forge with his stepdaughters grew stronger with each passing day.

Phil finally got back on his feet financially, landing a full-time position as a program administrator and division chief in state government with Child Support Services, where he supervised a staff of 20. An expert in computer systems, he was in charge of automated child support collection for the entire state. Interviewed in the wake of the bank massacre, his boss described him as an "outstanding manager" who had an uncanny ability to motivate his employees and improve morale.

In addition to his full-time job, Phil decided to moonlight as a security guard for United Bank—something else he'd kept secret from his sisters. Having held several senior-level positions at three different banks, never in a million years did he imagine he'd one day be sporting a guard uniform for yet another. But he was more than happy to work the graveyard shift at $5.42 an hour if that meant his wife and stepdaughters would have a little more comfort in their lives. His first day on the job was March 12, 1991, just over three months before an armed madman ended his life.

Ann and the girls tried in vain to suppress their tears as Phil's bullet-ravaged body was lowered into the earth at the

Congregation Emanuel section of Fairmount Cemetery. As per Jewish tradition, they'd be back again just before the first anniversary of his death—the first *yahrzeit*—to unveil his grave marker, which contained the words of the 1934 poem, "Immortality:"

> *Do not stand at my grave and weep,*
> *I am a thousand winds that blow,*
> *I am the diamond glints on snow,*
> *I am the gentle autumn's rain,*
> *I am the soft stars that shine at night,*
> *Do not stand at my grave and cry.*

••••

Bill McCullom made quite the first impression. Despite his physically imposing presence, his kind, gentle spirit oozed through his pores, his smile radiating warmth and sincerity.

Though his mom, stepdad, and sister lived in Dallas, he was raised primarily by his aunt and uncle in Denver, where he graduated from George Washington High and the Community College of Denver with a degree in computer science. Unsure of what he wanted to do next, Bill enrolled in Barnes Business School. The private institution cost him a small fortune and led to a mountain of student debt—debt that would haunt him to his dying day. At the time of the massacre, he was 88 days delinquent on over $15,000 in unpaid loans.

Bill's one true love didn't come in human form. Indeed, he'd never been married, didn't have a girlfriend, and rarely dated. What got his juices flowing more than anything was working with computers. His tiny basement apartment was jam-packed with computer equipment, books, and manuals—nearly 150 publications in all. Oddly, he was also a connoisseur of junk mail, which he hoarded by the bundle, hoping to find the one sweepstakes mailer that would make him a fortune—or at least supply him enough dough to buy a car. He'd reached the age of 33 without ever owning one, relying on the city bus system to shuttle him around Denver.

At the same time, he realized that his most likely path to success—and vehicle ownership—was through hard work. He typically worked two jobs at a time, described by friends and family as a workaholic. Among his many jobs were positions as a courier for both Citywide Bank of Denver and American Express. By 1990, he was working for Great West Life Assurance as a senior mail clerk. He was later promoted to what he considered his dream job—computer operations.

Bill began his side hustle at United Bank in September 1990, the only time in his life he was employed as a security guard. Though he dutifully reported for work at 12:30 a.m. every Saturday and Sunday morning, it bothered him that he couldn't carry a gun for protection. As soon as he made enough money to pay down his debt—and perhaps buy a car—he planned to quit. Sadly, he never got the chance.

Just as he was the final slain guard to be found, Bill Mc-Cullom was also the last to be laid to rest. Nearly 200 mourners crammed into the Pipkin Chapel of Peace to pay their respects, tears streaming down many faces as a vocalist performed her rendition of Larry Graham's soulful single, "One in a Million You." Bill was eulogized as a kind, empathetic soul—"an angel without wings"—whose honesty and gentle nature were worthy of emulation.

Among those who took to the pulpit to share their thoughts was one of the few Caucasians in attendance, United Bank's longtime chairman, N. Berne Hart. Though Hart wasn't acquainted with Bill personally, he wanted everyone in the sanctuary to know how deeply sorry the bank was that such an awful tragedy had occurred on its premises.

"It was all so senseless and so needless," he said, striking a somber tone. "We pray that in the future these events do not have to take place to remind us all how close we are to God."

Standing beside her son's metal, flower-rimmed casket, Bill's mother, Nellie Wilson, put on the bravest face she could muster as she greeted friends and family members following the service. Finally making his way to the front of the lengthy line, one of Bill's coworkers at the insurance company wrapped the grieving mother in his beefy arms. Wiping tears from his face, he told her Bill was a good spirit who never complained. "All he had to do was smile at you," he said, "and you remembered him forever."

6

BIG BANK

The United Bank of Denver's ancestry extended all the way back to 1884—when horse-drawn carriages still roamed the city's streets—with the chartering of Denver National Bank. Twenty years later, a second ancestor was born: U.S. National Bank. The 1959 marriage of the two competing institutions created the Denver-U.S. National Bank, which occupied a four-story building near the corner of Seventeenth and Broadway. The combined entity instantly became the second largest bank in Colorado, with nearly $300 million in assets. In 1970, Denver-U.S. and several sister institutions merged into the newly minted United Banks of Colorado holding company, resulting in the signage on the downtown headquarters being changed to United Bank of Denver.

By then, the holding company had become a billion-dollar enterprise with 12 community banks in its stable. Through its subsidiaries, United Banks also began dabbling in mortgages and insurance. By 1978, the company had grown to 19 banks with more than $2 billion in assets and nearly 3,000 employees. "We are a company committed to excellence," United's chairman, N. Berne Hart, proclaimed at the time. "We never believe it when someone tries to tell us that 'it can't be done.' Instead, we learn how it can be done, and we set about doing it!"

Over the next 12 years, United exploded in both size and wealth, becoming a $6.4 billion operation with 3,600 employees—United Bank of Denver retaining its status as the company's flagship. As a symbol of its growing prominence, United transitioned its headquarters to the swanky 52-story tower on the corner of Seventeenth and Lincoln—just across the street—when the architectural marvel was completed in 1983. By 1990, 30% of all households in the state were served by one of the 40 United Banks, which also held a quarter of Colorado's commercial deposits. The company's astronomical growth made it a juicy acquisition target.

Some 700 miles away in Minneapolis—meeting in their own brand-new, 57-story skyscraper—executives lining the table in Norwest Corp's boardroom salivated over the prospect of adding Colorado's largest bank to its arsenal, which already boasted nearly $30 billion in assets, 1,270 branches, and 17,000 employees. By scooping up United, the Midwest behemoth—the 21st largest American bank—would finally be able to plant its flag in the last remaining state outside of Alaska and Hawaii where it didn't have existing branches. The Colorado legislature had recently relaxed the state's banking laws to make just such a takeover by an interstate suitor perfectly legal for the very first time. All the stars seemed to be aligning, the acquisition a veritable no-brainer.

On July 26, 1990, Norwest's $370 million purchase offer landed like manna from heaven at Seventeenth and Lincoln. By agreeing to the sale, United's top five executives stood to reap a tidy $3.5 million windfall, nearly $1 million of which would be doled out to Chairman Hart alone. Agreeing to the sale was an even bigger no-brainer for his coterie than their counterparts in Minnesota.

But there would be consequences to this deal—severe to many of United's employees. The company announced its intention to jettison ten percent of its workforce by eliminating 350 positions before the takeover became final. The hundreds of pink slips, Hart explained to the media, would shave $9.5 million from the bank's $102 million payroll. Upon expected approval by regulators, he added, there would be further cuts to eliminate redundancies between Norwest's Minneapolis hub and United's headquarters in Denver.

United's prized residential mortgage unit would yield to Norwest's similar operation in Des Moines. Because there was no need for a credit card fraud operation at both locations, United's would be the one to go. Flesh-and-blood human beings—Todd Wilson, for example—would be affected by these decisions in ways that were impossible to fathom as executives from both companies stroked their signatures across the closing documents in April 1991.

But that is not the lens through which Norwest's chairman, Lloyd P. Johnson, viewed the impending merger. "When D-Day comes," he told reporters while visiting Denver in late March, "it should be smooth. It's never as smooth as you would like it to be. There are always glitches." There were no immediate plans to change United's name to Norwest. "United is a great name," he said. It's well recognized, and rightly so," adding that he didn't see any big changes in the offing.

Despite those soothing words, the runup to Johnson's "D-Day"—an eerily prophetic metaphor as things turned out—was filled with changes of every variety. Disarming United's security guards proved to be one of the most consequential. Before the company had even become a twinkle in Norwest's eye, guards at the United Bank of Denver were not only permitted to carry guns, they were encouraged to. Within 50 feet of where Phil Mankoff, Scott McCarthy, and Todd Wilson were pumped full of lead, no fewer than 22 .38-caliber Smith & Wesson revolvers sat in a storage locker—Locker 22—that had only recently become off limits. At an earlier time, guards had begun their shifts by checking out the Smith & Wessons as routinely as key rings and two-way radios.

Yet in the aftermath of the massacre, Chairman Hart painted a very different—most misleading—picture, contending that unarmed guards had been the "longtime policy" of United Banks. "We have long had a tradition of non-escalation of violence," he said. "When guns are present, violence does tend to escalate."

The reality was that United's upper management had become well aware of Norwest's own decision—years earlier—to disarm its guards all across the country. As management teams from each institution worked side-by-side to grease the wheels for their impending merger, Norwest's personnel persuaded their counterparts at United that guns needed to be phased out at each of the latter's 40 banks.

Why was Norwest so dead-set against guards carrying weapons? Did its executives really fear an escalation of violence? Not likely. Beginning in the 1980s, insurance companies started jacking up premiums for banks that continued to rely on armed security guards—convinced they faced greater risks under their policies with the presence of guns. Between more expensive insurance and the likelihood of being sued by customers maimed by stray bullets, the financial costs of relying on guns for security were considered too significant for banks like Norwest to swallow.

The concept that armed guards might deter would-be bandits from entering a bank in the first place had apparently never crossed their minds. Nor had the grim reality—painfully driven home to four grieving families—that unarmed guards would be sitting ducks to a bank robber packing heat.

7

POPCORN KERNELS

By late Father's Day afternoon, the Denver Police Department (DPD) was hard at work investigating three distinct crime scenes: one in the guard monitor room, a second in the cash vault, and a third in the incinerator room in the lower concourse. Within minutes of the first officers arriving at the bank, investigators with the DPD's Yankee 91 mobile crime lab were setting up shop in the monitor room and cash vault. Following the discovery of Bill McCullom's body at 5:45 p.m., additional investigators were dispatched to the incinerator room.

While crime lab technicians scoured each location for fingerprints, blood, bullets, shell casings, shoeprints, and other items of forensic significance—DNA analysis, still in its infancy, not part of their protocol—bank security personnel provided detectives a tutorial on the two computer systems that served as the brains behind the bank's security apparatus.

The Mosler system recorded in its memory when and where door alarms and motion detectors arrayed throughout the bank complex had activated, as well as when they were turned off and reset. The Marcham Control computer recorded each use of a Markey card to gain access to a mantrap, office, or department—and which employee's card had been used. All of that information would prove vital in reconstructing the timeline of events and determining how the perpetrator had weaved his way through the bank during his 42-minute murderous rampage.

Though detectives were hopeful the bank's surveillance cameras had captured him in the act—even in the grainy black-and-white video they churned out—their hopes were quickly dashed. The footage filmed by each camera had been recorded onto old-fashioned VCRs—12 of them to be exact. Investigators lit up with excitement when they discovered a bank of the machines in the U-shaped security console in the monitor room. But that excitement evaporated in mere seconds, as the cassette decks to all but one of the VCRs had been popped open, revealing that the killer had absconded with 11 of the 12 VHS tapes. The only one he'd left behind was in a VCR connected to a camera filming a motor bank on Sherman Street, one block east of Lincoln Street.

The perpetrator demonstrated his knowledge of the bank's security system in other ways as well. Twelve sets of keys were stolen off the hooks on the mahogany board where they ordinarily hung—the only ones that contained master keys, known as "MK1" keys. He'd also ripped out the top three pages of the blue three-ring binder that served as the logbook in which security guards recorded their activities by hand: when they went on rounds or were dispatched to escort bank personnel, the time and location any alarms triggered, and so forth. The only pages investigators found still in the logbook were blank—though they could see markings on the top page created by pen strokes that had pressed against the now-missing pages.

A DPD document examiner was consulted to enhance those markings by using a forensic technique known as an "ESDA lift," which revealed portions of the guards' handwriting in a manner similar to invisible ink being exposed by a fluorescent light. The first legible entry bore the time of 9:14 a.m. and indicated that Bill McCullom had been "dispatched to escort Bob Bartwell." Just beside that entry was the name Mankoff, the guard who'd apparently written it. Another entry revealed the time of 9:23 a.m. and the dispatch of Todd Wilson to investigate an alarm.

Contacted by the DPD, the real Bob Bardwell (spelled

with a "d")—one of the bank's 78 vice presidents—quickly eliminated himself as a suspect by establishing he'd been at his parents' home in the western Colorado mountains to celebrate Father's Day. Perhaps coincidentally, Bardwell told investigators he'd lost his Markey card in June 1990 and had it replaced that August.

Investigators also zeroed in on the Mountain Dew can that had propped open the monitor room's inner mantrap door—what had rendered the outer door inoperable—hoping the murderer had left his fingerprints on its aluminum surface. They slipped the can into a plastic bag to be analyzed by the lab. Fingerprints were also lifted from several additional surfaces, including one of the VCRs, and a palm print was lifted off the door jamb at the battery room's entrance.

A copper-wrapped .38-caliber bullet was recovered from the floor near the battery room's doorway. A computer keyboard was found damaged by a bullet strike, with a bullet fragment lying between two keys. Another fragment was found lying on the floor near Todd Wilson's right shoulder. Yet even though a dozen bullets had been fired inside the monitor room, not a single shell casing was located.

The most significant discoveries in the monitor room, apart from the victims, centered on the locked supervisor's office, which none of the keys on the guard key ring—not even an MK1 key—could open. Several telltale clues made clear the killer had attempted to break into the supervisor's office in multiple different ways. First, he'd fired a bullet at the exterior doorknob, badly denting its rounded surface. Yet it was the bullet, not the doorknob, that proved to be weaker, shattering into 11 fragments investigators found lying on the floor.

The perpetrator had also tried to karate kick through the plexiglass window beside the door, leaving a distinctive shoeprint on its surface. But just like the doorknob, the glass held firm. Finally, he attempted to kick in the drywall outside the adjacent storage room, but encountered sturdy plywood behind it that kept him from breaking through the wall. Investigators found torn drywall hanging below the gash the murderer had made with his foot, with more debris lying on the floor beneath it.

Why had the armed invader been so determined to break into the supervisor's office? With the help of bank security personnel, detectives developed a working theory. Prior to Norwest's takeover, a portable surveillance camera had been installed inside the monitor room to try to catch guards eating or drinking—a huge no-no management was trying to deter. Unlike the cameras arrayed throughout the three bank buildings—whose video footage was recorded by the VCRs in the security console—the portable camera policing the guards themselves delivered its footage to a VCR inside the locked supervisor's office. The killer had apparently believed that the VHS tape in that VCR would be his undoing if he failed to get his murderous hands on it.

What he clearly didn't know, however, was that after Norwest completed its takeover in April, the portable camera had been replaced by a permanent one that fed into one of the VCRs in the security console—not the VCR inside the supervisor's office. Thus, though the murderer's desperate attempts to get to that VCR had been thwarted, the VHS tape that had likely captured his image—quite possibly the bloodshed too—was one of the 11 he'd successfully absconded with. Luck, as it turned out, was on his side, not the detectives'.

• • • •

Crime-scene investigators in the incinerator room made important discoveries of their own. A piece of dot-matrix printer paper in the front right corner of the room bore a partial shoeprint. Even better prints of the killer's shoes were lifted from the dust covering the floor, which appeared to match the one found on the plexiglass in the monitor room. Though Bill Mc-Cullom's portable radio was found beneath his body, both his key ring and his Markey card were missing.

With that knowledge, as well as information gleaned from the ESDA lift of the guard logbook and a review of the Mosler system and Marcham Control computer, detectives were able to reconstruct a timeline of events, starting with Phil Mankoff dispatching Bill McCullom at 9:14 a.m. to take the freight elevator to the loading dock on Lincoln Street.

The person waiting for him when the elevator doors opened—who'd called into the monitor room requesting an escort from a phone beside the freight elevator—wasn't actually Bob Bardwell. Rather, it was the perpetrator, who had used his gun to take control of McCullom and force him to descend to the lower concourse. When the elevator doors opened again, he marched the muscular guard about 70 feet down the hallway to the incinerator room, used the MK1 key on McCullom's key ring to open the locked door, and then shot him to death near the far wall.

At 9:20 a.m., the murderer entered Stairwell C—the closest set of stairs to the incinerator room—triggering an alarm that flashed across a screen in the security console in the monitor room. He then climbed a flight of stairs to the concourse level, came through the proof department, proceeded down a hallway, entered the risk and bank security department with McCullom's MK1 key, and then turned left to reach the mantrap leading into the monitor room.

Meanwhile, at 9:23 a.m., Todd Wilson, already on his rounds, was dispatched by radio to investigate the Stairwell C alarm. His path hadn't crossed—not at that point at least—with the killer's.

At 9:24 a.m., the murderer arrived at the monitor room, using McCullom's Markey card to enter through the outer mantrap door and his MK1 key to open the inner door. Because Mankoff and Scott McCarthy had been expecting the other two guards to return—their backs to the mantrap as they watched TV—they wouldn't have been surprised to hear the sound of a key opening the door. The killer approached them from behind, marched them into the auxiliary battery room, and executed them in cold blood.

At 9:26 a.m., Todd Wilson actually did return, using his Markey card on the outer mantrap door and MK1 key on the inner door. Within seconds of his arrival, however, he was gunned down near the security console. All three victims were found still in possession of their Markey cards, though only

Wilson still had his key ring, which was discovered in his pants pocket. Each of their two-way radios had been swiped as well, as had three additional radios from the monitor room.

From that point, the timeline revealed a 22-minute gap before the murderer entered the cash vault. There were three pretty obvious explanations for his delay: (1) the 11 VHS tapes, 14 sets of keys, and six radios he had to gather and store for his eventual getaway; (2) his desperate attempts to break into the locked supervisor's office and storage room; and (3) his use of the Mountain Dew can on his way out to ensure that the outer mantrap door would be disabled when the police arrived.

Finally, at 9:48 a.m., the killer used McCullom's Markey card to enter the outer and inner doors to the cash vault's mantrap. Eight minutes later, he exited through those same doors—again with two swipes of McCullom's Markey card. With his leather satchel containing the loot in hand, he presumably scooped up whatever he'd used to store the VHS tapes, key rings, and radios and headed to Elevator #3, the only elevator available to the weekend guards. To operate the elevator, he had to use the correct key on McCullom's key ring—which wasn't marked.

He then rode the elevator to the seventh floor of the parking garage, where he'd presumably parked his getaway car. When the doors opened, he used the elevator key to lock it in place—"key it off" in guard lingo—to prevent responding law enforcement officers from accessing it.

The killer left one final clue before vanishing into thin air. Not far from the elevator bay on the parking garage's seventh floor was a trash bin. What did investigators find when they dumped it out and rummaged through its contents? A pair of matching latex gloves.

● ● ● ●

Despite all of the helpful evidence detectives and crime scene investigators uncovered, one particular discovery would haunt the investigation from its inception—one that didn't fit detectives' working timeline or theory. Something that was so confounding, they'd never be able to make much sense of it. The 9:20 a.m. Stairwell C alarm wasn't actually the first to have triggered that Father's Day morning.

Rather, at 5:04 a.m., the Mosler system recorded a motion detector being set off in an L-shaped tunnel in the concourse that stored boxes of paper records predating the bank's ability to archive records electronically. What had caused the motion-activated alarm to trigger at 5:04 a.m.? Had the killer actually entered the bank hours before 9:14 a.m.? Did he perhaps have an accomplice who'd been biding his time in the tunnel until his partner in crime finally arrived?

According to the Mosler system's notations, someone in the monitor room had manually turned off the motion detector—without investigating its cause—shortly after it activated. That wasn't standard protocol, as a guard should have been dispatched to the records tunnel to determine what had happened. Even more confounding, the motion detector had been rearmed at 9:33 a.m.—*after all four security guards were dead.* How on earth did that happen? Detectives couldn't make heads or tails of these pieces of evidence. Not on Father's Day. Not ever.

••••

Based on everything they learned in the hours and days following the 42-minute crime spree, DPD detectives would arrive at a critical conclusion from which they'd never waver: the use of Bill McCullom's Markey card to enter both the monitor room and the cash vault had to mean that the gun-toting robber who'd stolen nearly $200,000 from the latter was the same man who'd murdered McCullom in the incinerator room and Mankoff, McCarthy, and Wilson in the monitor room. And they were now on an urgent mission to figure out who he was—and bring him to justice—as fast as humanly possible.

8

BOYS IN BLUE

The robbery of a federally insured bank is a federal crime, the investigation of which is typically conducted by the FBI. Murder, on the other hand, is generally considered a state offense over which local police departments and district attorneys have jurisdiction. Because the Father's Day massacre was both a bank robbery and a quadruple homicide, the FBI and DPD joined forces, forming a task force to investigate the crime, one that would swell to 40 FBI agents and 30 DPD officers in just two weeks.

As of June 1991, the Special Agent in Charge (SAC) of the FBI's Denver field office was Bob Pence, a silver-haired, media-savvy lawman nearing his thirtieth anniversary with the Bureau. The Pennsylvania native had begun his service as a 24-year-old in 1962 under the FBI's first—and legendary—director, J. Edgar Hoover, who'd already been running the Bureau for 38 years when Pence arrived.

Pence assumed command over the Denver field office in 1986, following a six-year stint as SAC in Charlotte, North Carolina. From his spacious digs in Denver's downtown Federal Building, the highly experienced agent supervised more than 100 special agents assigned to the mountainous expanse of Colorado and Wyoming—some 200,000 square miles. He was telegenic and articulate whenever a TV camera was pointed in his direction, a reassuring voice in times of crisis.

Ari Zavaras's law enforcement career had spanned nearly the same time period as Pence's—his 25 years with the DPD commencing in 1966. The bespectacled Denver native projected a studious appearance, his thick mop of chocolate brown hair always neatly parted to the side and trademark mustache immaculately trimmed. He was muscular—a physically imposing presence—but also loved to banter and crack jokes. Zavaras was part of a proud and successful Greek family. Two years before the bank massacre, his son Clint, a pitcher for the Seattle Mariners, made his big-league debut against future Hall of Famer Nolan Ryan.

By June 1991, Zavaras had four years under his belt as Chief of Police for the City and County of Denver—one of the few municipalities in America holding the double distinction. He wasn't the type of chief who was comfortable behind a big desk, always preferring to be out in the field, particularly at a new crime scene. Though the geography of his jurisdictional footprint was but a tiny fraction of Pence's—a mere 153 square miles—Chief Zavaras had 1,200 officers under his command providing protection to the county's half million residents.

Pence and Zavaras were actually together Father's Day morning—chasing their golf balls across the fairways and greens of Denver's Overland Golf Course. While chowing down on their lunch, each noticed his pager vibrating—their relaxing day off about to devolve into a hellish nightmare. They watched in shock and disbelief as one light-blue body bag after another was removed from the bank and loaded into a waiting hearse. Before day's end, both men would meet with the media in an effort to reassure the community that law and order would soon be restored.

Quoted in an article on the front page of the *Denver Post,* Pence said, "It's the most bizarre bank robbery I've experienced during my entire career"—which was saying a lot considering all he'd witnessed during his three decades with the FBI. "It appears that the four homicides were unnecessary," he added, labeling the crime "inhuman." Whoever was responsible was to be considered "incredibly dangerous and heavily armed. We're reminding officers and agents that the person has not been reluctant at all to take lives. This is not the traditional, ordinary bank robbery."

• • • •

Even though the modern internet and social media hadn't yet been born—cellphones dumb as a post and the size of bricks—news of the bloody massacre bombarded the local population from every direction in the days and weeks following Father's Day. Denver's local TV news stations—Channels 2, 4, 7, and 9—led their morning, noontime, afternoon, and evening news broadcasts with updates on who'd been killed, the victims' funerals, details about the robbery, interviews of demoralized bank executives, and tiny morsels the DPD and FBI considered appropriate to reveal. Day after day, news about the sensational crime was splashed across the pages of the *Post* and *Rocky Mountain News*—known locally as the *Rocky*—the two papers combining to publish nearly 50 articles on the subject in the second half of June. The deluge of information about the horrific crime was impossible for Denverites to avoid.

The anguish gripping the city was growing more palpable and desperate with each passing day. After all, a mass murderer was on the loose. Even Bob Pence was stoking that fear with his comments to the press. "We have to consider the possibility that he could do it again with very little provocation," he told a reporter for the *Post* five days after the massacre. "That's what is creating the need to do this expeditiously." On another occasion, seated beside Chief Zavaras at a news conference with TV cameras rolling, he said, "Nobody is more aware that there is a killer on the streets of Denver or elsewhere than we are." He assured citizens the task force was working tirelessly to follow up on every lead.

Between the incessant news stories and a $100,000 reward put up by United Banks, the FBI and DPD were swimming in "tips" called into their hotline—most of which were useless. Officers and agents fanned out to meet with anyone who could possibly shed light on the events of June 16. Several set up shop at the bank proper on Seventeenth and Lincoln to facilitate interviews with bank employees, some 50 of whom willingly took polygraph tests to help establish they hadn't been involved. Investigators spoke with past and present security guards, janitors, maintenance crews, delivery truck drivers, and the private security guards who worked for the bank's landlord.

"We're trying to account for as many people who could be conceivably involved with access [to the bank], then try to eliminate them as having any involvement in the crime," Pence explained to the *Post*. "We're trying to whittle down the large numbers of people that have to be accounted for so we can start to focus the investigation on possible suspects."

But the answers weren't coming fast enough for journalists or the public. On June 30, the *Post* ran a front-page story with the headline, *Bank Killer Still at Large as Trail Grows Cold*. The article declared, "The FBI and Denver police appear no closer to an arrest today than on the day of the holdup, one of the bloodiest in Colorado history. And some law enforcement experts now question whether the gunman will ever be caught." The newspaper quoted a "veteran federal lawman who requested anonymity" as saying, "It's beginning to look like they have a dry hole."

To SAC Pence, Chief Zavaras, and the dozens of agents and officers under their command, the constant drumbeat of the media continued to ratchet up the pressure to solve the crime, make an arrest, and set the community at ease. Everyone involved was all too aware that time was ticking. "It's a complex investigation that is going to require a lot of endurance, patience, and a certain amount of innovation and ingenuity," Pence defensively told the media. He and Zavaras vowed the case would be solved.

• • • •

Not long after Father's Day, a 36-year-old police officer named Jonathyn Priest—who'd been with the DPD for 11 years—emerged as the lead detective on the joint task force. Standing 6'3", Priest carried himself with a confident, charismatic swagger, his gravitas enhanced by movie-star good looks—his lush brown mane perfectly coiffed à la John Travolta. During his early days cutting his teeth in the patrol unit, his fellow officers had actually nicknamed Priest "Hollywood" shortly after he'd dyed his hair blond. Yet he was more than easy on the eyes. Priest was also whip smart, thoughtful, and articulate. A consummate professional. Precisely the type of leader the DPD was trying to mold.

But this was new territory for the young detective, who hadn't yet earned his sergeant stripes. He'd spent the majority of his career in the vice and narcotics bureau, only joining the homicide unit in 1989. Never before had he assisted in directing a bank robbery investigation.

Yet what he lacked in experience, Priest made up for in tenacity and grit, burning the candle at both ends for days on end. He was determined to learn every nook and cranny of the concourse levels of the bank complex and master the intricacies of the bank's surveillance and security systems. He even had a 3D scale model constructed so he and his colleagues could spitball theories and test them out.

Not having to face the media onslaught on a daily basis like Bob Pence and Ari Zavaras, Jon Priest was able to focus like a laser on actually solving the crime. Deep in his gut, he knew it was only a matter of time before he and his team followed the available clues straight to the killer.

9

INSIDE JOB

Within days of the joint task force first assembling, Detective Priest and his FBI and DPD colleagues had all but concluded that the brutal murders and armed robbery bore all the hallmarks of an inside job. Only someone intimately familiar with the bank's layout, procedures, and security systems, they reasoned, could possibly have pulled off the bloody massacre and heist—in 42 minutes no less—and vanished into thin air without a trace.

For starters, only bank employees—not many of them at that—would have known that enormous sums of unsecured currency floated around the cash vault on Sunday (but not Saturday) mornings. Indeed, many of the patrol officers who received the 10:53 a.m. simulcast urgently directing them to Seventeenth and Lincoln had chuckled at the notion someone would try to stick up a bank on a Sunday.

Moreover, the killer/thief's timing suggested he knew precisely when the armored cars from Loomis and Wells Fargo arrived and departed. He'd clearly designed his plan to ensure entry into the vault not only after the couriers had delivered their cash-stuffed bags, but also after they were long gone. Why? Because he likely knew that arriving while they were still there would have led to a gunfight, since the couriers were always locked and loaded. He'd also timed the stickup to occur well before the day's million-dollar haul was locked up in a safe. Priest and his team figured none of that had happened by accident.

Judging by his very first act that morning—posing as a vice president and seeking an escort by calling into the monitor room from the loading dock phone beside the freight elevator—the killer demonstrated knowledge no outsider could possibly have possessed. Whoever was making that call would have noticed a surveillance camera a short distance away aimed directly at him—surely a deterrent to any rational person intent on the violence about to be unleashed. A present or former guard, however, would have known that the camera was horribly out of focus, the dark, blurry images it delivered to the monitor room's security console virtually useless.

Calling into the monitor room to induce a guard to meet him at the freight elevator also implied the murderer had ridden the elevator in the same circumstance on prior occasions—either as a guard or as a bank executive. What happened next established pretty convincingly the man couldn't possibly have been an executive. The lower concourse hadn't been actively used in years. It was, however, one of the floors guards routinely patrolled. Further, the only way the killer could have obtained entry into the incinerator room—where he shot and killed Bill McCullom—was by using an MK1 key. A bank executive wouldn't have been able to pick an MK1 key out of a lineup.

Further buttressing the conclusion that the man who'd ridden the freight elevator with McCullom had to be a present or former guard was that the light switch to the incinerator room wasn't located anywhere near its entry door. Since the killer had fired six shots into McCullom's head and torso with sniper-like accuracy—in the far corner of the room—he'd obviously accomplished that feat with the lights on. A guard who'd been in that room before would have known where the light switch was and how to find it through the darkness.

That the murderer knew which stairs to climb to get to the concourse level and how to navigate the labyrinth of hallways and offices all the way to the monitor room—using McCullom's Markey card and MK1 key in all the right places—was compelling evidence he had abundant knowledge only some-one trained in bank security would have possessed. That he'd done all of that—and four murders too—in 12 minutes flat had to mean he knew the entire layout like the back of his hand. It seemed reasonably clear to Priest and his colleagues that the man they were trying to identify had traversed the exact same areas—clad in a guard uniform—dozens of times before.

His actions once inside the monitor room, after his ruth-less killing spree was finally over, pointed to that conclusion as well. How could anyone who hadn't been a guard have known which VHS tapes to steal and which one was harmless enough to leave behind? And which of the key rings contained MK1 keys? Who could possibly have known the significance of the handwritten scrawls in the guard logbook other than someone who'd jotted entries in that same journal himself? Could anyone who hadn't been a guard have known that a soda can wedged between the inner mantrap door and door jamb would render the outer door inoperable?

The perpetrator's frantic attempts—with both his gun and foot—to break into the supervisor's office seemed to be a dead giveaway all by itself. Anyone who'd worked as a guard during the prior two years would have known that a VCR in-side the supervisor's office recorded activity inside the moni-tor room. The worst possible evidence the killer could have left behind—had that VCR been in operation that morning—would have been a videotape capturing him in the act.

Moreover, it would have been nothing short of a miracle for someone lacking intimate familiarity with the cash vault to have located it in the first place, let alone to have made his way inside. The outermost door—which led into an employee locker room—was located next to Elevator #3. An outsider never would have known that particular door led into the cash vault as it bore no signs or markings whatsoever—utterly in-conspicuous by design. But the murdering bandit had clearly been aware of its significance.

Between the employee locker room and the vault itself was another mantrap—and a tricky one at that. The prior Sep-tember, the bank had installed an "in-out" card reader outside the outer door and another one inside the mantrap, beside the inner door. An authorized employee on his way in had to insert his Markey card in the outside reader and allow the door to close behind him before inserting his card into the inside reader. The slightest mistake would have resulted in him being locked inside the mantrap.

The thief who'd penetrated the cash vault and absconded with nearly $200,000 in loot had properly used Bill McCullom's keycard in both card readers on his way into the cash vault at 9:48 a.m. and again on his way out at 9:56 a.m. He obviously knew what he was doing.

Both his words and actions while inside the cash vault—during the robbery—further established he was an insider. He specifically chose the word "mantrap" to direct the tellers to a room from which he clearly knew they couldn't escape. He instructed David Barranco to fill his satchel with "strapped money," rather than "bait money" or "loose money."

Even his getaway pointed to his prior service as a guard. The elevator he used—Elevator #3, just beside the cash vault—was expressly reserved for the weekend guards. He was able to pick out that particular elevator key from among the more than dozen unmarked keys on McCullom's key ring.

Like a jigsaw puzzle whose pieces were finally falling into place, the clear image staring back at Detective Jon Priest as he considered his next steps was that of a United Bank security guard—past or present. But there was still a portion of the puzzle that couldn't be filled in, and a critically important one at that: the one revealing the face of the monster who'd mercilessly slaughtered four defenseless guards.

10

DO YOU SEE WHAT I SEE?

During the armed robber's eight-minute rampage through the cash vault, David Barranco, Maria Christian, David Twist, Kenetha Whisler, Chong Choe, and Nina McGinty had each studied his appearance as carefully as they could from their respective positions and angles—Barranco having had the best opportunity considering he was with the gunman the longest. By mid-afternoon that same day, all six tellers were at police headquarters describing to detectives what the man looked and sounded like, their statements memorialized for posterity on videotape.

What quickly became clear, however, was that the intruder's disguise had severely interfered with the tellers' ability to describe him—as opposed to his wardrobe and props—in any particular detail. Considering that his hat, sunglasses, mustache, and left-cheek band-aid covered the majority of his head, there was precious little the tellers were able to discern beyond the color of his skin, shape and color of his mustache, and length, color, and condition of his sideburns.

Barranco told the detectives the robber stood anywhere from 5'10" to 6', was of average build, somewhat husky, and was wearing a tweed or plaid hat with dark colors and a flat brim and dark mirrored sunglasses. He reported the man wearing a dark-colored plaid or herring-bone sport coat, black casual pants, and black shoes with a thick rubber sole. Barranco didn't believe he'd been wearing a tie.

The bandit's only exposed hair, he recalled, was cropped in a salt-and-pepper crew cut, the same color as his sideburns and mustache. He remembered seeing a bit of space between the man's nose and mustache whiskers, which he described as "shiny." He wasn't sure whether the stache was real or glued on. The adhesive on his left cheek, Barranco said, was just below his left eye. He told detectives the man had a very calm demeanor with a stern, deep voice and no accent. He distinctly recalled a bit of silver peeking through the chamber of his black revolver.

Maria Christian recalled the robber wearing a black "gangster-type" hat whose brim came down half an inch above his eyebrows. She described the hair protruding beneath his hat as salt-and-pepper with "some grays." The man's sideburns weren't very long, she said, and his mustache was also salt-and-pepper. She pegged him at 5'9" or 5'10", 185 to 190 pounds, and noted his face appeared "fat." Unlike Barranco, Christian distinctly remembered him wearing a multi-colored, striped tie. As for his voice, she described it being soft, monotone, and calm.

David Twist recalled the gunman being about 6' tall, 180 to 200 pounds, heavy set with a pudgy stomach and rounded face, and somewhere between 45 and 50 years of age. To him, the man's exposed hair and mustache appeared gray. He told the detectives the intruder's hat had been dark gray, Bogart-style, and completely covered his forehead. Like Christian, Twist recalled the man wearing a tie, though he couldn't recall the color. He described his facial complexion as "clear" and noted the band-aid on his left cheek had been placed below his cheekbone, parallel to his nose.

Kenetha Whisler's description departed significantly from her fellow tellers. She remembered the thief being as tall as 6'2" and as heavy as 250 pounds and believed he was younger, perhaps in his late 30s or early 40s. She told the detectives the man had worn a derby-style black hat with black sunglasses that had a piece of tape on the nose bridge. She described his mustache as being salt-and-pepper, perfectly groomed, and thick. It looked so perfect, Whisler said, "it could have been fake." She too recalled the robber wearing a tie, though couldn't provide any description. Like Christian, she recalled the man's voice being very calm. What she remembered most about his gun was a silver pin sticking out from under the barrel.

Chong Choe confided in the detectives that her ability to describe the gunman in any detail was limited because, as a Korean woman, Caucasian people all looked pretty similar to her. She recalled the man speaking in a soft, calm voice and that he'd been wearing an English-style hat with black sunglasses and had a mustache. Though she initially pegged his height at about 5'8", she also described him as being nearly as tall as Barranco, who stood 6'2". Unlike Christian, Twist, and Whisler, Choe didn't believe he'd been wearing a tie.

From her hideout in her booth, Nina McGinty had been able to focus on the intruder more intently than her fellow tellers. But she'd only been able to see him from waist up, and just his left side. Her recollection of the man's hat was different from the others. To her, it appeared dark brown with a beaded, multicolored band encircling it and a yellow feather sticking out of the band.

McGinty reported the man's sideburns as being very thin, well-manicured, salt-and-pepper or silver, and extending all the way down to his earlobes. She felt certain he'd been wearing a tie, which she described as black and blue with a diagonal, narrow, maroon stripe. She estimated his age as between 40 and 50 and his height as 6'2". His demeanor, she said, had been calm, though he'd spoken to the tellers in a "very, very authoritative" voice.

• • • •

At just 26 years of age, John Kirk had a babyface so soft and round, it seemed years away from sprouting its first whiskers. Despite his youthful appearance, he had a gun strapped to his hip and an official-looking badge identifying him as a special agent with the FBI, a position he'd held for all of eight months.

On Thursday, June 20, the rookie agent was seated in one of the bank's conference rooms for what would turn out to be one of the most consequential events in the four-day-old investigation. Just outside the conference room, five of the six tellers made small talk as they awaited their turn to meet with Kirk. The only eyewitness who wasn't present was Nina McGinty, who was still far too traumatized to be anywhere near Seventeenth and Lincoln.

Resting on the table in front of Agent Kirk were two three-ring binders. The red-colored binder was filled with 15 three-hole-punched pages containing headshots of current United Bank guards, one per page, numbered 1 through 15. The 35 pages in the blue-colored binder, numbered 1 through 35, each contained a photo of a guard who'd recently worked for the bank, but no longer did. All of the photos were black-and-white, the quality of most pretty poor. The notebooks had been assembled by a couple of clerks in the FBI's Denver field office, who'd been provided DMV pictures on microfiche for some of the guards and headshots from the bank's files for the remainder.

By this point in the investigation, there was unanimity within the joint FBI-DPD task force that the man they were looking for was a present or recent guard. That conclusion narrowed the universe of potential suspects to the 50 photographs in the two notebooks. Detective Priest and his colleagues felt confident that one or more of the eyewitnesses would fixate on the image of the thief who'd robbed them at gunpoint like a Bloodhound alerting on the scent of human remains.

Yet what was being requested of the tellers who were about to join Agent Kirk in the conference room bordered on the impossible. After all, the intruder they'd seen in the cash vault had been heavily disguised—his hair and the shape of his head concealed by a hat, his eyes and top portion of his face hidden by sunglasses, and his left cheek covered with a band-aid. Whether his mustache was even real, or part of his disguise, was anyone's guess. They were now being asked to match the few facial features they'd been able to discern— hopefully still fresh in their memories four days later—with those displayed in 50 different images of uncertain age and dubious quality.

Agent Kirk summoned Kenetha Whisler into the room first. After studying each photo as carefully as she could—those of female and elderly guards requiring little of her attention—she found herself unable to make a positive identification. She told the agent that the mustache of the man depicted in Photo 1 in red book appeared identical to the robber's, but that his facial features weren't correct. The cheeks of the man in Photo 8 were correct, she said, but the mouth wasn't right.

Frustrated she couldn't be more helpful, Whisler asked the special agent whether she could draw a hat and sunglasses on the photos so they'd more closely resemble what she recalled from the robbery. Kirk told her she couldn't. He thanked her for her time and effort and politely escorted her to the door.

Barranco entered the conference room hopeful he'd be able to isolate the image most closely resembling the gunman's features, well aware of what was riding on him making a positive identification. Like Whisler, he noted that the face in Photo 8 in the red binder was similar to the robber's, but told Kirk that the pictured man's hair and mustache didn't match the gunman's. Barranco's gaze also lingered on the face displayed in Photo 16 in the blue binder. "This one has very similar features," he finally said. "The mustache and hair look close, but the robber's face was a little fuller." Like Whisler, he departed the conference room dejected, unable to make a firm identification.

Maria Christian came in next, hoping to flip to a photograph of someone with a fat face and dark hair with some gray in it—just as she recalled the bandit. Yet she too couldn't convince herself that any of the 50 images matched her recollection. She did, however, pause on Photos 10 and 17 in the blue book, telling the rookie agent the man pictured in each had similar features to the thief. Like Whisler and Barranco, she also made note of Photo 8 in the red book, commenting to Kirk that the face and mustache were similar to the gunman's, but that the mustache in the image was too thick.

David Twist was invited into the conference room next.

Although he wasn't able to make a positive identification, like Christian, he spent considerable time analyzing Photo 17 in the blue binder. "This one is similar to the face I saw in the vault," he said. "Especially the mustache and rounded face."

Last to enter the room, Chong Choe confessed to Kirk how all 50 images looked pretty much the same to her and apologized for not being more helpful. The rookie agent excused her, frustrated the hours-long process had proven an exercise in futility.

Six days later, he met with Nina McGinty at her apartment. She too was unable to pinpoint a picture that corresponded with her mental image of the robber. She also lingered on Photo 8 in the red book—the fourth eyewitness to do so—telling Agent Kirk the face and nose were similar to the gunman's, but that the neck was too bulky. She found some similarities in the nose and cheeks in Photo 29 in the blue book, but not the pictured man's other features. And though Photo 34 in the blue book reminded her of the robber, she had difficulty articulating why.

•••

John Gedney had a babyface that rivaled Agent Kirk's. The redheaded special agent had just passed his one-year anniversary with the FBI. On June 21, he met with David Barranco and Kenetha Whisler, the two tellers who'd informed Agent Kirk they had vivid recollections of the gun the bandit had pointed at them. Gedney placed four different black revolvers on a conference-room table, three Smith & Wessons and a Colt .38. He summoned Whisler into the room first.

When Whisler's eyes settled on the Colt .38, she had a visceral reaction. "That's the one," she told Gedney, her hand shaking as she pointed at it. The frightening memory of the robbery came flooding back as she stared at the weapon. She couldn't get out of the room fast enough. When Barranco's turn came, though he didn't have the same instinctive response as Whisler, he also selected the Colt .38 as the gun most closely resembling the weapon the robber had pointed at him while he was loading the black satchel with cash.

••••

George Noble was old enough to be John Kirk's and John Gedney's grandfather. The silver-haired special agent's duty station was at FBI headquarters in Washington, D.C., where he specialized in graphic arts. During his 30 years with the Bureau, his main role had been to listen to eyewitness descriptions of criminals and sketch out composite drawings to match their recollections. His forensic artwork often proved vital in paving the way for the arrest of a criminal suspect.

After Agent Kirk's meetings with the six tellers had concluded in abject failure, the FBI-DPD brain trust decided to fly Noble to Denver to try his hand at a composite drawing. Noble had been through the same drill hundreds of times before, always preferring to remain ignorant of any prior eyewitness accounts, artist renditions, or photos of potential suspects. He relied on a catalog called an Identi-Kit, which allowed eyewitnesses to select from numerous shapes, sizes, and iterations of facial features, such as hair, eyebrows, eyes, ears, noses, chins, mustaches, and beards—like a child playing the game Mr. Potato Head.

Summoned to meet with Noble first, David Barranco spent more than four hours making selections from the Identi-Kit and commenting on the artist's composite drawing as it was coming into focus. Noble made every change Barranco requested until the lanky vault manager appeared satisfied he'd captured the essence of the bandit's face. At that point, Kenetha Whisler and Maria Christian were invited into the conference room to offer their suggestions, resulting in the forensic artist making slight adjustments until all three tellers agreed the face staring back at them was that of the disguised gunman.

The completed composite drawing depicted a middle-aged man with a rounded face and chin and a perfectly manicured salt-and-pepper mustache that curled downward on both sides—like an upside-down canoe. Noble had drawn a tweed, fedora-style hat with a narrow brim covering the subject's entire forehead. Large, dark sunglasses concealed the pictured man's eyes and eyebrows. The little bit of hair he'd drawn in beneath the hat was salt-and-pepper, with sideburns running down to the subject's earlobes. For some reason, the sketch didn't include a band-aid on the subject's left cheek.

The special agent from D.C. next paid a visit to Nina McGinty's apartment. McGinty found the drawing a "remarkable likeness" of the man who had her cowering in fear under the counter. Chong Choe had the same reaction. Before flying back home on July 1, Noble had David Twist provide his impressions. Twist requested minor alterations to make the subject's face a little fuller and to add a necktie to the shirt collar.

After those changes were made, the finished product made its way to the desk of Jon Priest. The lead detective had been eagerly awaiting the big reveal since Noble's plane touched down at Stapleton Airport four days earlier.

As he examined the forensic artist's handiwork, however, it quickly became apparent that Noble's and the tellers' efforts had amounted to a colossal waste of time. Flipping through the pictures in the red and blue binders — the composite drawing resting by their side for comparison — the detective shook his head dejectedly. *This drawing doesn't help in the slightest,* he thought. Indeed, the likeness Noble had captured didn't reveal sufficient information about the robber's face to make a reliable comparison to any of the images in the two books.

Rather, all the sketch accomplished was to underscore how heavily disguised the killer had been. Flying a highly skilled FBI artist clear across the country hadn't altered that reality one iota. Priest and his colleagues were no closer to identifying the culprit — not by facial appearance, anyway — than they'd been the moment first responders had arrived at the bank Father's Day morning. Fifteen grueling days following the savage mayhem — with the media and public clamoring for an arrest — that realization was a bitter pill to swallow.

PART TWO

ZEROING IN

11

FIRST SUSPECT

By Father's Day afternoon, the three employees most responsible for weekend security at the downtown bank had gathered with detectives to share their insights and brainstorm potential suspects. Tom Tatalaski served as the manager in charge of security operations and Jim Prado and Neil Tubbs were the weekend guards' direct supervisors.

Prado was deeply shaken by the news of what transpired that morning. While training Todd Wilson the prior week, the college student had asked what would happen if someone confronted him. "I'm not a very good fighter," he'd confessed at the time.

Prado looked him square in the eyes. "We go home," he'd said reassuringly. "There's nothing wrong with running away." He next worked with Wilson that Friday evening. But the Metro State College student *didn't* go home on Sunday, instead leaving the bank in a body bag.

Scott McCarthy was weighing on Prado just as heavily. While working with Wilson in the monitor room Friday evening, the 21-year-old had called his best friend to find out if his paperwork had gone through—so he could start his training. When McCarthy answered in the negative, Wilson handed the receiver to Prado.

"Can I come in with Todd tomorrow just to start learning the layout?" McCarthy pleaded with him.

"Well, we probably won't be able to pay you since you're not technically on the payroll," Prado said. But he told McCarthy to come in on Sunday morning, since that's when a new pay period began; they could make his pay retroactive once his paperwork was completed. "You can shadow Todd while he's making his rounds," Prado said before handing the receiver back to Wilson. He made sure McCarthy had a Markey card waiting for him when he arrived on Sunday morning. *If only I'd waited,* he lamented.

The DPD detectives seated across from Prado, Tatalaski, and Tubbs shared the initial description the cash vault tellers had given of the disguised gunman: about 6' tall, thick build, salt-and-pepper hair, and a bushy mustache of the same hue.

An image instantly flickered across Prado's mind. "That sounds an awful lot like Mike McKown," he said. McKown had been one of his most reliable weekend guards, his tenure spanning from February 1988 until June 1990. During that stretch, McKown had trained more than 30 of his fellow guards due to the incredibly high turnover in the low-paying position. Though he'd been permitted to carry a weapon while on duty—and owned a .357 Smith & Wesson and 9-millimeter Luger—Prado told the detectives McKown had chosen not to.

"The guy was in the Air Force and did two tours in Vietnam," he said. "I remember him saying he was dropped into enemy territory and had to assassinate some bigwig Commie. So he's apparently killed before." Prado added that after leaving United Bank, McKown had worked as an armored courier for Wells Fargo, noting that he'd seen both sides of the bank's vault operation.

Tubbs chimed in. "I agree with Jim. That description sounds just like Mike. It wasn't much of a secret that he dyed his hair black. But it actually was salt-and pepper. He also grew his mustache out real thick and bushy." McKown's height and weight also matched that of the gun-toting bandit—6'1" and 190 pounds.

Tatalaski concurred. "My gut says either him or Paul Yocum, who's far more deranged. But Mike's the one who fits that description."

"Is he still in town?" one of the detectives asked.

"Actually, he's not," Prado said. "I think he relocated to the Seattle area a few months ago. Said something about moving in with his sister."

••••

Special Agents David Sousa and Daniel Boyd worked out of the FBI's Seattle field office. The tandem drew the assignment of meeting with 43-year-old Mike McKown at his workplace on Monday, June 17, the day following the bloody massacre. Since Seattle was located a good 1,300 miles from Denver, the agents' primary task was to confirm McKown had been in the Emerald City—not the Mile High City—on Father's Day.

McKown informed Sousa and Boyd he'd learned of the murders and robbery from his ex-wife—who still lived in Denver with their two daughters. She'd called him shortly after seeing the horrific news on TV. Less than 24 hours later, McKown had already developed his own theory. He felt certain the crime had been an inside job, he said, as only someone with intimate knowledge of the bank's layout and security system could have pulled it off. He told the agents that, during their downtime, guards would frequently "war-game" how to rob the bank, speculating the killer had likely followed the same steps they'd war-gamed on numerous occasions.

McKown mentioned a former guard named Bob Hoffman, who worked at the bank in 1989. "Bob would give these elaborate details about how to rob the bank—even killing the guards if necessary. He talked about it all the time. I'd definitely take a look at him."

"Do you keep up with him or know where he lives?" Sousa asked.

"I don't," McKown said. "The only one I still keep up with is Jim King. We worked together a bunch and he became a good friend. He quit not long after I did—for exactly the same reason. We both felt the security there was dreadful, which made it a dangerous place to work. Unlike me, Jim always carried a gun." As requested, McKown provided the agents King's address: 665 Juniper Street in Golden. "I just visited with him a couple of weeks ago when I was in town for my daughter's graduation."

When the agents provided McKown the cash vault tellers' description of the gunman, he chuckled. "That sounds exactly like me."

"Was it you?" Boyd asked, the deadly serious question sucking the levity out of the room.

"That would be physically impossible," McKown replied. "I was in the Seattle area all day."

"Where were you Saturday night?" Sousa asked.

"I went to see *Robin Hood* at the Sea-Tac Mall. Got home about ten o'clock, spoke with my sister, and went to sleep."

"What about yesterday morning?"

"I slept in until about noon," McKown sheepishly admitted. "I hung out with my sister and my nieces after that and waited all day for my daughters to finally call me for Father's Day. You can talk to my sister or check the phone records if you want. I'm not the guy you're looking for."

Convinced he was right, Sousa and Boyd thanked McKown for his time and left.

• • • •

While that interview was occurring in Seattle, Jon Priest was at his desk putting the finishing touches on a photo lineup. Although all six men depicted in the black-and-white array had mustaches, only one bore any affiliation with United Bank of Denver: Mike McKown, who was pictured in the fourth position—the first photo in the second row. When the "six-pack" was ready for prime time, Priest had it delivered to the bank, where an FBI agent was meeting with Maria Christian, David Twist, and Chong Choe. It would be another three days before they'd get a chance to look through the binders of present and former guards.

Christian, Twist, and Choe were shown the McKown lineup individually, each studying the images displayed carefully. All three told the FBI agent the photos—including McKown's—weren't consistent with their recollection of the armed robber.

Priest wondered whether David Barranco—who'd seen the gunman's face the longest—would have a different reaction. He personally drove out to the vault manager's home and dropped the six-pack on his dining room table. Though Barranco desperately wanted to pick out the robber, he didn't recognize any of the six faces. Nor did Nina McGinty when one of Priest's colleagues had her examine the lineup in her living room.

With a solid alibi four states away and a shutout with the photo array, Priest felt confident he could cross Mike McKown off the list of suspects. Nevertheless, 36 hours into the investigation, that list was continuing to grow.

12

CARNAGE

While DPD officers and Yankee 91 investigators scoured the crime scenes at the bank, a pair of medical examiners at the Denver General Hospital morgue—Drs. K. Alan Stormo and Thomas Henry—were analyzing the most important evidence the murdering bandit hadn't been able to abscond with: the corpses of the four slain guards. Both doctors had decades of experience in the field of forensic pathology, choosing to spend their workdays up close and personal with deceased patients in morgues rather than live ones in examining rooms.

Each bullet-ridden body was stripped of its bloody attire and splayed on a steel table. Dr. Stormo drew the assignment of performing Bill McCullom's and Scott McCarthy's autopsies. He discovered that McCullom had been shot four times in the head and twice in the back, concluding that two of the bullets had caused sufficient internal damage to result in his immediate death. The lethal shot to his head had penetrated just above where the top of his right ear attached to his face. That bullet had pierced his skull and plunged into his brain, tunneling from one side clear across to the other before running out of momentum. Dr. Stormo removed the slug with his forceps, setting it aside for subsequent analysis.

Another bullet had penetrated McCullom's face from the opposite direction, entering just above his left eye on a downward trajectory, shattering his orbital bone, then plowing into the flesh beside his left nostril. That projectile was recovered from the mucous membrane near his mouth. The victim's scalp revealed graze wounds where two additional bullets had channeled across his head from front to back. Dr. Stormo extracted a bullet fragment embedded at the rear of one of the channels. Based on his examination, the pathologist concluded McCullom had been facing the shooter when each of those four bullets had been fired.

The two shots to the 33-year-old bachelor's back, by contrast, had occurred when he'd been facing away from the shooter. Both entry wounds were located on the left side of his mid-back, inches apart. The bullet Dr. Stormo considered fatal had fractured a rib, passed into the decedent's left lung, sliced through the upper two chambers of his heart, entered his right lung, broke another rib, and lodged in the muscles over his right chest wall. The second bullet had also advanced through a rib before burrowing into his spine. Dr. Stormo dug both bullets out of McCullom's body and set them beside the three he'd recovered from his head before moving on to the next cadaver.

Scott McCarthy had been a bit more fortunate, suffering only two gunshots, both to the head. The first bullet had grazed across his right palm, near his thumb, before entering the front left side of his neck. That projectile had traveled in an upward trajectory, penetrating his spine just below the base of his skull—obliterating his spinal cord—exiting his body through the muscles of the right side of his neck. In Dr. Stormo's opinion, that shot had been fatal.

The second bullet had entered the 21-year-old newlywed's right cheek, just under his eye, shattering the mastoid bone behind his right ear, ending up embedded in its bony mass. That was the only slug Dr. Stormo extracted from the second cadaver. Judging by the orientation of the entry wounds and the graze wound to the victim's palm, the pathologist surmised that McCarthy had turned to face his killer—trying to protect his face with his right hand—just before he'd been shot.

Dr. Henry, the chief medical examiner, handled the autopsies of Phil Mankoff and Todd Wilson. He concluded that Mankoff's right hand had been behind his head when the killer fired his first shot. The bullet entered his palm near the base of his pinky, exited below his right thumb, and then plowed into the rear of his head—tunneling through nearly the entirety of his brain, in an upward trajectory, before lodging above his right eye. That bullet was found in two separate pieces—its copper jacket and lead core. With his forceps, Dr. Henry carefully removed each fragment. In his opinion, that blast to the head had been one of two fatal shots.

The second had penetrated the 41-year-old father's back, near his right armpit. That bullet had sliced through his liver, diaphragm, right lung, and heart before coming to rest on the left side of his chest, just beneath the skin. A third bullet, not fatal in Dr. Henry's opinion, had entered near the midline of the victim's lower back and burrowed into one of the lower vertebrae in his spinal column. The chief medical examiner removed both fully intact slugs, carving his initials in each before moving on to the final cadaver.

Like Bill McCullom, Todd Wilson had been shot with six separate bullets—three in the head and three in the back. Dr. Henry couldn't tell which flurry had occurred first.

Starting with the decedent's head, he found two entry wounds located side-by-side—an inch or so apart—between his left ear and cheekbone. Both had been fired in an upward trajectory, each exploding through the entirety of the decedent's brain from left to right before exiting through the same hole at the top right of his head. Either of those bullets would have caused Wilson's instant death. Dr. Henry also found a superficial graze wound that scraped across the right side of his scalp, from rear to front, piercing and exiting through the top of his ear.

The three bullets fired into the 21-year-old's back had caused even greater destruction. One had entered near his right armpit on a downward angle, ripping through his right lung, diaphragm, and liver before exiting through his right chest wall. Another had entered near the midline of his back, mid-spine, cutting through his spinal column like a knife before penetrating his left lung, diaphragm, and stomach. That projectile exited Wilson's body just above his left rib margin.

Somewhat miraculously, Dr. Henry found that slug in the left shirt pocket of his bloody guard uniform.

The sixth and final bullet wreaked havoc on several internal organs. It too entered through the mid-back, just right of the midline, sawing though Wilson's spine before shredding his pancreas, small bowel, colon, and stomach. Dr. Henry dislodged that projectile from the small tissue by the left rib cage. He also noted scrapes on the victim's left and right forearms, a bruise on the knuckle of his right index finger, and a small scrape over the front of his left leg—all of which had been caused when he tumbled to the floor after absorbing the rapid-fire shots to his head and back. By that point, however, the Metro State College student was already dead.

Between them, Drs. Stormo and Henry had conducted several thousand autopsies as of Father's Day 1991. Analyzing cadavers had become as routine and monotonous as brushing their teeth. Yet there was nothing routine or monotonous about their work in the hospital morgue on this particular occasion. Each would need a stiff drink—perhaps two or three—before closing his eyes for the evening.

13

BULLISH ON BULLETS

A specialist in firearms and ballistics, Detective Frank Kerber had worked in the DPD's crime lab for the past eight years and as a cop for nearly 20. His primary role in the investigation was to analyze the bullets recovered from the autopsies and monitor room and to determine, as best he could, what type of gun had fired them.

Kerber concluded that each bullet was .38 caliber and bore markings demonstrating a "left twist," meaning they'd rotated in a counterclockwise direction as they exploded through the barrel of the gun. Each was consistent with having been shot by an old-fashioned revolver—a six-shooter—rather than a semi-automatic weapon like a Glock. Only a handful of revolvers were capable of firing .38-caliber bullets with a left twist, among them a Colt model like the one David Barranco and Kenetha Whisler had picked out of a four-gun lineup on June 21. Kerber was convinced that the same gun, most likely a Colt, had fired each of the bullets he examined.

His conclusion that the killer's weapon of choice was a revolver solved the mystery of why no shell casings had been found. Revolvers don't expend spent shell casings as the gun is fired, like semi-automatic weapons do. Instead, the casings remain in the cylinder as it rotates to ready the next bullet for discharge.

Once all six bullets are fired, the spent shell casings are

removed manually by opening the cylinder—with the barrel pointed upwards—and pushing down on an ejector rod. That forces the six "empties" to drop from the cylinder in unison—typically into the shooter's hand. Fresh bullet cartridges can then be inserted with a small, circular device called a "speed loader." The speed loader's six slots line up with those in the cylinder to allow the new bullets to be loaded in one fell swoop, rather than one at a time.

Detective Kerber's most significant finding related to the ammunition the killer had used. He determined that the assassin had fired three different types of bullets, most of them having concave, hollow tips—"hollow-point" bullets—rather than solid, pointy tips known as "round-nose." Behind the hollow-point tip is a soft lead core wrapped in a copper jacket, rendering the bullet as a whole "semi-jacketed."

The cavity on the forward end of a semi-jacketed hollow-point causes the projectile to expand rapidly upon impact. The design is intended to increase the bullet's stopping power, making it more effective for self-defense than round-nose bullets. In addition, most of the bullets Kerber inspected were designated as either +P or +P+, meaning extra gunpowder had been loaded inside the cartridge to create significant pressure, producing higher velocity and energy than a standard bullet.

The specimens recovered from McCullom's corpse were Remington-Peters, 110-grain semi-jacketed hollow-point +P. Though Mankoff and McCarthy had also been shot with 110-grain semi-jacketed hollow-points, the ballistics expert concluded they'd been manufactured by either Winchester-Western or Federal. More significantly, there was a crucial distinction between those bullets and the ones pulled out of McCullom's body: their designation was +P+, not +P. Why was that important? Because unlike +P bullets, which were widely available to the public, +P+ bullets were specially manufactured for a distinct group of people: law enforcement officers.

The two bullets recovered from Todd Wilson's bloody corpse—including the one found in his shirt pocket—were of a different composition altogether. In his report, Kerber classified them as Winchester-Western 158-grain lead Lubaloy, with a copper "wash" rather than a jacket. They bore round noses solid to the tip rather than hollow points and weren't highly pressurized +P or +P+.

The detective was also supplied the shirts of the four slain guards to examine them for evidence of gunpowder residue. Each tested negative, leading Kerber to conclude none of the victims had been shot from close range.

•   •   •   •

The discovery that the slugs plucked out of Mankoff's and McCarthy's bodies—and the one found in the doorway to the battery room—were +P+ bullets specifically manufactured for police departments sent a shiver down Frank Kerber's spine. *Could the killer have been a police officer?* he asked himself, shuddering at the thought.

There was something else that left the detective scratching his head. The base of the hollow-point bullets removed from Bill McCullom's corpse had the shape of a ring. He had a vague memory of seeing ammo like that before, but not for quite some time. Kerber acquired a handful of bullets the DPD had issued in the mid-1970s from a couple of older cops and studied them closely. Bingo! They too had the exact same ring shape at the base.

As Jon Priest pored over his fellow detective's written report, his heart began to race. Who carried Colt-model revolvers? A large swath of his colleagues with the DPD, both past and present. What was issued to every cop who carried a revolver? Two speed loaders and a total of 18 bullets—six to fill the cylinder and 12 to fill each slot in the speed loaders. Officers had to requalify at the firing range every summer. After they did, they'd receive precisely 18 rounds of the department's newest ammunition.

Quickly doing the math on the entry wounds revealed by the autopsies, plus the additional shot fired into the doorknob of the guard supervisor's office, the lead detective arrived at the total number of shots the perpetrator had fired: 18. A perfect match. Not only that, the three varieties of bullets Kerber identified were all consistent with ammo issued to DPD officers since the 1970s—most notably, those classified as +P+. Priest shook his head, his stomach suddenly queasy. *Is one of our own the murdering bandit?*

14

GETAWAY CAR?

By June 1991, Denver's Stapleton International Airport was bursting at the seams. The circa-1929 facility, situated more than a mile above sea level, served as a hub for both Continental and United, gates for every major airline except Southwest dotting its four terminals.

Just three miles east of downtown, the aging complex had proven far too cramped to accommodate the demands of modern air travel to the wildly popular mountain destination. Plans to build a new airport had been in the works since the early 1980s. With the federal government agreeing to kick in $500 million, ground was broken in September 1989 on what would eventually become Denver International Airport, located 23 miles northeast of downtown. The first flight wouldn't land at the $4.8 billion facility—second largest on the planet—for another five-and-a-half years.

Father's Day 1991 wasn't particularly busy at Stapleton, just a normal, lazy Sunday before the workweek cranked up. Lloyd Quintana had been working at the ground transportation center, stationed between two sets of baggage carousels, since early that morning. His job was to field questions and assist confused travelers, pointing them to where they needed to go. At about 12:30 p.m., he was approached by a well-dressed man he thought to be in his early 50s. When questioned by a police detective and FBI agent two days later, Quintana estimated the traveler's height at somewhere between 6' and 6'1".

Because the man wasn't wearing a hat or glasses, Quintana was able to glimpse his hair and facial features. He observed salt-and-pepper hair and a thick gray mustache with a reddish tint. He distinctly recalled a strawberry birthmark or cancer scar on the left side of the man's face and a significant overbite as he spoke. Quintana noticed him clutching a twin-handled, light-brown leather bag.

"I need to rent a car," the gentleman told him. "I've got $100,000 on me, so money is no object." Based on his comment, Quintana assumed the leather bag was stuffed full of cash. Though he found the man's request and behavior most odd, it didn't dawn on him that the traveler might be a bank robber attempting a getaway. Indeed, news of the downtown massacre wouldn't break for several more hours, Quintana first learning about the bloodshed the following day.

Seeking to be as helpful as he could, he walked the gentleman over to the counter of National Car Rental. On their way, the man told him he'd already met with a Superior Rental Car agent, who refused to rent him a vehicle because of his plans to travel out of state.

"Well, they should be able to help you at National," Quintana said, politely excusing himself as the gentleman walked up to the counter.

"May I help you?" agent Phyllis Martinez asked. She would later describe the traveler's appearance a bit differently from Quintana. She recalled him being in his 40s or 50s, standing about 6'2" or 6'3" with grayish hair on a balding head, a reddish sunburned face, and one of his eyes off to the side, unable to focus.

"I need to rent a car with cash," he said. "I have over $6,000 with me."

"I'm so sorry, sir," Martinez replied. "But it's our policy, on weekends, to require a major credit card. I can't rent out a vehicle for cash." She never got so far as to ask him for his driver's license. When she learned of the United Bank murders later that day, Martinez made no connection to her encounter with the strange man.

Frustrated but undaunted, the traveler slid down the counter to an Avis agent named Doug Peterson. "Will you take cash instead of a credit card?" he asked.

"Yes, sir," Peterson answered.

The man's body language softened with the affirmative response. "I've got more than $1,000 on me," he said. "Cash won't be a problem."

Peterson would later tell a DPD detective the gentleman was wearing a tan or brown sport coat, dress pants, and light colored shirt with no tie. He estimated his age at 40 to 45, his height at either 6'1" or 6'2", and his weight at 200 pounds. Peterson described medium-length gray hair and a salt-and-pepper mustache and also recalled the man carrying a black or brown briefcase. He found the traveler calm and composed, not in any particular rush.

"In order to rent a vehicle for cash," the Avis agent told him, "I'll need to see your airline ticket and a valid driver's license."

"Oh," the gentleman said, disappointment washing over his face. "That's not going to work. Could you possibly rent me a car in Los Angeles instead? That's where I'm heading."

"I'm sorry, sir," Peterson said. "Maybe one of the other companies can do that."

The traveler picked up his bag and trudged further down the rental-car aisle. A few minutes later, he reappeared at the transportation center, explaining to Lloyd Quintana that he'd struck out with both National and Avis.

Quintana scrunched his face as he pondered how he could help. "Let's give USA a try," he finally said. He escorted the man to USA Rent A Car, where agent Scheree Parrish was typing on a computer terminal behind the counter. She shifted her gaze to the two men.

"Scheree, this nice fella has been trying to rent a car for quite some time and hasn't had any luck," Quintana said. "Do you think you can help him?" It was now a little after 1:00 p.m.

"I'll certainly try," Parrish said, offering a friendly smile. Interviewed four days later, she described the traveler as a well-built man in his early 50s, about 6' tall, 160 to 170 pounds, with short salt-and-pepper hair and a similar-colored mustache, and wearing a coat and tie.

"He wants to rent a car with cash," Quintana said. "Can USA do that?"

Parrish shook her head, conveying an empathetic expression. "Actually, no, we can't. We require a major credit card during the weekend. I'm so sorry."

The mysterious traveler thanked Quintana for his efforts and walked away. Exactly where he went, no one seemed to know.

• • • •

Jon Priest sat at his desk, poring over the reports of his colleagues' interviews of Quintana, Martinez, Peterson, and Parrish. *How bizarre,* he thought. Their descriptions were eerily similar to how the cash vault tellers described the well-dressed man who'd robbed them at gunpoint and absconded with nearly $200,000 in loot. *This guy was even bragging about how much cash he had!*

But as he reflected more deeply, a conflicting thought emerged that left him puzzled. *Why would the bank robber have needed to rent a car?* Priest distinctly recalled observing the contents of the trash bin beside Elevator #3 on the seventh floor of the bank's parking garage—and the pair of latex gloves an investigator had plucked from the pile. There was unanimity among his DPD and FBI colleagues that the murdering thief had ridden the elevator to the seventh floor to make his escape—in a car he'd presumably parked there earlier that morning. *Why on earth would he need to rent a second car two-and-a-half hours later?* That didn't make any sense.

Priest flung the pieces of paper across his desk and leaned back in his chair. As the number of questions continued to mount, not a single answer was coming into focus.

But that was about to change.

15

SUSPECT NUMBER TWO

Like most inner cities, Denver suffered from its fair share of drug-related crime. In an effort to combat the problem, a neighborhood drug-watch program had sprung up—the Unsinkables—which focused on the downtown area. Jodine Lang served as the program's co-chair. She was up early on Father's Day morning, keeping an eye out through her open living-room window.

At about 8:45 a.m., Lang noticed a middle-aged man crossing the street and walking toward her Pearl Street apartment building near the corner of Thirteenth Avenue. She'd seen him in the neighborhood before, but didn't know him personally. The man was wearing an off-white dress shirt and dark-colored pants and dress shoes. A dark suit jacket was draped over his left arm. When Lang hollered for her husband to get out of the bathtub—because they were going to be late for a Father's Day visit with her dad—the man on the street looked up at her and waved.

That's when Lang got a really good look. The gentleman wasn't wearing a hat and had short dark hair that was graying at the temples and curly around the ears and shirt collar. Dark-colored sunglasses shielded his eyes and a five-o'clock shadow covered his face. The man's right hand was clutching the twin handles of a small, dark nylon duffel bag, its shoulder strap left to dangle near the sidewalk. He was also carrying an umbrella.

At about 9:00 a.m., Lang headed over to the 7-Eleven adjacent to her building, at the corner of Thirteenth and Pearl, where she encountered the man again as he waited to cross the street—still heading in the direction of downtown. By the time she departed the convenience store, he was gone.

When news of the bank massacre broke, Lang didn't make any connection to the man she'd observed that morning. But after more than a week of the crime going unsolved, her observations had begun to gnaw at her. She decided to call the DPD. By the time a police detective and FBI agent were seated in her living room on June 27, the joint task force was well aware of the man's identity and possible connection to the crime, not to mention the theft of United Bank of Denver he'd been tried for the prior August. Indeed, they'd already met with Paul Yocum at his Pearl Street apartment on several occasions.

• • • •

Now 50 years of age, Paul Tillman Yocum, a lifelong bachelor, had led a troubled life. At just ten years of age, he and his family had been attending an air show at the Flagler Harvest Festival when a plane suddenly fell from the sky and crashed, remnants of its fuselage and wings ricocheting in every direction, killing 19 people. Both he and his seven-year-old sister had been struck with debris, which instantly claimed his sister's life. By a stroke of luck, he'd survived the catastrophe with only mild brain damage and a slight speech impediment.

Yocum's father worked for the First National Bank of Flagler his entire adult life, retiring as a senior executive after a 51-year career. He and his wife did their best to raise their son, which became considerably more difficult following the airshow tragedy.

As an adult, Yocum held down a series of low-paying, menial jobs before landing a position as a weekend guard at United Bank of Denver in August 1985, which he held for five years. He'd lived at his Pearl Street apartment—11 blocks from the bank—for 13 years. Unlike Mike McKown, Yocum had a gun strapped to his hip during every shift.

His life began to deteriorate over the 1990 Memorial Day weekend, when $29,600 disappeared from a collection bin in a secure room behind one of the bank's twin ATM units. Though no surveillance footage had caught him in the act, the FBI charged him with the crime largely because he was the guard who'd discovered the missing cash. After making a partial confession, he quickly recanted, lawyered up, and took the case to trial. Without a solid eyewitness identification, the federal prosecutors struggled to make the charges stick. The jury needed only 90 minutes to return a not-guilty verdict.

Amazingly, the bank hadn't fired Yocum in the lead-up to the trial, suspending him without pay instead. The day after his acquittal, he begged Jim Prado to let him come back to work. But Prado told him that Tom Tatalaski and other senior bank officials felt certain he'd been the culprit—despite having beaten the rap—and would make his life a living hell if he came back. Much to his dismay, Yocum had little choice but to resign. It was of little consolation that the bank sent him $2,073 in back pay. He remained unemployed for several months before securing part-time work as a stocking clerk at an equipment store, earning all of $125 a week.

●●●●

Jon Priest had been well aware of Paul Yocum's 1990 larceny charge—as well as his acquittal at trial—since Tom Tatalaski shared his gut feeling about the former guard. Thus, in addition to having the McKown lineup prepared, Priest had another six-pack assembled featuring Yocum's black-and-white DMV photo in the third position.

When Agent John Kirk met with the cash vault tellers on June 20 to have them review the red and blue photo binders, he also showed them the Yocum lineup, asking each teller whether they recognized any of the men displayed in the six-pack. Even though none of them did, Priest wasn't convinced Yocum could be eliminated as a suspect—not yet, anyway. He asked his FBI colleagues to pay the former security guard a visit.

At about 1:00 p.m. on Monday, June 24—eight days after the bank massacre—Yocum was exiting his apartment complex at 1200 Pearl Street when a pair of special agents, Bill McMath and Robert Klimt, approached him and flashed their badges. Minutes later, the three men were sitting in Yocum's cramped living room discussing the quadruple murder of four of his successors.

Yocum told the agents he'd learned about the heist at about 1:45 p.m. Father's Day afternoon, when a former guard called him to share the news. He didn't know any of the victims, he said. When McMath and Klimt brought up the 1990 ATM theft, Yocum claimed to have no hard feelings against bank officials about being charged with the crime or having to stand trial. During the interview, he mentioned taking medications for both a heart condition and epilepsy, his first epileptic seizure having occurred during his trial. Though he owned a car, he usually took the city bus to get to work and around town, he said, because his medication made it difficult for him to drive.

The agents had Yocum speculate about who might have committed the crime. He came up with only one name: Doug Bagley, a former guard who'd been fired for propping open the inner door to the monitor room's mantrap with a soda can.

McMath and Klimt asked the former guard whether he owned any firearms. "I do," Yocum said. "They're locked in that closet over there." He pointed at a set of double-doors near his apartment's entrance.

"Can we take a peek?" McMath asked.

"Sure," Yocum said, leading the agents to the closet. Oddly, the doorknobs were secured by a pair of handcuffs. When he unlocked them and swung the doors open, an arsenal the likes of which the young lawmen had never seen in a residential setting came into full view. *Wow!* McMath thought, instantly sensing Yocum's possible connection to the murders.

Inside the closet were two 12-gauge shotguns, a .45-calbier Colt semi-automatic pistol, and a Ruger mini-14 rifle as well as numerous boxes of .38, .357, .22, .223, and .45-caliber ammunition—many of the rounds semi-jacketed hollow-points. Yocum explained that the .38- and .357-caliber ammo was for a .357 Smith & Wesson revolver he kept at his boyhood home in Flagler, the weapon he carried while working at the bank. He recounted visiting his mom there over the weekend.

There were several additional items of interest in Yocum's closet: a large collection of loaded and unloaded speed loaders, a police scanner, and several military-type duffel bags and backpacks. Tucked in the corner of the closet floor was a small green spiral notebook that appeared to be some type of handwritten journal or diary. Surveying the apartment, McMath and Klimt also spotted two police batons, thumbcuffs, another pair of handcuffs, replica police badges, and an assortment of disarmed hand grenades.

When the three men returned to the living room, their discussion finally turned to Yocum's whereabouts Father's Day morning. He claimed to have been at his apartment until about 11:00 a.m., dubbing jazz composer Dave Brubeck's tracks onto audio cassettes. He'd taken the city bus to have lunch at a restaurant named Skippers, he said, after which he'd gone to a bookstore before returning to his apartment at 1:45 pm. His chronology didn't bear the slightest resemblance to the timeline Jodine Lang would recount three days later.

••••

After speaking with the longtime bank guard for a little over an hour, McMath and Klimt thanked him for his time and returned to the FBI field office. The pair immediately contacted Jon Priest to fill him in, fairly certain the man they'd just interviewed was the murdering bandit himself.

Holy Toledo! Priest thought, his heart thumping as he listened to the agents' play-by-play. *This guy had the motive and means—plus the inside knowledge to pull it off.* Eight days into the investigation, this was by far the most significant lead to come across his desk. He raced over to the field office to meet up with the federal agents. A third agent, Neil Hoener, joined the group on their short ride to 1200 Pearl Street.

Priest was itching to size up the former security guard for himself, hoping he'd be a dead ringer for what the eyewitnesses in the cash vault had described. But when the door to Yocum's third-floor apartment cracked open, the detective's excitement began to wane. The man standing across from him couldn't have been a millimeter taller than 5'8", 140 pounds dripping wet. He had a full head of light brown hair, with a slight bit of gray around the temples. With his Dumbo-like protruding ears and pudgy face, he bore a striking resemblance to Yoda from *Star Wars*.

"I'm on the phone with my lawyer," Yocum informed the foursome, asking them to remain just inside the doorway until he completed his call. He eventually handed the receiver to Agent Hoener, explaining that his attorney wanted to know their purpose in returning. After a few minutes on the phone, Hoener set the receiver on its cradle.

"We need you to sign this consent form to allow a search of your apartment," Hoener said, holding out a pen and a legal-looking document. "If you refuse, we can have a judge issue a warrant. Your choice."

Even though his lawyer had advised him not to, Yocum took the pen from the special agent's hand and scribbled his signature on the piece of paper. Adrenaline now coursing through their veins, the lawmen made a beeline for the double-doored closet. The treasure trove they found inside was just as McMath and Klimt had advertised.

Crouched beside the closet, Priest and his colleagues gathered the green spiral notebook, pistol, ammunition, and about a dozen speed loaders and stuffed them into a blue United Bank bag lying on the closet floor. The detective zipped up the bag, hollering to Yocum—who was again on the phone with his attorney—that they were leaving.

"Wait just a second," Yocum said. "My lawyer wants to speak with you." This time, he handed the receiver to McMath.

"I told my client *not* to let you conduct a search," the attorney said. "You do not have his consent to remove anything from his apartment. I'm directing you and your colleagues to leave his residence immediately."

Shoulders slumped, Yocum's guests followed his attorney's instructions, exiting his apartment empty-handed. Their next step would be a formal search warrant. Priest called in the DPD's Metro SWAT team to keep Yocum's apartment under tight surveillance while he had the warrant prepared.

At 8:30 p.m., Yocum's front door suddenly swung open. Carrying an Army-like green duffel bag, he made it only three steps before the SWAT team engulfed him.

"Drop the bag and hands against the wall," an officer commanded, his gun drawn. Trembling in fear, Yocum did precisely as he was told. A second officer patted him down, pulled his hands behind his back, and slapped on a pair of handcuffs. When Jon Priest arrived a few minutes later—search warrant in hand—he was more than a bit surprised at the spectacle.

"What did you do with the bag we filled up this afternoon?" he asked.

"It's inside the duffel bag. My lawyer told me to get rid of it," Yocum confessed. Priest squatted down to unzip the duffel bag, unearthing the blue bag he and his FBI colleagues had stuffed full of incriminating evidence that afternoon. Sure enough, everything they'd removed from Yocum's closet was still inside.

With their prime suspect detained in the hallway, DPD officers scoured his apartment, finding still more items to add to their haul. They also impounded his 1974 Ford Mustang hatchback for a thorough search downtown.

••••

The following day, Priest had another search warrant issued for Yocum's childhood home in Flagler, where his mother still lived. In his personal bedroom, officers discovered five speed loaders filled with .38-caliber bullets; an ammunition pouch containing two more speed loaders; a jar of spent slugs; two buckets filled with empty .38-caliber cartridges; two plastic bags of 158-grain, .38-caliber bullets; a box of Western .38-caliber bullets; a metal box of additional rounds of .38-caliber ammo and gunpowder; and nearly 40 additional loose bullets.

Dozens of newspaper clippings piled all over his room—including accounts of his larceny trial—were also seized.

In the backyard, one of the officers discovered a rusty, corrugated iron barrel containing what appeared to be fresh ashes, suggesting something had recently been burned in it. As he sifted through the charred contents, he was able to identify a piece of paper with the words "United Bank of Denver" printed at the top. He also pulled out what appeared to be letters Yocum had written to his mother, which were too badly fire-damaged to decipher.

• • • •

The former bank guard's personal diary turned out to be even more incriminating than his fortress of munitions—making clear he'd lied when he told Agents McMath and Klimt he didn't have any hard feelings over being charged with the May 1990 ATM theft.

On several pages, Yocum spewed his contempt for United Bank officials, complaining they'd ruined his life. He labeled his supervisors "assholes," stating he'd "never recommend them as employers to anyone." He saved his most caustic words for the bank's security manager, Tom Tatalaski. "That lying Tatalaski can fry in hell and go to confession 24 hours a day and the Lord will have his way," he wrote. "There is plenty of room in hell for him. He's the one who needs to be in the federal pen raking rocks with a 16-pound hammer, not me."

Yocum described United Bank as being "like any Jew outfit. The pay is low and they expect you to bust your ass to earn what little you get."

"My accusers will be judged by a higher authority," another entry began, "and may he have mercy on you. I will not... I have a character flaw—I don't forget who screwed me. I have another flaw in my character—patience. I am patient to a fault. I have the patience to do it. I may wait 50 years, but I will get even eventually."

Yocum also lamented how the larceny charges and relat-

ed legal expenses had destroyed his relationship with his father. His dad—the longtime bank executive—had loaned him
$12,000 so he wouldn't need to rely on a public defender at
trial. Though he'd been able to repay $1,000 after his acquittal
with money from his backpay check, he hadn't been able to
make good on the remainder. He felt certain that his father
would "gripe about it until the first shovelful of dirt is tossed
onto his grave."

That entry was prophetic. The elder Yocum died in January 1991, five months before the United Bank massacre.

At his desk at DPD headquarters, Jon Priest flipped over
the last page of the spiral notebook, shaking his head in disbelief. *Incriminating as hell!* he thought. *Nobody had more of a
motive to wreak havoc on the bank than Paul Yocum.* But just as
he was about to convince himself he had the crime solved, a
countervailing thought gave him pause: *The eyewitnesses are
dead certain he's not the guy.*

• • • •

Well aware he was now the prime suspect in a quadruple
homicide, Yocum decided to take to the airwaves to defend
himself. On June 25, the day after he was detained outside his
apartment and his arsenal was seized, he agreed to sit for an
interview with Paula Woodward, a highly respected investigative reporter for KUSA-TV, known locally as 9NEWS.

"Did you stage the Father's Day bank robbery," she asked
him bluntly.

A TV camera aimed at the former guard captured his response. "No, ma'am, I did not," Yocum said in a wobbly, halting voice. "I think I'll be vindicated eventually." He also told
the journalist he hadn't been involved in the ATM theft. "I'm
just a 50-year-old man who gets along as best he can."

Half of metro Denver tuned in to Woodward's interview,
including Jon Priest—who had an epiphany as he watched the
broadcast. The TV interview provided a far better depiction of
Yocum than the black-and-white still image he'd included in
the six-pack shown to the tellers. Not only was Yocum's face

displayed in vibrant color, his voice, facial expressions, and mannerisms were all captured as well. *If any of the tellers had seen Yocum on the news, maybe, just maybe*, the detective thought, *something might have clicked*. It was certainly worth finding out.

Priest had an FBI agent contact all six tellers by phone. As it turned out, four of them had seen the interview. Maria Christian told the agent Yocum neither looked nor sounded like the robber and that he appeared "clumsy," unlike the smooth manner in which the armed robber had conducted himself.

David Twist agreed, noting how unstable Yocum appeared compared to the robber's calm voice and steady demeanor. David Barranco said Yocum didn't "fit the image" still ingrained in his memory. Nina McGinty was even more emphatic: "That guy's not even close."

Although Kenetha Whisler hadn't seen the TV interview, she had come across Yocum's picture in the newspaper. She too felt certain he wasn't the man she observed in the cash vault, describing his face as having a "fish mouth"—the sides drooping down—not at all similar to the robber's.

Though he still wasn't certain Yocum could be crossed off the list, Priest decided to abandon the round-the-clock surveillance on his apartment. The lead detective was frustrated the Dumbo-eared, fish-mouthed former guard—who had an obvious motive and stockpile of weapons and ammo—was about to be pushed to the periphery of his and his colleagues' radar. Fortunately, he wouldn't have to wait long for another suspect to emerge—one who fit the physical description of the murdering bandit far better than Paul Tillman Yocum.

16

A HANKERING FOR CHESS

James W. King, a 54-year-old retired Denver cop, was piddling in his backyard in Golden, Colorado—at the edge of the foothills of the Rocky Mountains in neighboring Jefferson County—a sweaty T-shirt and shorts clinging to his 5'11", 180-pound frame. With the back of his hand, he wiped the perspiration beading up on his forehead just below his neatly trimmed, 1950s-style light-brown flat-top.

It was June 23, one week since the bloody massacre. King was mildly surprised nobody on the joint task force had reached out to him to brainstorm. After all, he'd spent 13 months in the bowels of United Bank—until August 1990—and knew its security system better than just about anyone. Two days earlier, he'd written a letter to his good friend Mike McKown—the guard who'd trained him—lamenting how law enforcement was "of course" blaming past and present guards for the tragedy. "The Police and FBI have not yet questioned me," he wrote, "but I guess they'll get around to it soon."

Though his prediction turned out to be eerily prophetic, the gentleman who interrupted his gardening that Sunday afternoon was on the payroll of a newspaper, not the DPD or FBI. John Ensslin, the police-beat reporter for the *Rocky*, was working his way down a lengthy list of former United Bank guards as he pieced together a story for Monday's paper. After the two exchanged pleasantries, King invited him inside, offering the journalist a cold beverage. The two men chatted in the living room as a gray poodle, yapping furiously, tried to dominate their conversation.

King told Ensslin he was stunned upon hearing news of the robbery and felt "sorrow" for the slain guards and their families. "They should have been armed," he insisted. He shared that he was one of the few guards on the weekend crew who carried a weapon, boasting he'd done so without first receiving the bank's authorization. "No one challenged me," he said. King voiced his intense displeasure over United Bank and its new parent company, Norwest, creating an environment in which security guards weren't able to protect themselves.

"Security at the bank was shitty," he added, noting how bank officers wandered through secure areas whenever they pleased. They would regularly call downstairs to the monitor room to receive an escort via the freight elevator, he said, claiming to have misplaced their keycards. He told Ensslin it was obvious the killer possessed detailed knowledge of the security system.

"Do you have any idea who it might have been?"

"I can't imagine who would have done such a horrible thing," King said with a shake of his head.

Thirty minutes after entering the retired cop's cramped bungalow, Ensslin headed back to his car—parked on the dirt road beside the house—another former guard now crossed off his list. The interview hadn't unearthed anything close to a bombshell—nothing even worthy of mention in the article that would appear under his byline the next day. Not even King's name.

••••

John Gedney and Kevin Knierim were working through their own list of former United Bank guards that Monday morning. Unlike John Ensslin, however, they weren't sitting in James King's living room because they were writing a newspaper article. Rather, the two 20-somethings were special agents with the FBI. King's premonition to Mike McKown had been dead on the money. The agents carefully studied King's bushy salt-and-pepper mustache, which they found similar to the description provided by the bank tellers. They also noted that his hair was beginning to gray around the temples and down his ultra-thin sideburns.

As he did with Ensslin, King expressed his disapproval of Norwest's decision to disarm the guards. He informed the agents he was writing a book about police procedures and bank security. He became particularly animated as he described United Bank's woeful security procedures, noting that was one of the reasons he'd decided to quit.

The ex-cop was particularly upset, he said, because bank employees would be permitted to enter the facility on weekends without having to show any identification. Even maintenance employees could freely enter the guard monitor room. King told Gedney and Knierim he was convinced that the crime had been committed by an insider, someone who possessed thorough knowledge of the bank's security systems.

As for his own whereabouts on Father's Day morning, King recounted that he'd risen from bed at 8:00 a.m. and driven out to the Capitol Hill Community Center at approximately 9:30 a.m. to seek out a game of chess. He returned a short time later, he said, because the facility was closed. Upon returning home, he ate breakfast with his wife and then accompanied her to visit her father's grave at the cemetery. They stopped for frozen yogurt on the way back. When they returned home at about 1:00 p.m., he washed his car.

Asked whether he owned any guns, King identified three: a 12-gauge shotgun, a .22-caliber bolt-action rifle, and a .22-caliber handgun. As for his .38-caliber police revolver, he told the young agents he'd gotten rid of it because it had a cracked cylinder. When the lawmen asked if he'd be willing to take a polygraph, King nodded affirmatively, without displaying the slightest hesitation.

A few days later, Gedney and Knierim's report made its way to police headquarters. As Detective Priest perused the document, several items virtually leapt off the page. First, though King lived 11 miles from United Bank's downtown facility, he placed himself just over a mile away—at the community center on 1290 Williams Street—at the same time a homicidal maniac was brutally murdering four security guards. Second, the community center hadn't hosted the Denver Chess Club in over three years, a fact confirmed by Priest's subordinates. *Why wouldn't he have known that?*

Even more significant, Priest couldn't comprehend how a cop could casually discard the revolver he'd carried for 25 years. He considered his own service weapon part of his identity, no different from his badge. Most retired officers he knew had placed their guns and badges in display cases to memorialize their service. He'd also never heard of a crack forming in the cylinder of a .38-caliber revolver. James King's story didn't add up. In the blink of an eye, he leapfrogged Paul Yocum to the top of the detective's list of suspects.

••••

Detective Calvin Hemphill drew the assignment of conducting a follow-up interview of King. He'd spent the last 16 years with the DPD, nearly ten as a detective. Though he'd overlapped with King for more than a decade, he didn't have the foggiest clue who he was.

On July 2, Hemphill stood on the former cop's front porch alongside another FBI agent, Alfonso Villegas. When the front door cracked open, the middle-aged man across from them appeared clean shaven, his bushy salt-and-pepper mustache suddenly gone.

Hemphill and Villegas flashed their credentials. "May we have a word with you?" the DPD detective asked.

King's eyes darted from Hemphill to Villegas, and then back again. "No," he finally said. "My lawyer told me not to speak with the FBI or DPD."

"Listen," Hemphill said, attempting to charm his way inside by appealing to King's ego. "We're here because you worked as a guard at United Bank and also with us on the force. You're not a suspect. We want to tap into your experience to see if you can help us solve the crime."

The detective's ploy worked. King opened the door wide, directing the lawmen to a couch in the living room as he took a seat in an easy chair.

Their conversation began with a review of his employment with United Bank. The longtime cop explained that he'd worked 12-hour shifts on Saturdays and Sundays, carrying his .38-caliber Colt Trooper revolver on a Sam Browne belt. The belt contained a pouch for two speed loaders. King acknowledged wearing the gun even after learning it had a cracked cylinder. After he quit, he said, he dismantled it—because it was dangerous—and threw it in the trash. His wife really didn't like having guns around the house anyway.

Without much prompting, King launched into a stinging critique of the bank's security procedures. For starters, the surveillance cameras were never cleaned, the footage they captured always out of focus. Though the freight elevator supposedly had a dedicated key, he said, virtually any key on the guard's key ring would work. He explained how he'd once mistakenly used the wrong key to operate the elevator and it worked just fine. It was such a serious breach of security, he noted the problem in the guard logbook. "But they didn't care," he told the lawmen, with evident disgust.

Furthermore, anyone who wanted to gain access to the bank during the weekend could just call down to the monitor room and be allowed in without any identification. The weekend guards felt compelled to let employees enter the bank even if their names weren't found on the computerized list. "If we told them we couldn't let them in without proper identification," he said, "they would complain and we would get into trouble."

When King finally took a breath, Hemphill asked, "How would you know if the person seeking access to the bank was really who they claimed to be?"

"You wouldn't," the ex-cop said with snicker. "You wouldn't know if they were a vice president or a secretary."

"Are you familiar with the name Bob Bardwell?"

King shook his head. "No, I'm not." As he resumed his

rant, Villegas jotted in his notes that he displayed "animosity" toward the bank, the FBI, and the DPD.

The former security guard acknowledged being aware of a camera that filmed the guards as they worked in the monitor room and that it fed footage into the VCR in the supervisor's office. "They spied on us to see if we were eating or drinking," he said, his tone dripping with disdain. "Of course I ate and drank during my shifts, and I couldn't have cared less if they caught me."

King shared with the lawmen additional details about his activities on Father's Day—a few of which didn't mesh with his June 24 interview. He now claimed that he'd eaten breakfast with his wife *before* leaving for the community center at 9:30 a.m. He told Hemphill and Villegas no one was there when he arrived and that he therefore came back home without playing chess, returning at about 10:20 a.m. His wife and youngest son were there, he said, and they all went to the cemetery together.

Hemphill asked what prompted him to play chess that morning. King explained that he used to play all the time, but hadn't been to the community center for a game since 1986. He said he decided that very morning to start playing again, noting he'd met his attorney, Walter Gerash, years earlier when they'd competed against each other at the center. "He's a close friend of mine," he said. "I don't think he's going to bill me for this."

King really perked up when the discussion shifted to his book on police procedures. He told the detective and special agent he'd been writing one chapter per year and had completed eight of the 23 he planned to write. He took the job at United Bank, he said, in part to obtain background information for a chapter about bank security. But since quitting his job there, he'd changed his mind. The book wasn't going to include a chapter on bank security after all.

Before leaving, Hemphill asked King to confirm—a second time—that he'd be willing to take a polygraph.

"Actually, I'm not," the retired cop said, pursing his lips. "The polygraph scares me and I'm nervous as it is. I just don't trust it."

• • • •

Hemphill and Villegas raced back to police headquarters to share with Jon Priest what King had told them. After hearing their summary, the lead detective was even more convinced they were closing in on the killer. He asked Sergeant Doug Hildebrant, a fellow detective, to conduct a third interview. Hildebrant called King the next morning, July 3.

King repeated to Hildebrant what he'd said the prior day, though with slight adjustments: that he left for the community center at 9:30 a.m. and that the facility was closed when he arrived. He told Hildebrant he got back home between 10:20 and 10:30 a.m. Between 11:00 and 11:30 a.m., he and his wife visited Mount Olivet Cemetery, where her parents were buried. On their way back, they stopped for some ice cream. At 1:00 p.m., he drove to a car wash and then came back home. He learned about the bank heist, he said, watching the six o'clock news on TV.

Later that afternoon, Hildebrant and Lieutenant Tom Haney paid King yet another visit. The detective asked if any of King's neighbors could verify his whereabouts on Father's Day morning. The ex-cop replied that he didn't know any of his neighbors and hadn't seen any of them when he left for the community center or when he returned home.

Hildebrant inquired whether anyone had seen him at the community center who could corroborate his alibi. King recounted that he parked in the back, walked around to the front, but didn't see anyone to let him in. The place was closed and locked. A well-dressed gentleman was standing on the front porch, he said. He asked the man if he knew where the chess club was meeting, but he didn't know. Yet the stranger couldn't serve as his alibi, as King had no idea who he was.

He told the officers that he'd played a lot of "correspondence" chess, but hadn't played an over-the-board game in several years prior to seeking out a game on Father's Day. Asked what clothing he had on at the time, the longtime cop said he was wearing a white T-shirt, khaki pants, and white slip-on tennis shoes. He also mentioned that he was writing two books in addition to the one on police procedures—an autobiography and a science-fiction novel.

••••

While Hildebrant and Haney were drilling down on King's story, Dick Penington, another police detective, was at the downtown Weight Watchers interviewing his wife, who worked there as a receptionist. Carolyn King told Penington that her husband worked the noon to midnight shift at United Bank on weekends and holidays until about June 1990. To the best of her recollection, he quit because Sunday was the only day the two of them could spend together based on her work schedule. In addition, she said, he had back problems and wanted to be fully retired.

Carolyn told Penington that her husband carried a big black gun while on duty at the bank, which he kept in his gun belt in his bedroom closet. After he quit, she said, he kept the gun in a lockbox in the den. She made no mention of any aversion to having guns around the house.

Her recollection of Father's Day morning was that she and her husband had eaten breakfast together, after which he left to play chess at about 9:15 a.m. He hadn't told her exactly where he was going. Prior to that morning, the two of them had discussed what he wanted to do on Father's Day and he'd shared his desire to play chess, since he hadn't played in about three years. When he returned at about 10:00 a.m., he told her that no one was there to play chess with him. They left their home at 11:30 a.m. to visit her parents' graves at Mount Olivet Cemetery, she said, and stopped at the Dairy Queen before returning home at 1:00 p.m. She told Penington her other two sons arrived about 2:30 p.m. to celebrate Father's Day.

Penington expressed curiosity about why King had shaved off his mustache. His wife recounted that he'd been breaking out with pimples underneath the mustache and was trying to obtain some relief. She confessed it was hard getting used to him without it. She described him as "a loner" who didn't have any friends at United Bank, volunteering that he didn't talk about the massacre unless she brought it up. She made a point of telling the detective that he'd complained to her repeatedly about the bank's security because the guards had to let employees in on the weekends—no matter what.

● ● ● ●

Jon Priest decided to prepare yet another six-pack, this one featuring James King in the middle of the first row—position number two. Based on everything he'd learned from Hemphill, Hildebrant, Haney, and Penington, he was all but convinced that the ex-cop from Golden and the madman who ruthlessly executed four defenseless security guards were one and the same. Yet he also knew that, on June 20, none of the eyewitnesses had selected King from the blue binder of former guards—despite his DMV photo appearing on page 16. *Maybe his hair and forehead threw them off,* Priest speculated, well aware those features had been hidden by the gunman's hat.

To address that possibility, the homicide detective decided to crop each of the images in the new lineup just above the pictured individuals' eyebrows—to simulate the portion of the robber's face David Barranco and his subordinates were able to see. Each of the six black-and-white photos—the other five consisting of mugshots from neighboring counties—was also cropped tightly around the ears and just below the chin. The men displayed were wearing different types of glasses and sported mustaches of varying shapes and thickness. Priest tasked his fellow detective, Jim Rock, with ushering the brand-new lineup to the residence of David Twist.

Rock and a female FBI agent knocked on Twist's door at about 3:00 p.m. on July 3. The detective centered the six-pack on the bank teller's kitchen table, instructing him to pay particular attention to the facial structure of the men staring back at him. "If you can," he said, "try to picture them wearing sunglasses and a hat. It's perfectly okay for you not to choose anyone at all."

While Rock and the FBI agent stood off to the side, Twist ran his fingers across all six faces, studying them intensely for nearly ten minutes.

"Number two looks really close," he finally said, pointing to King's photo. "It's the roundness of the face. The way the ears are sitting." Twist explained that the "hair color is not quite right, but I can't tell because of the way the picture is. It doesn't show enough of the hair."

What really struck him, the 25-year-old told his guests, was the intensity of the man's gaze. "The expression on his face almost exactly matches the face that I saw the day of the robbery. The serious appearance. The features are almost exactly identical."

Rock had him circle King's picture and sign and date the six-pack. "Please don't talk with anyone about this lineup, especially the other tellers. We don't even want you mentioning it to your wife."

"I won't," Twist promised. He had no idea the man whose face he'd just circled had spent a quarter century protecting him and his fellow citizens as one of Denver's finest. Or that he'd briefly overlapped with the former cop when both were employed at United Bank—during the last three months James King patrolled its hallways.

"Someone will be in contact with you soon," Rock said, politely excusing himself, ecstatic the investigation had just reached a new milestone. The six-pack bearing David Twist's signature would shortly land on Jon Priest's desk, the engine of justice about to throttle into overdrive.

17

WINDMILL TILTER

God broke the mold when Walter Louis Gerash emerged from his mother's womb. The flamboyant criminal defense attorney was known as much for his courtroom antics and showmanship as for his withering cross-examinations and spellbinding closing arguments. He'd sometimes arrive at the courthouse sporting a cape and beret—even purple or green velvet suits. He'd seek out newspaper and TV reporters to denounce the injustices being visited upon his clients, making his points in his unmistakable New York accent. He had a moxie and a schtick all to his own. Clients who engaged Walter Gerash didn't just get a lawyer. They got a warrior.

Always brash and gruff—unapologetically combative—the bald-headed attorney's booming, baritone voice would thunder across the courtroom, sometimes so loud the windows would rattle. He'd employ sarcasm like a surgeon's scalpel, always pushing boundaries. When his theatrics irked prosecutors and judges, he'd wear their disapproval like a badge of honor. Though he was regarded as Colorado's version of the famed Melvin Belli—and actually worked on cases with the King of Torts—that he ended up in the Centennial State was a pure accident of fate.

Gerash was born in the Bronx in November 1926, three years before the stock market crash that triggered the Great Depression. His parents were among the tidal wave of Russian Jews who fled persecution in Eastern Europe to emigrate to the Big Apple. In the mostly Irish neighborhood where the Gerash family settled, Walter was bullied for being short and Jewish. He'd eventually top out at just 5′6″, his diminutive stature belying the inferno lurking just beneath the surface.

When he graduated from James Monroe High in 1944, the country was mired in World War II. Just 17, he enlisted in the Army, both to fight the ugly scourge of fascism and also to take advantage of the GI Bill so he could afford college. In the summer of 1945, his infantry unit was stationed in Hawaii—poised to be shipped off to Japan—when the nuclear bombs dropped on Hiroshima and Nagasaki brought the worldwide conflict to an abrupt end. He continued his service until his honorable discharge in August 1946.

Because his parents had moved to Los Angeles during the war, Gerash enrolled in college at UCLA, where he became enamored by the teachings of Karl Marx and radicalized by the Communist Party. After obtaining his bachelor's degree, he decided he wanted to be a history professor, moving to the Windy City to enroll in the master's program at the University of Chicago. Though he successfully completed his degree, he was told there was no room for him in the doctoral program, extinguishing his dream of becoming a college professor. He returned to L.A., where he became a union organizer instead. It was at a rally protesting the execution of Julius and Ethel Rosenberg that he met his first wife.

"You love to argue and you're good at it," she told him one day as he pondered his future. "Why don't you become a lawyer?" Having never seriously considered the idea, Gerash enrolled at UCLA's law school. By his second year, however, his ongoing ties to the Communist Party had become a serious problem, several professors going out of their way to make his life miserable. He began to doubt he'd be allowed to sit for the California bar exam. Thus, with his wife and one-year-old son in tow, he migrated to Colorado—where McCarthyism hadn't yet taken root—completing his legal studies at the University of Denver.

Though he'd gone to law school intending to become a

labor lawyer, his first legal job had him working at the right hand of an experienced criminal defense attorney. Not only did he enjoy the work, he realized he could achieve social justice just as readily practicing criminal law as labor law. Two years out of law school in 1958, he opened his own firm on the twentieth floor of the 23-story Mile High Center on Seventeenth and Broadway, the tallest structure in Denver at the time. Right beside it was the four-story bank building that would later bear the name United Bank of Denver. Not only did he do his banking there, he'd eventually appear in one of its TV commercials.

The rebellious streak that led to his membership in the Communist Party continued to animate Gerash throughout his legal career. He was an unabashed crusader and champion of unpopular causes. During the 1960s and 1970s, his vast pro bono clientele included civil rights and Vietnam War protesters, student radicals, members of the Black Panther Party, and Chicano activists accused of mailing letter bombs. He successfully defended the "midnight rapist" who was believed to have raped more than 30 women, a teenager who murdered his parents, and a heavyweight boxer who shot and killed his former trainer.

When actors with the San Francisco Mime Troupe were arrested mid-performance in September 1966 for using "obscene gestures" and "filthy words" to rail against the Vietnam War, Gerash was the lawyer who came to their defense, persuading a jury following a ten-day trial to render a not-guilty verdict. During the height of the Iranian hostage crisis in 1979, he represented an Iranian college student who'd been home with his wife when a band of teenage hooligans smashed in their front window with baseball bats. As the ruffians fled, the student fired shots at their car, killing one of the boys and wounding two others. He was hauled off to jail, charged with murder. Gerash took the case to trial—and won.

When he was representing someone accused of a crime, Walter Gerash didn't have the slightest hesitation to rail against prosecutors, cops, and even judges—both in media interviews and even to their faces—if he sensed them attempting to tilt the playing field unfairly. There was nothing he despised more, and found more anathema to a system of justice, than the government overreaching at the expense of ordinary citizens. "Seeking justice is a constant struggle," he once told a reporter, "and where there's no struggle there's no progress." He believed the government exploited "the overwhelming majority of the people" and that the law was a method "to help mollify this oppression."

An avid swimmer and skier, Gerash took pride in his physical fitness and appearance. He'd go biking and roller-blading across city parks wearing gym shorts to showcase his ultra-toned legs. He drew immense pleasure from music, particularly by classical composers such as Mozart. Like his wardrobe, his taste in vehicles bordered on the eccentric. His was the only red Cadillac in town with an antiwar sticker emblazoned across its rear bumper.

A member of the Denver Chess Club since 1958—serving one year as its president—Gerash was one of the most formidable players in the city, competing in tournaments every month despite his busy law practice. But he got just as much satisfaction playing pickup games with strangers at the concrete tables lining the Sixteenth Street Mall—sometimes shirtless—and competing against his chess buddies on his personal ivory and mahogany set. He considered chess his "respite and escape from the storms" of his "personal and professional struggles."

• • • •

Apart from his prized Cadillac, the material possession Gerash cherished most was the sandstone townhouse—circa 1888—he purchased in 1979 and converted into a law office. The two-story, Queen Anne Victorian on the 1400 block of Court Place had been owned by a mobster at the turn of the century, the red light hanging in the foyer still there to remind guests of its unsavory past. As developers tore down buildings all around it to make room for more modern structures, Gerash refused to sell. After all, the Victorian was the oldest remaining residential structure in the central business district, protected from demolition as an official city landmark.

On Monday morning, July 1, 1991, he was behind his desk in his second-floor office toiling away on one of his cases when his secretary shouted at him from her workstation—their version of an intercom. She let him know a potential client was on the phone. "His name is James King. He says he has to speak to you immediately and that he used to play chess with you."

The name didn't register or trigger a memory. The attorney pushed his work aside and picked up the receiver. "This is Walter Gerash. Can I help you?"

"Mr. Gerash, this is Jim King," the man said, sounding a bit anxious. "We used to play at the Denver Chess Club at the Capitol Hill Community Center at Cheesman Park." He told Gerash he'd been a police officer when they last played, but was now retired. As he spoke, a faint glimmer of recognition set in. Gerash vaguely recalled playing chess against a cop in the late 1970s or early 1980s, but had no memory of the man's name.

King explained that after retiring from the DPD, he'd worked as a security guard for United Bank. In the past few days, he said, the FBI had been questioning him about the robbery and murders. "I think I might need a lawyer."

Along with the rest of metro Denver, Gerash hadn't been able to escape the intense media coverage of the bank massacre, fully aware the DPD and FBI appeared stymied in their investigation. *They're going to charge a retired cop?* he thought to himself. *No way.* Though he'd seen the DA's Office do some pretty outrageous things, he considered it far-fetched that the man on the other end of the line was about to be fingered as the savage beast who'd annihilated four defenseless men.

"Do you still play chess?" Gerash asked.

"I do," King said. "In fact, I was trying to play a game on Father's Day morning and drove out to the community center, but the place was closed."

"The chess club moved out of that building *years ago.*" Gerash chuckled. "I'm surprised you didn't know that. We now play at VFW Post 501 on West Colfax." He paused to think.

"I'll tell you what," he finally said. "They've got a tournament starting tomorrow night at seven o'clock. Why don't you come down, play a game or two, and we can talk afterwards."

"That sounds great, Mr. Gerash. I really appreciate it."

"Please call me Walter. I'll see you tomorrow, Jim. Looking forward to it."

As he placed the receiver back on its cradle, Walter Louis Gerash couldn't possibly have known that he was about to embark on the biggest case of his illustrious career. One that would place him in the glaring media spotlight—and consume his law practice—for an entire year.

18

PULLING THE TRIGGER

District Attorney Norm Early was still licking his political wounds. Fifteen days following his bitter defeat in the race to become Denver's first Black mayor, he'd all but vanished from the face of the Earth, telling one of his chief deputies, Craig Silverman, he'd "gone fishing." With the clock about to strike five on Wednesday, July 3, the DA's Office was a veritable ghost town, most everyone having left early for the long holiday weekend. Silverman, a 6'5", third-generation Denverite, was about to head home to spruce up for a date when his phone rang.

"Craig, this is Jon Priest," he heard from his end of the line. "I need you to come to police headquarters right away." The homicide detective explained that, between David Twist's positive identification, James King's dubious claims about his whereabouts Father's Day morning and disposal of his service revolver, and a host of circumstantial evidence, the joint task force was on the verge of making an arrest.

"I need your help preparing the affidavits for the search and arrest warrants," Priest said. "Hopefully there's at least one judge left in this city who can sign them before the holiday."

So much for my date, Silverman lamented, his plans for the evening unexpectedly scuttled. *At least I'll get to play golf tomorrow.*

With the chief deputy DA's fingers clacking away on the keyboard, Priest and an FBI agent described their reasons for believing James King was the criminal who'd committed the atrocities at the bank—what was necessary to establish the requisite probable cause for the warrants. Priest signed the affidavits a little after nine o'clock. Though they'd prepared an arrest warrant, the lead detective planned to keep it in his hip pocket, a game-time decision dependent on the evidence uncovered at King's residence.

Silverman jumped into the unmarked car of another homicide detective, Joe DeMott, the duo now on a mission to locate a judge who hadn't yet skipped town. They were in luck. When they rang the doorbell to the stately home belonging to Judge Aleene Ortiz-White, the jurist appeared at the front door and welcomed them inside. After reviewing the warrants, she scribbled her signature across the blank lines at 9:51 p.m.

DeMott radioed Priest from the judge's living room. "Mission accomplished," he said gleefully. "We should be there in ten minutes."

• • • •

Fireworks from the Jefferson County Fairgrounds had been exploding across Golden, Colorado's pitch-black sky since 9:30 p.m. The event brought the local community together for an evening equal parts patriotism and celebration—children staying up well past their bedtimes to participate in the annual ritual. Dozens of locals had set up camp on the circular, dead-end portion of Juniper Street—just across Sixth Avenue—their backs to the bungalow owned by James and Carolyn King.

The onlookers seated on lawn chairs and blankets were about to be treated to not one, but two grand finales. Behind them, a parade of squad cars crept along as if in a funeral procession, ultimately congregating in the driveway and dirt road fronting 665 Juniper. After exiting their vehicles, a small army of uniformed and plainclothes officers and FBI agents assembled in the front yard—a show of force unlike any the Mile High City had seen in years.

Among the lawmen gathered on the property were FBI Special Agent in Charge Bob Pence, Denver Police Chief Ari Zavaras, and Detective Jon Priest. Investigators from the Yankee 91 mobile crime lab readied their equipment and supplies. There was even a dog from the DPD's K9 unit patiently awaiting its turn to assist with the search. Craig Silverman soaked in the action from DeMott's unmarked car with as much fascination as the locals watching the fireworks display down the street.

At 10:05 p.m., Sergeant Doug Hildebrant led a group to the front porch, search warrant in hand. James King was in the living room, the TV tuned to the evening news. When he flipped on the porch lights and opened the door, he glimpsed several familiar faces, men with whom he'd worked side-by-side for decades. Yet by the looks of it, they were now on very different sides.

"What's this all about?" King asked, eerily calm despite the jarring circumstances. A white T-shirt and khaki pants hung loosely over his 180-pound frame.

"We have a warrant to search your home and vehicles," Hildebrant said, all business, holding out the paperwork. "You're going to be detained on the front porch." He signaled the crime-scene investigators to advance inside, patting King down to make sure he wasn't armed. Hildebrant removed a pair of handcuffs from his duty belt—identical to the ones King himself had carried for 25 years—snapping one end around the ex-cop's right wrist and leading him to a small table on the porch.

"You're going to sit here while we search your home," the officer declared, clasping the other metal ring around the post at the center of the table and sliding a lawn chair under King's rump. He pulled up a chair to sit beside the ex-cop, his job the remainder of the evening to babysit him while his colleagues did their jobs.

Another officer rousted Carolyn King from bed to inform her that her home was being searched and that she couldn't remain inside. She was permitted to throw a robe over her nightgown before being marched outside, instructed to sit across the table from her husband and not say a word. She was mortified, painfully aware her neighbors and locals attending the fireworks show were craning their necks to gawk at the spectacle.

Watching her shiver in the crisp evening air, King begged Hildebrant to fetch her a blanket—a request that, in his view, took far too long to honor. Once a blanket was finally draped over his wife and her shivering ceased, he sat in his chair impassively, seemingly nonplussed by the frenetic activity engulfing him.

••••

Two dozen detectives and crime-scene investigators performed their tasks in teams, dividing the property into several zones, including the outdoor areas and vehicles. Photographs were taken to document the condition of each room and vehicle, as well as any items determined to be of particular significance.

As his colleagues turned the house upside down—quite literally, as the contents of drawers and cabinets were dumped onto the floor—Priest was hoping to unearth the VHS tapes, key rings, handheld radios, and pages from the guard logbook the murdering thief had absconded with. Yet none of those items were found. Nor were the doctor's satchel, hat, sunglasses, sport coat, or tie the tellers had described in their interviews. Bill McCullom's Markey card would have been a knockout blow all by itself, but it too wasn't located.

In the master bedroom, officers did find a stack of cash in the night stand adjacent to King's side of the bed, $500 in all. Another $295 was removed from his wallet. But when the $795 in currency was sent to the crime lab, David Barranco's fingerprints didn't appear on a single bill. Beyond that cash, there was no sign of the nearly $200,000 in stolen loot.

An investigator rifling through a filing cabinet in King's den did make a seemingly significant discovery—a manila folder labeled "Plans" that contained blueprints of the bank. One of the pages depicted the layout and dimensions of the concourse level, specifying the location of the elevators, stairwells, monitor room, and cash vault.

Though King claimed to have discarded his Colt Trooper, Priest had investigators scour the residence for any sign of it—or any other potential murder weapon. Officers located a 12-gauge Winchester shotgun, a bolt-action .22-caliber Winchester rifle and, in the same nightstand where they'd found $500 in cash, a .22-caliber North American Arms revolver. Yet none of those weapons were capable of firing the .38-caliber ammo removed from the victims.

Recalling that Carolyn King had informed Detective Penington about a lockbox in the den where her husband stored his service revolver, Priest stepped outside to ask her about it. She told him that, to the best of her recollection, her husband's gun belt and gun were in a gray box in the den. Priest headed back inside, only to find a combination lock securing the metal container. He sent one of his men to the porch to retrieve the combination from King himself, who, under no compulsion to do so, provided the correct sequence of numbers.

The lead detective's adrenaline surged as the combination lock finally clicked open and the lid was pulled off the box. Yet the big reveal turned out to be no reveal at all, the container completely empty. He scooped it up and carried it outside.

"Is this the right box?" he asked Carolyn, now a bit irritated. "When we opened it, there was nothing inside."

"That's the one," she said. "That's where I remember Jim keeping his gun."

Not only were investigators unable to locate the Colt Trooper and police belt, they couldn't find the speed loaders King had carried in the belt's pouches. Officers searching the closet in David King's bedroom did find several rifles, which were laid out on his bed to be documented. But they too clearly had nothing to do with the crime.

Over two hours into the search, no smoking gun—quite literally—had been found. The blueprints for the bank's concourse level, while certainly incriminating, didn't provide enough of a connection to the crime to make an arrest. It was beginning to look like the evening would end with the retired police officer sleeping in his own bed. But Jon Priest was still holding out hope about an additional piece of evidence of singular significance to the crime: the shoes worn by the killer.

The lead detective had carefully studied the impressions of the shoeprints lifted from the plexiglass in the monitor room and from the dusty incinerator room floor. He'd examined them so many times, the sole pattern was indelibly etched in his memory: parallel grooves running across the width of the shoe from heel to toe.

Between midnight and 1:00 a.m., just when it was beginning to look like the entire evening would be a bust, a crime-scene investigator tugged on Priest's shirt. "You've got to come see this," he said. He led Priest to the door between the kitchen and the garage. There, resting on the floor, was a pair of size-8 Comfort Lite black shoes. Priest picked them up and flipped them over. *I'll be damned,* he thought, his face lighting up with childlike glee. The sole pattern was exactly what he recalled from the shoeprint impressions—parallel grooves from heel to toe.

"Bag them up!" the detective said. "We'll ship them off to the FBI crime lab to confirm the match."

Before long, the investigator marched back outside through King's front door—hoisting the clear plastic bag like a first-prize winning marlin—his Cheshire-cat grin a dead giveaway for the shoes' forensic significance. Right on cue, Sergeant Hildebrant rose from his chair to unlock the metal cuff securing King to the table.

"Stand up and hold out your hands," he said, snapping the open steel bracelet around King's left wrist. He began reading from a small police-issued card: "You have the right to remain silent. Anything you say can and will be used against you in a court of law. You have a right to speak with an attorney and to have an attorney present during any questioning."

Due to the lateness of the hour and tight-lipped nature of the operation, not a single journalist, photographer, or TV camera was on hand to document the moment for posterity—or capture King's perp walk to a waiting squad car—the culmination of the joint task force's tireless efforts over 18 days. Once the sun peeked over the horizon a few hours later, news of the former police sergeant's arrest would spread like wild-fire, not only across metro Denver, but throughout the Centennial State as well.

King was taken to the Denver City Jail, where he was booked, fingerprinted, and processed, his T-shirt and slacks swapped out for a drab gray jumpsuit. In the mugshot released to the media on July 8, his wide-open, ocean blue eyes stared defiantly at the camera—as if to say, "You have the wrong man"—his tightly pursed lips forming a narrow slit between his nose and chin. Not a whisker of hair appeared below his eyebrows, his mustache having vanished a week earlier.

Whether this was the face of the monster who'd executed Bill McCullom, Phil Mankoff, Scott McCarthy, and Todd Wilson in cold blood would now be up to prosecutors in the DA's Office to prove. The battle had only just begun.

19

KING ME

To say that James King's childhood lacked stability would be a severe understatement. His mother, Doris Keplinger, was born and raised in Delta, Colorado, about 250 miles southwest of Denver. When she was 14, her nuclear family migrated to Berkeley, California, near San Francisco. Five years later, while dating a man named James William Ette, Dorothy learned she'd become pregnant. At the time, abortion was neither safe nor legal. The couple hastily arranged a shotgun wedding, exchanging vows in November 1935. James William Ette, Jr. sucked in his first breaths of air on July 10, 1936. Three years later, he was joined by a brother named Thomas.

James Sr. was physically abusive, at first directing his venom—and hands—toward his wife, and later, his namesake. Not long after Thomas's arrival, Dorothy scooped up the boys and fled, leaving divorce papers in her wake. Ette would never see his children again. In 1942, Dorthy waltzed down the aisle a second time to wed a man named Harold Scott King. Prior to meeting his bride-to-be, King had completed a three-year stint in the Navy and had become a civil servant for the federal government. Unlike Ette, he would never lay a finger on Dorothy or her kids.

With World War II raging in the Pacific, Harold held down a series of government posts in the U.S. territories of Hawaii and Guam, Dorothy following him to each. The couple left James and Thomas in the care of their maternal grandparents in Northern California.

In July 1943, while Harold was stationed in Hawaii, he and Dorothy welcomed a daughter, Myra. Later that year, he petitioned the Hawaii courts to adopt James and Thomas as his own children. Their surnames were legally changed from Ette to King when the petition was granted. The King boys joined their mom, adoptive dad, and half-sister in Hawaii, bouncing back and forth between the Pacific islands and Northern California over the next several years.

As a youngster, James King was quite the looker with his curly blond locks and big blue eyes. His education was somewhat of a mess, however, as his family's nomadic lifestyle meant constant transitions to new schools. He ultimately attended over a dozen, three in 1950 alone. The moves also made it difficult for him to get involved in sports. James filled his spare time with two activities he could do anytime and anywhere: reading comic books and playing chess.

By 1951, the King family had settled in Oakland, California, where James attended Castlemont High. His grades were average, mostly Bs and Cs. His favorite parts of the school day were mechanical drawing and the ROTC, in which he served as an officer. By then, chess had become an outright obsession. During his senior year, he proudly held the mantle of president of Castlemont High's chess club.

Upon graduation in June 1954, King enlisted in the U.S. Army. At his basic training in Monterey, his light-brown hair was shaved down to the flat-top he'd wear like a badge of honor throughout the decades that followed. When the 18-year-old signed up to be a military police officer, the Army shipped him off to Georgia for specialized training. In December 1954, he was assigned to a top-secret installation in Siegelsbach, Germany that assembled nuclear warheads.

Military life suited King to a T. He had no inclination to break the rules—the same ones he enforced as an MP—mortified when his fellow soldiers drank to excess, smoked pot, and cavorted with prostitutes. His existence in the barracks, and in the years that followed, was rigidly straight-laced and squeaky clean—sans booze, drugs, and women. He rarely even resorted to foul language.

King remained at the nuclear weapons facility until his honorable discharge in July 1957 at the rank of private first-class. Upon his return to the States, he enrolled at Long Beach City College in Southern California. While attending school, he held several part-time jobs, including, very briefly, as a cadet with the Los Angeles Police Department. After two years in Long Beach, he transferred to the University of Colorado in Boulder, where he majored in economics and math. To afford his tuition, he worked part time as an insurance investigator and cab driver.

After two years of classes in Boulder—still a distance from snagging his diploma—King grew restless. Rather than continuing his education, he decided to embark upon a career in law enforcement, a logical progression from his service as an MP. In his application to the DPD, he rated himself "excellent" with automatic weapons, revolvers, and rifles. Thanks to his military training, he also touted his skills in boxing, wrestling, and Jujitsu. Upon his admission into the police academy in September 1961, he plunked down $61.93 for a .38-caliber Colt Trooper, which he wore proudly on a leather police belt.

Two months later, the 25-year-old graduated first in his class of 37 cadets. As he slipped his navy blue uniform over his ultra-slender frame—running his fingers across the ridges of his gold badge—James King felt like a million bucks. One day, he believed, it was his destiny to become the Chief of Police.

● ● ● ●

Carolyn Ann Guida—"Carol" as James called her—was all of 17 when she and King sized each other up on their first date in the summer of 1961. By the following June, they'd been married two months and were already expecting their first child. James Jr.—whom they nicknamed "Jimmy"—was born in March 1963. He was followed by Greg in April 1964 and David in October 1966. While their dad was climbing the career ladder, the responsibility for raising them fell largely to their mother.

As a young officer, King grew self-conscious about his babyface, which made him look more like a high school student than a hard-nosed cop. To project a grittier image, he decided to grow a mustache. The thick pile of brown hair that sprouted above his lips made him appear considerably older and more rugged, bestowing upon him instant gravitas. He groomed his mustache meticulously, molding it into a shape that resembled a bat with outstretched wings. His trademark stache would adorn his mug for the vast majority of his quarter century on the force.

Though his police career began with tremendous potential, it didn't pan out quite like King had planned. His mild-mannered, at times aloof, demeanor made him somewhat of an oddball among his peers, many of whom gravitated to policework craving physical altercations and gunfights with the bad guys. Unlike them, King didn't seek out flashy or dangerous assignments.

Indeed, during his many years on the force, he didn't rack up a single notable achievement, so anonymous the majority of his fellow cops couldn't have picked him out of a lineup. He simply did his job without commotion, blended in as best he could, and went home to his wife and family, rarely taking time to socialize.

Like all new officers, King's first assignment after the academy was with the patrol division. After two years on patrol, he began a six-year stint as a dispatcher in the radio room—a desk job—followed by a position in the traffic division that had him patrolling Denver's streets on a three-wheel motorcycle. In 1975, he was promoted to sergeant and assigned another desk job in the identification bureau, where he worked with fingerprints and other forms of identification—including the IDs issued to cops—for another six years. Toward the end of his career, he spent four years augmenting Stapleton Airport's security detail, often during the graveyard shift.

King also held down several part-time jobs to afford the middle-class lifestyle to which he and his wife aspired. The most glitzy was as a traffic announcer for KLZ-FM, the radio affiliate for Channel 7 TV. He also served as a security guard for Beth Israel Hospital and as a traffic control officer for The Bank of Denver, which bore no relation to United Bank. In 1973, while working off duty in his police uniform, he actually subdued a bank robber. His commendation from the DPD — the only one he'd ever receive — noted that the "quick, decisive and efficient manner in which the arrest was effected" resulted in no injuries and no monetary loss.

• • • •

King's obsession with queens, rooks, knights, and bishops continued unabated throughout his police career. From time to time, he even sat across the chess board from the Chief of Police. In 1977, he joined the Denver Chess Club, where he played in numerous tournaments and "rated games." He had an official ranking with the Colorado State Chess Association, his name regularly appearing in its *Colorado Chess* magazine. He also served as a club director for the U.S. Chess Federation.

By August 1981, King had become enamored with correspondence chess, in which players send moves to their opponents by postcards through the mail. Games would take weeks or even months to complete and King had several going at any given time — at one time keeping up with 18 games simultaneously. Over an eight-year stretch, he competed in 244 rated postal games. During that time, he let his membership in the Denver Chess Club lapse, eschewing across-the-board chess tournaments and formal games altogether. But he continued playing casual games — "skittles" in chess parlance — at the club's rented space in the Capitol Hill Community Center until the mid-1980s.

To the extent he had free time that wasn't spent plotting out his next move, King enjoyed building model ships, trains, airplanes, and bridges. When the weather was nice, he'd putter around his yard gardening and feeding the birds and squirrels.

Once personal computers came along, his eldest son, James Jr., purchased one for him and installed a chess program that allowed him to play against the machine. It was during one such game he had an epiphany that made him sick to his stomach—leading to him quitting correspondence chess cold turkey. It wasn't the recipients of his postcards against whom he was actually competing in his postal games, he realized. Rather, it was their computers.

• • • •

Due to a creaky back, by 1980, the 43-year-old police sergeant was no longer physically able to work side jobs to supplement his income. Making the mortgage payments on the family's two-story home was becoming increasingly difficult. Though he'd tried for some time to advance to the rank of lieutenant, he failed the oral exam on multiple occasions. With his soft-spoken, measured disposition, he was told, he lacked the imposing presence required to instill fear and obedience in subordinate officers. King simply didn't possess the machismo the department considered essential to earning a lieutenant's badge. Chief of Police material he was not.

His failure to achieve a promotion led to significant financial distress. He and his wife resorted to credit cards to help make ends meet. When they maxed out their cards, they decided to downsize. In June 1985, after all three sons had completed high school, they moved into much smaller digs, a 1,500-square-foot bungalow in the Pleasant View neighborhood of Golden—665 Juniper Street. Their youngest child, David, made the move with them. Because David, a mechanic, liked to tinker with used cars, several would litter their modest lot on any given day.

By September 1986, King had put in the required 25 years to earn a full police pension—about $1,600 per month. He left the force without any fanfare, accolades, or even the slightest recognition, much as he'd spent his entire career. He was content with a simple dinner with his family to mark the milestone.

The retired sergeant quickly picked up work as a draftsman for the city's leading cartographer, Pierson Graphics, where his primary responsibility was to label street names in tiny lettering on foldout city maps. Between his pension, salary at Pierson, and the money his wife was pulling in as a receptionist and weigher for Weight Watchers, he figured they'd have ample cash flow to pay their bills. As it turned out, however, his calculations were far off the mark.

The financial dam finally burst in 1987, about a year after his retirement. King and his wife sought protection from their spiraling debts in U.S. Bankruptcy Court. At the time, they owed $65,216 on their mortgage—on the home they'd just purchased for $65,000—as well as nearly $25,000 in credit card debt. The only assets of any consequence listed in their petition were King's 1978 Ford Fiesta and his wife's 1978 Honda station wagon, the combined value of which was just under $1,000. In March 1988, an order entered in the bankruptcy court allowed them to restructure their debts.

In addition to his financial problems, King was also experiencing an array of health issues. His physician had diagnosed him as having high cholesterol and prescribed medication in an attempt to lower it. He was told to exercise more frequently, at least three times a week for 30 minutes in order to elevate his heart rate to 140 beats per minute. His wife even bought him a pedometer as a birthday present, so he could count his steps and focus on his exercise.

King was also experiencing growing difficulties with his vision. Though he'd been wearing prescription glasses since 1984, his incessant work with tiny lettering led to significant degradation of his eyesight. By July 1989, he was left with little choice but to quit his job. He was fitted with bifocals to help with both close-up and distance vision, though he preferred not to wear glasses when he didn't absolutely need to.

Realizing he had to continue making money to help pay the family's bills, King applied for a position as a security guard with United Bank of Denver. His letter to the HR department detailed his prior work as a military police officer, Denver cop, and security guard at a bank and hospital. He requested shifts during weekend nights and holidays.

He was offered a position the same day the bank received

his application, first donning a guard uniform on July 20, 1989. When he finally quit 13 months later, not a single weekend guard then on staff had been employed at United Bank of Denver as long as James W. King—or knew their way around its innards or bowels better than he did. He was also the only weekend guard who kept a loaded gun strapped to his hip at all times—just in case he needed to use it.

20

MEDIA FRENZY

July 4, 1991, marked the 215th anniversary of America's independence. As significant as that milestone was, it was barely a blip on the radar as Denver's media outlets scrambled to catch up with the jaw-dropper they'd completely missed the prior evening. The DPD had just arrested one of its own for the most horrific crime to have hit the Mile High City in decades—one that had the entire population living on a knife's edge for 18 harrowing days.

Though James W. King was now behind bars, the dozens of journalists who'd been covering the story since Father's Day didn't have the slightest inkling why he'd been arrested. It was certainly welcome news that the sprawling investigation had finally borne fruit. Yet there were so many questions that remained unanswered. Why would a retired cop who'd never been in trouble before—a dedicated public servant who'd devoted his entire career to protecting citizens from crime—suddenly go on a murderous rampage? What clues had led to his arrest? Was he the lone culprit, or were more arrests imminent?

Fortunately, Denver's press corps didn't have to wait long to seek answers. A hastily arranged news conference was scheduled for 8:00 a.m. at DPD headquarters. Satellite trucks from the local TV stations began filling the parking lot before dawn, a slew of journalists for the *Post, Rocky, Associated Press,* and other news organizations filling the standing-room only crowd. As the witching hour drew near, cameramen maneuvered their tripods to get the best angle for footage that would be beamed live all across metro Denver.

At the table positioned at the front of the room, Ari Zavaras claimed the middle seat, flanked by Craig Silverman to his left and Bob Pence to his right. Questions to the three men came fast and furious.

"What tipped you off about James King?"

"Did King confess to the crime?"

"Has the murder weapon or the money been found?"

Zavaras and Pence took turns dodging the journalists' inquiries, providing only the most cryptic of details. "Any facts of the case, any of the information," the police chief said. "I know it's frustrating—we're not going to detail today."

There hadn't been any "significant bombshell tips" leading to King's arrest, Pence revealed. Just good old-fashioned, "minute, extensive, step-by-step investigation by teams of FBI agents and Denver detectives." He pointed to inconsistencies in some of the evidence, but wouldn't divulge what they were.

"Why won't you tell us what you know?" a frustrated reporter asked. "The citizens of Denver have a right to know what's going on."

"It's just a good, sound investigative decision not to release information," Zavaras said. "There's still a lot of investigation to be followed up on and a lot to be done. This case broke extremely fast. Now we'll be in a mode of trying to do things very quickly."

"Do you personally know Sergeant King?" Zavaras was asked. "Your police careers overlapped for decades."

"I do know who he is," the chief confirmed. "But I never worked with him directly." Everyone within the police department, he said, was deeply troubled by one of their own being arrested for such an atrocious crime. He told the assembled media—and those watching at home—"a crime like this happening in your city greatly disturbs you, and we're happy to be at this point in the investigation." He stressed that the investigation was "far from over."

"Do you anticipate making any further arrests?" another reporter asked. "Is Paul Yocum still considered a suspect?"

"We don't have any immediate plans to make any further arrests," Zavaras replied. "But we also haven't cleared anyone either."

"When will charges against Sergeant King be filed? Will they be filed in federal court or state court?"

Because those were legal questions, Craig Silverman leaned forward to answer them. "Any decisions about filing charges will likely be made next week," he said. What he didn't say was that the person responsible for making those decisions—DA Norm Early—hadn't been seen at work since his defeat in the mayoral election on June 18.

As the news conference drew to a close, Zavaras made an urgent plea. "Mr. King is going to have his initial appearance later this morning. We have several witnesses who still haven't seen him in a lineup. It's absolutely imperative that no photos of him appear publicly in any way, shape, or form. It would severely impact what's to follow in this case."

To make sure the media honored the chief's wishes, Silverman asked the judge presiding over King's initial appearance to prohibit cameras in the courtroom—advocating that position at the precise moment he was supposed to be smacking his drive down the first fairway. So much for his July 4 golf game.

With Walter Gerash concurring in the motion, the judge precluded the assembled journalists from taking pictures or filming the defendant, who sat beside his attorney for the short proceeding. The judge, however, refused Silverman's request to ban the media from publishing photos of King they'd already acquired by other means.

When the hearing concluded, Gerash stepped outside the courthouse to make his first public comments about the case. Shielding his eyes from the morning sun, the combative defense attorney pulled no punches.

"They invaded his house, they made it a shambles," he complained to a Channel 7 reporter. "And I'd like to know what they found. I'd like to know what probable cause they had to search." He went even further with a *Post* reporter: "From what little I've seen, they don't have a case."

While Gerash was making his comments, another TV camera was filming King's eldest son, James Jr., in the front yard of his parents' home. "I think, you know, he was caught in circumstances," the 28-year-old told a wide-eyed 9NEWS reporter named Tom Costello. Precisely what "circumstances" his dad had been "caught in," he didn't specify.

Jimmy added that his father was "a great guy, you know. He doesn't even speed on the highway." He expressed optimism he'd be cleared of any wrongdoing.

"Is he the kind of guy who could kill four people?" Costello asked.

"No. Not even," Jimmy said, shaking his head vigorously, repeating "not even" a second time. A strange answer to be sure.

$\bullet\bullet\bullet\bullet$

Apart from meeting with his client at the city jail, appearing in court with Craig Silverman, and denouncing the investigation to the media, Walter Gerash spent part of his July 4 holiday haranguing DPD detectives, insisting they bring the six eyewitnesses to the police station for an in-person lineup—confident they'd fail to identify James King as the man who'd robbed them at gunpoint. He filed a motion asking the judge to order a physical, "corporeal" lineup if the DPD refused his request.

Priest and his team politely declined the defense attorney's invitation, opting instead to rely on the same photo lineup they'd used with David Twist. It didn't make any sense to conduct an in-person lineup, they concluded, because King had significantly altered his appearance since Father's Day, his most distinguishing facial feature—a bushy mustache—suddenly gone. He'd likely shaved it off, the detectives believed, knowing how difficult his altered appearance would make it for the eyewitnesses to identify him.

Each of the cash vault tellers was instructed not to watch the TV news, listen to the radio, or read the newspaper until they had a chance to examine the photo lineup—just in case one of the local media outlets decided to publish King's photo despite Chief Zavaras's plea. Yet by the time they sat down with detectives, each was well aware an arrest had been made—even though none of them had seen any images of the man now behind bars.

Detective Hemphill met with Maria Christian at her home the afternoon of July 4, showing her the same six-pack from which Twist had identified King a day earlier. Christian initially selected both King's photo and the one directly beneath his, number five. But when she covered King's eyes with her hand, she decided he looked "very much like the man that robbed us."

The following morning, Detective Tony Widmayer met individually with David Barranco, Kenetha Whisler, and Chong Choe in a bank conference room. Barranco made an odd statement Widmayer had difficulty understanding. Pointing to King's photo, the vault manager told him, "It's him. The same man I picked out when I met with the FBI agent."

Though he hadn't made a positive identification when he met with Agent John Kirk on June 20, Barranco *had* commented about King's face—Photo 16 in the blue binder—the only one of the six tellers who'd done so. At the time, he'd said, "This one has very similar features," pointing out that "the mustache and hair look close, but the robber's face was a little fuller." He was now saying he was equally certain he'd fingered the robber on June 20 as he was now.

Whisler was visibly shaken as she studied the six faces, fighting back tears. "I don't need to tell you who it is," she told Widmayer. "You know who it is. It's number two. He's the man who came into the vault on Father's Day with a gun."

Choe told Widmayer she couldn't possibly select any of the images because she dropped to the floor the second the gunman entered the vault, her eyes never catching a glimpse of his face.

Because Nina McGinty was still too traumatized to come anywhere near the bank, Widmayer met with her at police headquarters. She placed the six-man display on her lap with the photos facing down, taking an ultra-deep breath before flipping it over. After about 15 seconds, Widmayer noticed her body beginning to convulse. With a trembling hand, she pointed at King's photo. "This is the man who … who came into the vault on Father's Day," she declared in a halting voice, tears rolling down her cheeks. She told the detective she was certain.

••••

Though he wasn't the least bit surprised to see news of his client's arrest on the front page of the *Rocky* that same morning—sans photo—Walter Gerash's eyes nearly popped out of his head when he glanced at a related headline on page seven: *King's Brothers were Notorious Robbers.*

According to the article, the DPD had confirmed that James King's brothers, Billy and Freddy King, had been two of Denver's most notorious robbers in the 1950s and 1960s. While fleeing a robbery in 1967, Billy had engaged in a gunfight with police officers. He was hauled off to jail and ultimately died in prison. Both brothers had been involved in a string of drug-store robberies in which they'd been heavily disguised. As of 1990, Freddy was still considered one of Colorado's "most wanted" men.

The article concluded by quoting a police source as stating that Sergeant James King never discussed his notorious brothers with his fellow cops. "But every time we'd arrest Billy or Freddy," the police source said, "we'd say, 'Oh, there go Jim's brothers again.'"

Gerash slammed the newspaper on his kitchen table. *How dare those sons of bitches!* his inner voice screamed. Whoever these notorious robbers were, they had nothing whatsoever to do with his new client—who Gerash knew had only one brother, Thomas, who lived a peaceful life in San Francisco. *How desperate are they to destroy Jim King?*

He flew out the front door in a rage, jumping behind the wheel of his red Cadillac. When he arrived at police headquarters, he demanded to speak with Ari Zavaras.

"Where on earth do you get off pulling a stunt like this?" Gerash said through gritted teeth, shoving the article perilously close to the police chief's face.

"I don't know what you're talking about, Walter."

"This article is total bullshit!" Though he was considerably shorter than Zavaras, Gerash's fierce intensity more than made up for his diminutive stature. "Do you have any idea how common the name 'King' is? These criminals aren't even distant cousins of Jim King."

"If that's true," Zavaras said, "it was up to the *Rocky* to confirm their facts. In case you haven't noticed, we run a police force here, not a newsroom."

Though the defense attorney succeeded in getting the *Rocky* to issue a retraction the following day, he was convinced the DPD and the media were conspiring to tilt the playing field against his client. Walter Louis Gerash wasn't about to let that happen.

• • • •

Norm Early was finally back in the saddle on July 5, telling reporters he'd soon be charging James King for the bloody massacre. He was also giving serious thought to seeking the death penalty. No further arrests were anticipated, he said, as the DPD had concluded King acted alone, without assistance from the slain bank guards or anyone else. For his part, Paul Yocum was now in the clear.

Early's first major decision was to swap horses, replacing Craig Silverman with his most experienced homicide prosecutor, 51-year-old Chief Deputy DA Bill Buckley. Buckley had been trying Denver's worst criminals since 1971—nearly 50 murder trials under his belt. Over those 20 years, his bushy mane of brown hair had turned nearly completely silver, his mid-section adding a bit more heft. Buckley was all business all the time, his expression deadly serious in the heat of battle.

Reared in Midland, Texas, he migrated to Denver to attend Regis College, where he received a Jesuit-based education. Following his junior year in 1961, his worst fears came true when his draft number was called. He ended up with the Army Air Defense Command in Fort Meade, Maryland. With the war raging in Vietnam, it appeared only a matter of time until he found himself on the battlefield being shot at by the Viet Cong.

But to his good fortune, the Defense Command had a chorus that sang gigs all over the country—donning red-jacketed tuxedoes rather than fatigues. With his Sinatra-like singing voice, Buckley snagged a coveted spot in the 25-member ensemble, racking up 64,000 miles on Trailways buses over the next 12 months—his golden voice his ticket to greener, bullet-free pastures. He even got to sing at Carnegie Hall and on the *Tonight Show with Johnny Carson*. Though he received orders to be shipped off to Vietnam when his year with the chorus ended, the six months left on his three-year contract proved too short to actually send him.

Following Buckley's honorable discharge, he played guitar and sang folk music five nights a week in Vail and Colorado Springs while finishing his course work and obtaining his bachelor's degree. Thanks to the GI Bill, he was able to attend law school through the University of Denver's night program while working full time in the Probation Office. Time and again, one deputy DA or another would tell him, "You need to get your butt over here when you pass the bar"—which is precisely what the 31-year-old newly minted attorney did. He planned to hang up his prosecutor's hat in five years to go into private practice, which he knew would be far more lucrative.

Yet fate would intervene again, this time in the cruelest of ways. Less than two years out of law school, Buckley's kid brother, a rookie prison guard in Arizona, was savagely murdered during a well-planned uprising—stabbed 44 times by numerous inmates. When he arrived the next morning, the warden gave Buckley access to the shower stall where the inmates had taken his brother to kill him. Blood was spattered everywhere, a trail leading to the door where his brother had tried in vain to crawl to safety. The gruesome image would be seared in his memory for the rest of his life.

On the plane back to Denver, Buckley vowed to spend

the remainder of his career prosecuting ruthless killers like the monsters who'd murdered his younger brother. He felt a deep sense of kinship with family members of murder victims, always able to forge an empathetic connection that meant the world to loved ones suffering the most horrific of tragedies.

Eighteen years following his brother's brutal slaying, four sets of families were now counting on him to deliver justice. William Patrick Buckley wasn't about to let them down.

• • • •

The career prosecutor didn't need to wait long for his first skirmish with Walter Gerash, which occurred the afternoon of July 5—hours after Buckley first laid eyes on the case file. He sat quietly at the prosecution table while King's attorney made his case for a live, in-person lineup.

"Photo lineups are statistically inaccurate," Gerash argued. He urged the judge to order the DPD to bring the cash vault tellers to the police station to confront his client. "They won't do it because they know the witnesses will exonerate him," the bald-headed defense lawyer insisted.

When Buckley claimed the podium, he informed the judge—Gerash as well—that it was too late. "They've already been shown a lineup with Mr. King's face, Judge. A physical lineup now—after they've already seen his face—would be completely inappropriate." He explained that the DPD had used a photo lineup because King had "shaved a mustache he had had for years and years. His appearance is different today than it was on Father's Day."

Reporters seated in the gallery perked up when the prosecutor revealed a juicy tidbit the DPD hadn't yet made public: King had posed for a new driver's license photo—sans mustache—on June 28, four days after his first meeting with FBI agents, reporting on a DMV form that he'd lost his license and needed a duplicate. Rather than using that brand-new picture, detectives had opted to include his prior DMV photo taken in July of 1989—the one displaying his bushy mustache—in the six-pack shown to the tellers.

The hearing wrapped up quickly, the judge concluding that the defense motion was moot because the eyewitnesses had already seen a photo array that included James King. There would be no corporeal lineup after all.

Bill Buckley 1, Walter Gerash 0.

21

BIGGER BOX, PLEASE

Even though James King was safely behind bars—now confined to a ten-by-ten cell in the county jail, held in isolation for his own protection—the investigation into his involvement in the brutal massacre continued apace. Detective Priest and his team were desperate to figure out where the retired cop had stashed the nearly $200,000 stolen from the cash vault. They'd searched records for 119 different banks in the Denver metropolitan area to determine whether any had received deposits of that magnitude—all at once or in dribs and drabs—in the days and weeks following Father's Day. No such luck. They went through the same drill in Mesa, Arizona, where King's mother lived, but struck out there too.

By a stroke of good fortune, however, they seemingly hit a forensic home run with First Bank of Westland in Golden, where King had a safe deposit box, the account having been opened in April 1988. Amazingly, on Monday, June 17, 1991, King decided—after three years and two months—that he needed a bigger box. He told the bank's safe deposit attendant, Elizabeth Peralez, he wanted to upgrade to a larger box "right away," the $10 exchange fee "no big deal."

Though the timing was highly incriminating all by itself, it was King's frequent trips to First Bank that had Jon Priest convinced it was where he'd stashed the loot. According to Peralez, the retired police officer had returned six times between June 17 and July 1, each time carrying an expandable, bright-green plastic folder. On at least one of those occasions, she recounted, the folder appeared "lumpy" in the middle. Every time he came to access the new box, King insisted on using a private room, rather than the stand-up booths utilized by virtually every other customer. What he did behind closed doors, Peralez had no way of knowing.

Armed with a search warrant, Priest had a locksmith break into the metal box on July 5.

But for a second time in less than three days, the big reveal turned out to be a spectacular flameout, not a single dollar of currency—stolen or legit—found in the container. The only items stored in the box were a notary seal, a few insurance documents, and some police ID cards. Priest asked Peralez for one of the smaller boxes, allowing him to confirm that the handful of materials easily fit inside, with plenty of room to spare. Clearly, those weren't the items that had motivated James King to seek out a larger box the morning after the bank massacre.

We got here too damn late, the detective thought, deeply frustrated. Something had obviously spooked King, causing him to remove the loot after he'd stashed it in the box.

Priest asked the attendant which of the six visits had been his longest. Peralez carefully reviewed the bank's records. "His box was checked out from 12:22 to 12:29 on June 24," she said. "That's the longest one."

And there's the proof, Priest reasoned, acutely aware June 24 was the *same day* FBI agents had first appeared on King's doorstep.

As for the six plastic police ID cards located in the box, as it turned out, they were fake. Only one of the six contained King's actual name. The names on the others were William Scott Goody, William S. Goody, William J. Keplinger, James W. Ette, and Oren W. Marshall. The date of birth listed on each ID was August 23, 1940—nearly four years later than the ex-cop's actual birthdate. Exactly what had motivated him to create the fake IDs—when he'd done so, why he'd put them in the new box—was anyone's guess.

• • • •

If King had gotten cold feet and removed the loot from his new safe deposit box, it had to be somewhere else. But where? Equally if not more important was the murder weapon, the .38-caliber Colt Trooper he claimed to have dismantled and thrown away. Jon Priest didn't believe his story for a second, his instincts imploring him to keep digging.

On July 8, a new set of warrants was issued authorizing several additional searches. Investigators armed with metal detectors, shovels, and hoes probed the turf and soil in King's front and backyard—attempting quite literally to unearth buried treasure. Another set combed through the interior of his residence a second time. Once again, however, no murder weapon, loot, or any other item of forensic significance was discovered. King's desktop computer—clunky CRT monitor and all—was boxed up for forensic examiners to analyze, his evolving manuscript on police and bank security of particular interest.

Meanwhile, scuba divers with flashlights strapped to their foreheads submerged themselves in the lakes of Mount Olivet Cemetery—where King and his wife had supposedly gone just before noon on Father's Day. Yet they too found nothing of any consequence.

• • • •

That same afternoon, Walter Gerash and his client—hands cuffed, legs shackled—were back in court on the defense law-yer's motion for the imposition of a gag order, his attempt to squelch the "false guerilla tactics" and "hysteria campaign" he claimed the media was waging against his client.

"They're publishing slanderous and libelous informa-tion," the Bronx-born attorney complained to the judge, the *Rocky's* article about King's supposed drugstore-robbing brothers his primary example.

He turned to face the journalists seated behind him in the gallery, wagging his finger. "They're getting these fake, anonymous tips and they're printing them as if they're the truth. They shouldn't publish illegal stuff!"

"And it's not so anonymous either," Gerash added, contending the DPD and FBI had been selectively feeding information to the media. "It's a calculated, planned script and operational procedure to prejudice whoever sits on the jury."

Bill Buckley sat at the prosecution table as a mere observer, Denver's media outlets having retained their own counsel to oppose any attempt to restrict their activities. When one of the media lawyers insisted to the judge that the public had a right to know what was going on, Gerash leapt to his feet, interrupting the attorney mid-sentence.

"Right to know what?" he barked. "Illegal evidence? Prejudice? Lies? Slander?"

Unimpressed by his theatrics, the judge denied the motion for a gag order.

Now seething, Gerash had one final parting shot as he walked by a row of reporters on his way out of the courtroom: "You're making millions by inflaming the public," he snarled.

But if the DPD and prosecution were going to have carte blanche to weaponize the media to their advantage, Walter Gerash wasn't beneath doing so himself. *Two can play at this game,* he thought.

"Their case has a stench of weakness," he said, taunting the prosecution in a TV interview later that day. That was precisely why the government was working so hard to bias potential jurors against his client. "They're inoculating the jurors with a virus."

• • • •

Tuesday, July 9, 1991, marked another milestone in the march to justice for the families of Bill McCullom, Phil Mankoff, Scott McCarthy, and Todd Wilson, with two blockbuster events taking place on opposite ends of downtown Denver's Civic Center Park. At Colorado's Supreme Court, the highest tribunal in the state released an opinion striking down the state's death penalty. Bombshell number one.

Across the park at the district court, DA Norm Early made good on his promise to file formal charges against James King—eight counts of first-degree murder (two for each victim), six counts of menacing with a gun (one for each armored teller), and a single count of aggravated robbery. Bombshell number two. Not exactly how the retired police sergeant had planned to mark his 55th birthday, which he'd be "celebrating" from behind bars the following day.

Speaking to reporters, the district attorney explained that the case against King met his longtime standard for charging a defendant: "There's a reasonable likelihood of conviction by a jury of 12 people beyond a reasonable doubt." He refuted Gerash's contention that the prosecution had a weak case.

"I would say that Mr. Gerash is inaccurate," Early said. "He's not seen the evidence. To make such statements without seeing the evidence, I believe, is inappropriate." He described the evidence against King as "voluminous."

For his part, Gerash was overjoyed when a *Post* reporter alerted him to the Colorado Supreme Court's decision, telling the journalist, "You made my day. There's no death penalty for my client. They can't pass any laws to change it. We're in good shape."

"Not so fast," the DA later told the same reporter. "If the Colorado Legislature moves quickly, passes a new death penalty statute prior to the trial … there's a possibility that the new statute and new procedures could be used."

Sheriff's deputies escorted King back to court on July 11, where he listened impassively as the judge listed the charges against him. After he was whisked away from the courtroom, Gerash unleashed yet another diatribe against the prosecutors, claiming they'd "violated massively" his client's fair trial rights.

"They've been orchestrating a scenario akin to a soap opera," he said derisively. "It's like the press and media are cheerleaders as to what is going to turn up next. The press is part of an orchestra playing the DA's song … My God, we have to stop this!"

Gerash returned to his Victorian office building down the

street to draft a motion for a "cease-and-desist" order, now asking the judge to order the DA and his staff to stop "the improper dispensation of information to the media." Yet that motion was also denied.

The drumbeat of news coverage about the imprisoned former cop—now a criminal defendant facing at least life in prison—would continue to build and build. There was precious little Walter Louis Gerash could do to stop it.

22

AUTHOR! AUTHOR!

Though the loot from the bank heist was nowhere to be found, another treasure trove of sorts was coming into clear focus as a team of specialists sorted through the hard drive of James King's computer. The longtime cop had apparently made good use of his spare time over the five years he'd been retired, banging out portions of three different books.

The first, entitled *The Police Officer's Guide,* was the manual he'd talked about extensively during his interviews with FBI agents and DPD detectives—361 double-spaced pages. Yet that constituted only a portion of the 23 chapters he planned to write. The completed chapters covered a wide range of topics, including community relations, crime prevention, mechanics of an arrest, disturbance calls, mentally disturbed persons, and medical emergency calls. Notably, however, he hadn't written a single word about bank security or working as a security guard—his purported reason for taking a weekend position with United Bank.

Exactly why the retired cop believed he had the background and qualifications—let alone literary chops—to craft a publishable police manual was anyone's guess. After all, he'd never advanced beyond the rank of sergeant, his police career mired in mediocrity by any objective standard. Perhaps it was the same hubris he possessed as a 25-year-old, convinced after graduating first in his class of cadets he'd eventually become police chief.

Priest had subordinate officers drill down on every word of King's tome, hoping they'd find incriminating nuggets to use at trial. Though most of the pages contained ultra-dry, unhelpful prose, more than a few passages caught their attention. In several chapters, he'd written about officers being ambushed and shot in the back of the head and in their backs—21 such instances in all—similar to how the United Bank killer had executed the four security guards. Was that merely a coincidence?

The ex-guard was also laboring on an as-yet untitled action-adventure, science-fiction novel with pornographic overtones. His heroine was a *Playboy* centerfold and also a female wrestler. During a televised bout, King wrote of her opponent yanking off her bra and exposing her ample breasts. Another female character, Anne Smith aka Eve, was a 5'3" brown-eyed beauty with protruding nipples who'd been gifted the art of pleasing by the goddess Venus. King had named a third female character Satan.

The wannabe author filled several pages of his novel with graphic descriptions of sexual bondage, torture, and vicious gang rapes—quite the opposite of his excruciatingly dull police manual—the writing pieced together in a clunky, amateurish style. One of the more fleshed-out scenes involved a sadomasochist using a burning cigarette to torture a bound, half-naked woman.

"The masked man touched the red-hot cigarette to Pauline's left nipple," King wrote. "There was an audible hiss and a tiny stink of burning flesh. Pauline shrieked desperately but her tormentor was viciously unmoved by her struggles."

"Scream as much as you please," he taunted his helpless captive. "I enjoy it, and no one can hear you."

To Priest and his fellow detectives, the combined effect of the sadomasochistic fantasies King narrated in his novel, and his callous descriptions of officers being shot in the back of the head in his police manual, spoke volumes about his psyche. Did he meet the clinical criteria to be labeled a psychopath? At the very least, in view of the cold-blooded manner in which the security guards had been slaughtered, King's writings seemed eerily prophetic. Certainly worthy of mention to the prosecution team as they assembled their evidence for trial.

His third book was perhaps the most significant of all, an autobiography he entitled *A Life! What For?* To Priest, the choice of title was most illuminating, indicating frustration, if not anger, over the ex-cop's underwhelming career and deteriorating financial condition. A self-recognition that his life as a whole had been an abject failure. He also found noteworthy that King didn't include a single mention of his wife or children in the three-page outline—which was as far as the book had matured. The outline was organized chronologically, chapters focused on the author's early years, his time in public school and college, his career as a police officer, and his retirement.

In the section outlining his retirement, King had jotted some notes about the United Bank of Denver. "After the theft from the North Vestibule ATM in May of 1990," he'd written, "I decided to quit working at the bank. The poor investigation of the approximately $30,000 money loss and the treatment of the guard employees was so bad that I decided to quit." Tellingly, he acknowledged remaining at the bank until that August "so that the bank would not try to accuse me of the theft also." Was this a tacit confession that he'd been involved in *that* crime? What did he mean by "also"?

Yet it was the final entry in the outline that virtually leapt off the page: "United Bank robbed. Four guards killed Sunday, Father's Day. Security seems to be worse than when I worked there with all their new bank alarm systems." What was his point in typing those words? Was he bragging about how much more he knew about bank security than United Bank's high-level security personnel? Was that why he'd killed the defenseless guards—to prove what bumbling idiots the bank's so-called security experts were?

Notably, King didn't express an iota of sorrow or sympathy for the loved ones of Bill McCullom, Phil Mankoff, Scott McCarthy, or Todd Wilson. How telling was that?

• • • •

To further explore the possibility that King's animosity toward United Bank security officials had morphed into a diabolical murder plot, DPD detectives thoroughly reviewed his personnel file for clues. Interestingly, in his self-evaluation, he touted his "strong background of knowledge of criminal law and criminal behavior" and wrote of his desire "to learn as much as possible concerning private security operations."

In the section of the pre-printed form entitled "Factors Limiting Performance," King complained of the "general lack of concern for real security by most bank employees that I come into contact with." He'd expressed those same sentiments—after four of his successors were ruthlessly annihilated—to the *Rocky*'s John Ensslin, FBI agents, and DPD detectives. Though he was outspoken about such concerns during his employment and had made recommendations for improvements, his superiors had completely ignored him. Were the brutal murders his way of teaching them a lesson?

Perhaps most significant of all, King's personnel file included a letter of reprimand regarding an incident that occurred in February 1990, some six months before he quit. Apparently, a moving crew had arrived at the bank one weekend morning seeking his assistance in entering a secured area. The writeup indicated that King had rebuffed their request after he'd been unable to get ahold of a supervisor to confirm the movers had been pre-cleared.

Thus, not only was he highly critical of the bank's "shitty" security procedures—particularly in allowing non-employees to roam freely through secure areas over the weekend—he'd actually been disciplined for trying to impose some semblance of security on his own.

Wow! Priest thought as he slid the letter to the corner of his desk. He closed his eyes, deep in thought, trying to remember what King had told Detective Calvin Hemphill just prior to his arrest. The words finally came back to him. "You wouldn't know if they were a vice president or a secretary," he'd said, referring to the pressure he felt to let strangers into the bank despite the obvious security risk in doing so.

At that moment, everything suddenly clicked together. *That's why he did it!* Priest reasoned. *He wanted to prove how wrong they were to have written him up. He needed to show them the bloodbath their reckless approach to security could cause.*

Unquestionably, the $200,000 stolen from the cash vault would have eradicated the financial mess King and his wife were facing following their bankruptcy. Yet that wasn't the true motive for the crime, Priest now realized. *It wasn't about the money.*

But that said, the lead detective was still dying to know where it was.

23

IF THE SHOES DON'T FIT ...

The most significant item discovered during the initial search of James King's home were the shoes Detective Priest believed matched the shoeprints the killer had left behind in the bank's monitor room and incinerator room. Indeed, the black shoes were the critical piece of evidence that had tipped the scales in favor of reading the ex-cop his rights and hauling him off to jail.

The footwear was shipped off to the FBI's crime lab in Quantico, Virginia, where a shoeprint expert conducted a detailed comparison to the prints discovered at the bank. Much to Priest's dismay, however, the report he received back from the FBI indicated that the sole pattern of the incarcerated suspect's shoes *didn't* match the prints left by the killer.

Though there was some similarity between King's shoes and the shoeprints—both containing a series of parallel grooves running from heel to toe—the spacing between the grooves on the soles was different from the spacing in the shoeprints. The actual shoes also had wear patterns not observable in the prints. The FBI expert couldn't even determine whether the footwear seized from King's home was the same size as the shoes that created the prints.

Even more troublesome, the crime lab technician couldn't confirm whether the shoeprint on the plexiglass in the monitor room precisely matched the prints left in the dust and on the printer paper in the incinerator room. The report noted the sole patterns were "similar" in design and design size, but that not enough detail existed in the print on the plexiglass to make a definitive match.

King's shoes were also tested in the DPD crime lab with the chemical phenolphthalein, which forensic technicians use to detect even microscopic quantities of blood. The result of that testing was also negative.

Thus, considering the conclusions of forensic experts in both Quantico and Denver, the "smoking-gun" evidence the DPD had relied on to arrest the retired police sergeant bore no actual connection to the massacre at United Bank. Unfortunate indeed.

• • • •

Priest and his colleagues had been holding out hope that fingerprints lifted from various surfaces in the monitor room—as well as the palm print discovered on the door jamb at the entrance to the battery room—would connect James King to the primary crime scene. Following King's booking and processing at the city jail on July 4, they had a fresh set of fingerprints to use for comparison. Yet not a single print lifted from the monitor room matched.

Of the six latent prints the DPD's fingerprint examiner considered usable, only one could be identified: a print on the cellophane wrapper of a vending-machine cookie that matched Scott McCarthy. The one latent print recovered from a VCR was determined to have no forensic value at all.

What about the Mountain Dew can that had propped open the inner mantrap door? A print lifted from its aluminum surface contained the ridge detail of a left pinky finger. Yet that print didn't match James King either. Rather, it matched an employee named Harry Glass, one of the security guards relieved by Bill McCullom and Phil Mankoff when they reported for work at 12:30 a.m. Father's Day morning. With shoulder-length, auburn hair and matching mustache, the bespectacled 25-year-old guard didn't bear the slightest resemblance to the gunman the six tellers observed in the cash vault.

At the time it was discovered, the palm print on the battery room's door jamb held so much promise—the impression crystal clear. From his jail cell, James King was ordered to dip his palm in ink to create a print for comparison. But it didn't match either.

Attempts were also made to harvest usable prints from the latex gloves found in the trash bin beside the elevator on the seventh floor of the parking garage. Like King's shoes, the gloves were sent off to the FBI's crime lab, where they were subjected to chemical processes designed to reveal fingerprints. But the FBI's fingerprint examiner found insufficient ridge detail to make a suitable comparison to King's prints. The examiner also provided a second opinion on the six latent prints the DPD's expert had analyzed—and came to the exact same conclusion: none of them had been made by the retired cop now behind bars.

• • • •

The trial was set for May 11, 1992, a mere ten months following King's arrest. Behind the scenes, Bill Buckley and his team were working feverishly to assemble the best possible case they could. But that wouldn't be easy, as it was now clear the crime-scene evidence would bolster the defendant's case, not their own. Walter Gerash was sure to play up each negative finding about the shoes, fingerprints, and palm print every chance he had—not to mention investigators' failure to recover the VHS tapes, keys, handheld radios, or pages from the guard logbook. Or the murder weapon or loot.

To be sure, the prosecution had five eyewitnesses who'd made positive identifications of James King. Buckley was well aware, however, the tellers' testimony would be subject to vigorous cross-examination that held the potential to sink their identifications altogether. Gerash would undoubtedly focus on the failure of each to identify King as the gunman when they'd first seen his photo four days after the massacre. Nearly as significant, the defense would force each eyewitness to admit how heavily the gunman had been disguised.

If jurors discounted the testimony of David Barranco, Maria Christian, David Twist, Kenetha Whisler, and Nina McGinty, the entire case would boil down to purely circumstantial evidence and the believability of the defendant himself were he to take the stand.

In view of all that, it's fair to ask whether the DPD and FBI made their arrest too hastily—jumped the gun, so to speak—perhaps succumbing to the intense hue and cry to hold someone accountable for the most horrific crime to have hit the Mile High City in decades. They'd only begun to focus on James King as a serious suspect on July 2—preoccupied with Paul Yocum until then—placing him under arrest less than 48 hours later.

Unlike Yocum, law enforcement officers hadn't surveilled King's activities for any appreciable length of time—giving him a chance to slip up and incriminate himself. If he had nearly $200,000 at his immediate disposal, wasn't it worth waiting for him to start spending it? Though they hadn't found any suspicious transactions in his bank accounts between June 16 and July 3, there had only been 13 banking days since the heist. If they had held off making an arrest for a few months, would the results have been different?

Moreover, if they had probable cause to search King's home and vehicles, they had equal probable cause to obtain an order allowing a wiretap of his telephone. Who knows what the ex-cop might have revealed to one of his sons, his wife, or perhaps even an accessory had they just waited him out and eavesdropped on his conversations.

Another option at their disposal was a "controlled call" with someone like Mike McKown—the former guard King considered his best friend—who could have been provided a script written by Priest and his colleagues. The reason why controlled calls often succeed is that the suspect believes he's talking to a friend, his guard completely down. Suspects don't readily notice that the friend's questions are born of more than idle curiosity.

Better yet, a sting operation could have been arranged to

get King talking to an undercover agent who either gained his trust or threatened to expose his criminal conduct. The FBI had employed precisely such tactics to catch criminals of all stripes—including dirty cops—since its founding.

Why didn't Bob Pence and his colleagues make similar efforts with James King? Wasn't it worth the wait to try to develop that type of evidence before pulling the proverbial trigger? With the former police sergeant now biding his time at the county jail, the ship to employ such tried-and-true investigative techniques had already sailed out to sea.

And to ratchet up the pressure on Bill Buckley and his prosecution team all the more, Norm Early had gotten his wish from the state legislature, which reinstated Colorado's death penalty on September 19, 1991. On December 4, the DA announced he'd be seeking the death penalty against James King after all. Consequently, the upcoming trial would, quite literally, be a battle to the death.

PART THREE

TRIAL OF THE CENTURY

24

BATTLE STATIONS

The mere sight of the Honorable Richard "Dick" Spriggs perched on the bench had more than a few Denver attorneys quaking in their tasseled loafers as they entered his courtroom. The hard-nosed judge appeared to delight in chewing out prosecutors and defense lawyers—an equal-opportunity offender—his tongue-lashings on full display to jurors, witnesses, and courtroom staff. He'd demonstrate displeasure by raising his voice, slamming down a pen, or wagging a finger, labeling even talented attorneys a "public embarrassment" if their tactics exceeded his rigid boundaries.

The bespectacled, 57-year-old jurist combed what little was left of his auburn hair over his otherwise bald head. A bushy beard of the same hue ran down the sides of his face, graying as it encircled his mouth. More often than not, he'd adorn his black robe with a stylish bowtie.

Spriggs' gravelly voice bore a passing resemblance to that of actor W.C. Fields. His demeanor, however, was more akin to Ebeneezer Scrooge—crusty, curmudgeonly, cantankerous—his temper boiling over on a near-daily basis.

Hyperactive in nearly every proceeding, Spriggs implored lawyers to "move it along"—patience not his strong suit—reframing questions he considered poorly constructed and sustaining objections whether they'd been lodged or not. It would drive him batty when attorneys weren't fully prepared or attempted to plow the same ground over and over again, his blood pressure particularly elevated when opposing counsel sniped at one another like schoolkids. "I'm the one in charge here," he'd admonish them sharply. "In this courtroom, you direct your remarks *to me*."

But Judge Spriggs also had a playful sense of humor, frequently injecting his whimsical quips into the ebb and flow, as much for his own amusement as to lighten the mood. He enjoyed trotting out the idiom—delivered with his own inimitable flair—"when pigs fly." He actually kept a picture of the farm animal adorned with wings at the ready, flashing it at lawyers to signal his rejection of a weak argument. Despite his often prickly demeanor, no one doubted his legal acumen, his rulings typically spot on, rarely reversed on appeal.

Like Walter Gerash, Spriggs hailed from the Empire State—the outskirts of Syracuse—earning his B.A. in English literature from Colgate and a law degree from Cornell. He first set foot in the Mile High City in 1961, two days after completing law school. Before receiving his judicial appointment in 1988, he'd spent most of the prior 27 years as a state and federal prosecutor, clashing with Gerash on numerous occasions. Outside the courtroom, the judge's lifelong passion was fly fishing, the Rockies' rivers and streams the only place he felt completely at peace.

• • • •

The trial of *The People of the State of Colorado v. James W. King* took place in Courtroom 16 on the top floor of the Denver City & County Building, a neoclassical granite structure completed in 1932. The visually striking, four-story edifice—fronted by three dozen Roman columns, an elegant clock tower rising from the center—seemed more befitting the streets of medieval Rome than a modern American city. The building housed the mayor, city council, city offices, and county and district courts.

Both counsel tables in the oddly configured courtroom were turned at a right angle to the bench—facing the jury box—

the prosecution table closest to the ultimate decision-makers, the defense table a row behind. The prosecutors and defense attorneys who weren't standing at the podium to examine witnesses had to pivot to their left—at least 90 degrees—to bring the witness, or judge, into their field of vision.

For their part, jurors had to crane their necks to see the witness stand, situated 30 feet across the room—to the judge's right. Compounding that problem, the court reporter's station jutted out halfway between the jury box and the stand, the stenographer directly in jurors' line of sight.

Even more bizarre, the jury room was located clear across the courtroom—some 50 feet from the jury box. Hence, when they entered and exited the courtroom, jurors had to parade by both counsel tables, the spacing so narrow they'd have to tuck in their elbows to avoid making contact with James King himself—who sat at the far end of the defense table, almost directly in their path. During the month-long trial, they'd get close enough to touch the accused killer at least ten times a day.

The courtroom's acoustics were downright dreadful, Judge Spriggs constantly having to remind witnesses to speak up and lean into the microphone. Making matters worse, church-like bells from the building's clock tower clanged every 15 minutes—loud enough to be heard all across downtown— additional chimes marking the top of each hour. Blaring sirens from police cars, ambulances, and firetrucks brought the proceedings to a standstill at least once a day.

Due to the intense public interest in the case, a slew of journalists attended the trial. A fledgling cable network in its very first year—Court TV—had successfully petitioned to allow its camera to beam gavel-to-gavel coverage all across America. Though the faces of jurors and the six eyewitnesses were deemed off limits, the camera was otherwise free to roam Courtroom 16 to zoom in on the lawyers, judge, defendant, witnesses, exhibits, and spectators.

Only a handful of seats were reserved for the media—situated just forward of the gallery in front of a stately mahogany partition, called the "bar"—the remainder of the press corps relegated to an overflow room down the hallway. The gallery could barely accommodate 100 spectators, limited further by the front rows being reserved for family members of the victims and of the defendant. Because the local community's demand to attend the trial far exceeded its limited capacity, sheriff's deputies began each morning raffling off the available seats, those having their names called celebrating as if they'd won the grand-prize lottery.

Bill Buckley was joined at the prosecution table by Detective Priest and Chief Deputy DA S. Lamar Sims. The mustachioed 38-year-old tall drink of water bore an uncanny resemblance to actor Billy Dee Williams. Before attending Harvard Law School, Sims had parlayed his movie-star good looks into cold hard cash, working as a fashion model. He'd been prosecuting criminals in Denver's district court since 1981.

Ever suave, Sims glided around the courtroom with elegance and grace—as if on a ballroom dance floor. Unlike most trial lawyers, he smiled and laughed as he went about his business, unflappable under pressure. Beloved by members of the DPD, Sims had instructed up-and-coming officers at the police academy for the past six years. He was also quite the athlete and a champion kayak racer.

Seated beside Walter Gerash at the defense table was his 42-year-old law partner, Scott Robinson, a Denver native who'd gone to college intending to become a novelist. Yet by the time he'd graduated from the University of Denver with a B.A. in history and English literature—a huge Dickens fan— he realized he'd die a poor man pursuing that avocation. He chose law instead, paying his way through law school at the University of Colorado driving a taxi at night. He finished near the top of his class in 1975.

After two years clerking for a judge on the Colorado Court of Appeals, Robinson was hired primarily to help Gerash with appellate work, though it wouldn't take long for the junior lawyer to become his right-hand man in the courtroom. By the time the King case was called for trial, the sign in front of the Victorian serving as their law office read "Gerash, Robinson & Miranda."

With his boyish mop of chocolate-brown hair, youthful appearance, and syrupy sweet voice—unfailingly polite and cheerful—Robinson could charm judges, juries, and even opposing counsel, an "aw-shucks" grin seemingly permanently plastered across his face. The happy warrior's courtroom skills were razor sharp, delivery smooth and polished. Robinson was particularly adept at mastering complex evidence and making it simple enough for jurors to understand.

He too was an excellent athlete, having completed the Boston Marathon in under three hours and Hawaii's ironman triathlon on multiple occasions. Though he arrived late to the game—taking his first glimpse at the King file after the Christmas holidays—Scott Robinson could hardly wait for the trial to get underway.

• • • •

The first stage of jury selection lasted an entire week, whittling a pool of 236 prospective jurors down to 80. Due to the pervasive media coverage of the bloody massacre and King's arrest, many would-be jurors had already formed intractable views regarding his guilt or innocence, resulting in Judge Spriggs excusing them "for cause."

Moreover, because this was a capital case that would end in a death-penalty phase were King to be convicted, the jury had to be "death qualified." Even if potential jurors hadn't formed an opinion as to guilt or innocence, those who held moral convictions preventing them from considering the ultimate punishment were automatically excluded.

The prosecution and defense took turns questioning the 80 who'd made the cut, each permitted to exercise 12 peremptory challenges without having to explain their "strikes." In his conversations with panel members, the mantra Lamar Sims returned to time and again was "don't judge a book by its cover." That aphorism was intended to acclimate potential jurors to the notion that just because King was a soft-spoken, mild-mannered, former public servant didn't mean he wasn't also the savage killer who'd brutally executed four defenseless victims in cold blood.

For his part, Gerash wanted the citizens seated in the jury box to understand that the entire case boiled down to whether the cash vault tellers had mistakenly identified the wrong man. A human being, he explained, can see something many times and still not be able to identify it correctly. To drive that point home, the defense lawyer asked would-be jurors if they could recall which way Lincoln is facing on a copper penny, despite having seen that image thousands of times. (The sixteenth president is facing to the right.)

After both sides exercised their allotted strikes, a jury of seven men and five women, along with one male and one female alternate, was empaneled to hear the evidence. Over the next several weeks, the 14 Denverites—nearly all under the age of 50—would become like family, learning virtually everything they could about one another. Two were Latino, one was a naturalized citizen originally from Iran, and the remainder were Caucasian. Six of the eight men sported mustaches, one of whom also wore a beard.

Four of the jurors worked at Stapleton Airport: two airline mechanics, an administrative assistant, and a woman who prepared meals for United Airlines. One juror worked for Coca-Cola and another for the Adolph Coors beer company. The jury also included a mental-health counselor, nurse, office manager for a national realtor, unemployed actor and writer, vacuum parts representative, electrician, architect, and a factory representative for Ford.

The group brought a wide variety of life experiences with them into the jury box. One had been shot during an armed robbery. Another had a brother-in-law who served as a police officer. The father of a third was an airport security guard. A fourth was a skydiving enthusiast and motorcross racer. Two of them enjoyed playing chess. An alternate juror even bore the surname, King.

In all, the 14 citizens who took their oaths just before lunch on Tuesday, May 19, 1992 comprised a representative cross-section of the Denver community, precisely what America's Founding Fathers had envisioned. In their hands, they now held the quest for justice that was all the families of Bill McCullom, Phil Mankoff, Scott McCarthy, and Todd Wilson had left. Equally significant, they would be the ones to decide whether James William King would walk out of the courtroom a free man, spend the remainder of his life in prison, or meet his maker in the execution chamber.

The stage was finally set for the highly anticipated showdown to begin.

25

CURTAIN UP

Spectators were crammed into Courtroom 16 like a can of sardines, nervous energy pulsating throughout the gallery, counsel tables, and jury box. In the wooden pew closest to the defense table, James King's wife, sons, and sister sat elbow to elbow, praying their long nightmare was about to end.

The defendant himself had been allowed to trade in his jail uniform for a crisp brown suit purchased just for the occasion, his hands and legs freed from the manacles he'd endured during his short ride over from the county jail. He was a shell of his former self, having shed 28 pounds since his July 4 arrest, his face as clean-shaven as on that fateful day.

Across the aisle from the accused killer's family sat the still-grieving relatives of the murdered security guards—wives, parents, siblings, in-laws, aunts, uncles, and stepkids. No matter what happened in the coming days and weeks, their nightmare would continue for the rest of their lives. By the same token, however, their quiet presence and stoic resolve would serve as a constant reminder to all participants that the trial's singular purpose was to obtain justice for the four slain guards.

On the judge's cue, Bill Buckley approached a well-worn, four-legged oak podium centered in front of the jury box, to which he'd remain tethered for the entirety of his opening statement. His presentation style and tone were akin to that of a college professor at the front of a lecture hall—unemotional, matter-of-fact—attempting to teach the jury large chunks of the information they'd need to know.

"You've all no doubt heard the adage, 'Don't judge a book by its cover,'" he began in his distinctive Texas twang, repeating the refrain Lamar Sims had employed repeatedly throughout jury selection. That saying, he told jurors, held particular significance for the evidence they were about to hear.

Gesturing to their family members in the gallery, Buckley provided brief biographies of McCullom, Mankoff, Wilson, and McCarthy, explaining where and how each was murdered. Rather than going home at the end of their shifts, he said in a somber tone, they'd left the bank building in hearses "because of the greed of one man. One man who entered the bank by trickery, using the precision of a *Mission: Impossible*-type plan."

The veteran prosecutor asserted that "the murderer/robber possessed too much insider information or knowledge not to have worked in the recent past as a security guard at the bank," and that the circumstances surrounding the crime "narrow down the possible suspects to a select few." Among those few, James King "showed a disordinate, excessive interest in learning about every nook and cranny of the bank—entering areas that had no relationship whatsoever to the regular duties of a weekend guard."

The timing of the killer's entry was critical, Buckley said, because coming earlier would have caused a confrontation with the armored couriers and the money would later be locked away in a safe. The defendant knew that using the name Bob Bardwell would elicit a response from a guard "from whom he could obtain the necessary tools to complete the task"—namely, a Markey card and key ring.

The chief deputy DA described the killer's desperate attempts to break into the guard supervisor's office—shooting the doorknob, kicking the window and then the sheetrock outside the adjacent storage room—his removal of all the VHS tapes except one, and all the key rings that contained MK1 master keys. Buckley noted the assassin had entered the cash vault through an unmarked door, using McCullom's Markey card to penetrate the secure area.

The robber's language inside the vault further illustrated his insider knowledge, the prosecutor said, "mantrap," "bait money," and "strapped money" all being terms of art familiar to bank employees. So too did his use of McCullom's Markey card to exit the cash vault and his ride up the #3 elevator to make his getaway.

Having fleshed out the crime, the lead prosecutor pivoted to King's interviews with law enforcement officers. On June 24, he told FBI agents he'd quit his job at the bank "because he felt security procedures were poor and also because he had heard that the bank intended to disarm the guards." At the time, the ex-cop offered his view that the crime had been committed by a current or former bank employee. When asked about his Colt .38-caliber revolver, "he told these two young agents that he had disposed of this gun because he discovered it had a cracked cylinder," Buckley said, his tone conveying utter incredulity. "So he threw it away."

The very same day he met with the FBI agents, the prosecutor revealed, King received a call from his old pal, Mike McKown. He told his former partner he'd just been visited by the FBI and was "in a bind" because he didn't have an alibi for the time of the crime. He also claimed to have been home alone on Father's Day because he'd dropped his wife off at work. Yet that wasn't true, Buckley said, because both his wife and son David spent the day at the house.

Detectives were immediately skeptical about King's purported reason for disposing of his gun, he told jurors. Why? Because a retired police officer wouldn't "dismantle and throw away the service revolver he had carried for 25 years—which represented safety and his identity as a police officer."

He provided jurors a tutorial on firearms and ballistics, noting that Detective Frank Kerber, who'd examined all the recovered bullets, had concluded they'd most likely been fired by a Colt-type revolver. "And so the police were interested in this fact—that the defendant's missing his longtime, lifetime revolver and Detective Kerber is saying that the bullets could well have been fired by a Colt revolver." Not only that, the three or four types of ammo used to kill the security guards were "consistent with the kinds of ammunition issued to Denver police officers during the duration of a police career."

An hour into his opening statement, Buckley finally turned to the subject of eyewitness identification, telling jurors about the red and blue notebooks the armored tellers had reviewed with Agent John Kirk. He acknowledged that "no one made any kind of a positive identification" and that King's DMV photo had been in one of the books. David Barranco, however, had lingered on King's picture, mentioning to Kirk that "the hair and mustache were similar to that of the robber."

The deputy DA explained that detectives later used a photo lineup of six men, which was different from the photo books because the foreheads and hair had been cropped to simulate what was observable at the time of the robbery. Five of the six tellers, he revealed, selected James King from that lineup.

Buckley circled back to the retired cop's Colt Trooper, telling jurors it had been fired regularly at the police range and was never reported to have a cracked cylinder or malfunction. In fact, in October 1989, King had taken the gun for minor repairs to a gunsmith, "who will tell you that it was in excellent shape and that all it needed was some minor timing work ... He'll tell you that cylinders on such guns don't crack." And also that any repair would have been "easy and inexpensive."

During his July 2 interview with Detective Hemphill and Agent Villegas, Buckley said, the defendant provided a second explanation for discarding his gun: that his wife "didn't want such a gun around the house." He also told the lawmen that because of the problems with the bank's surveillance cameras, security guards wouldn't know who they were letting into the bank, but felt compelled to do so for fear of a complaint being lodged if they refused.

During that same interview, he placed his return from the Capitol Hill Community Center at 10:20 a.m., 24 minutes after the armed robber had departed the cash vault. Buckley told jurors that Detective Priest had driven that route several times, and that on a Sunday morning with almost no traffic, the trip back to King's home would have taken only 12 to 15 minutes.

On July 3, he continued, the defendant was interviewed by Sergeant Hildebrant and Lieutenant Haney—who asked whether he had any information that could corroborate his alibi. King reiterated that he'd gone to the community center to try to play a game of chess. Conveying incredulity again, Buckley noted that "the Denver Chess Club hasn't met, or used, the Capitol Hill Community Center since 1984." Moreover, there were two men working there that morning "and they never saw anybody."

Not only did the former sergeant fail to offer Hildebrant and Haney anything to corroborate his alibi, Buckley recounted, he also told the officers he didn't believe any neighbor had seen him when he returned home. Meanwhile, his wife Carolyn was being interviewed by another detective and agent, telling them that the ex-cop kept his gun in a locked box in the den—rather than having discarded it—and that she'd never expressed any concerns to him about having guns at the house.

Buckley shifted to the July 3 search of the couple's home, sharing with jurors how a set of plans showing various parts of the bank's lower levels was found, as was a pair of shoes with a "very similar pattern" to the shoeprints found near McCullom's body and on the plexiglass window in the monitor room. He conceded, however, that the FBI lab had concluded they were "probably not the correct shoes."

Another item found at the house led detectives to the First Bank of Westland, the prosecutor explained, where King had shown up the day after the crime seeking a larger safe deposit box—which he needed "right away." He'd made several suspicious trips to access the larger box over the following two weeks, each time carrying a green accordion-type folder that seemed to be bulging. The money stolen from the cash vault "would have easily fit into that large box with room to spare."

The last item of evidence Buckley discussed was the anticipated testimony of a security guard named Dana Pappas. King had shared with Pappas how he would rob the bank—hypothetically speaking. "Dana Pappas will tell you the defendant told him that he would call up security to gain entry to the bank. That he would then kill the unarmed guards in the monitor room. That he would then go to the cash vault and rob the bank and that he would then exit the bank in an elevator to the parking deck"—precisely what transpired on June 16, 1991.

Despite having previewed a large swath of the evidence during his 85 minutes behind the podium, Bill Buckley resumed his seat beside Jon Priest without having said a single word about three critical subjects: (1) the fingerprints and palm print lifted from various surfaces in the monitor room, (2) the 5:04 a.m. alarm in the records tunnel, or (3) Paul Yocum. Not surprisingly, those were topics King's lawyers had every intention of highlighting during their opening statement.

• • • •

Scott Robinson stepped up to the podium sporting the first of what would amount to a closetful of double-breasted suits he'd showcase during the course of the lengthy trial. Unlike Bill Buckley, he didn't remain centered behind the podium, choosing instead to roam the well of the courtroom during his 90-minute presentation, which he delivered with a bit more passion than his adversary.

"On Father's Day last year," he began, "Jim King did not get out of bed, drive down to the United Bank, and coldly murder four security guards. During the next few weeks, you will be not just jurors, but also witnesses—witnesses to what happens to a person unjustly charged. You're going to hear a little bit—if not a lot—about what actually happened at the United Bank. What you're not going to learn during the course of the next few weeks is who murdered the guards, who robbed the tellers, or even how many people were involved."

Unlike Buckley, who'd refrained from discussing the eyewitness identifications for a solid hour, Robinson launched into that subject right out of the chute, describing in great detail the photo binders reviewed by the six tellers, "four days after the robbery, while the witnesses' memories were still fresh." He told jurors they hadn't been assembled by accident. "These books were not some sort of casual attempt to start getting information about what the robber looked like. These books were put together to take to the eyewitnesses and give them an opportunity to see if they could identify the man that robbed them at gunpoint."

The result? "None of them identified James King. He was *exonerated* of this crime almost a year ago … And by the time the trial comes around almost a year later, you will hear these witnesses tell you they are unwaveringly sure that James King is the man they saw." Now it was the defense attorney whose tone was dripping with incredulity.

He quickly pivoted to the forensic evidence. "The robber or robbers left something behind—something other than the memories of the eyewitnesses. What the robbers left behind were footprints, a palm print, and fingerprints." All of the scientific evidence, he declared, "*exonerates* James King."

He turned next to his client's alibi. "Almost a year ago on Father's Day, Jim King was away from home for about 45 minutes—a decision which has affected not just the ten months that followed, but truly the rest of his life. He went in search of a chess game on Father's Day. He decided to do something for himself. He never dreamed that that drive would bring him here."

Before the ex-cop left for the community center, Robinson said, his neighbor Roberta Trujilo saw him and yelled "Happy Father's Day, you old fart." That occurred at nine o'clock. "So we have Jim King at his home at about nine o'clock."

King had actually attempted to call the chess club a few days before Father's Day, the defense lawyer recounted, trying to find out where it met. Since he couldn't learn anything through that phone call, he drove out to the community center, parked, and tried to access the building—but to no avail. "Luckily for James King, yet another neighbor saw him return home," a man named David Bell, who recalled seeing him arrive next door at about ten o'clock.

Robinson revealed that his client didn't know any of the four men who'd been killed. But he was "horrified" when he heard about the massacre on TV. Why? Because "he had made numerous, numerous suggestions to anybody who would listen—any of his supervisors—urging them to improve security."

The very next morning, "James King did the first of several acts which he will always regret." He needed a larger safe deposit box because he was working on a book about police security on his computer and was backing up the project on floppy disks. His eldest son, James Jr., had urged him to store the disks in a safe place. He made several trips to the box to get it organized. "It never occurred to Jim King that his working on his book, and changing safety deposit boxes, would make him the focus of the police and the FBI."

Robinson noted how the longtime cop had spoken with a newspaper reporter about the deficiencies in security at the bank before FBI agents showed up on his doorstep. "Jim King was not the only guard who was worried," he noted. "Jim King was not the only guard who felt the security procedures were inadequate."

When he spoke to FBI agents on June 24, he told them he'd disposed of his gun nearly a year earlier. "The cylinder had cracked," Robinson said. "The gun had been promised to son David, but it was dangerous." It was 30 years old and "had been in for repairs several times. The cylinder, in fact, had been repaired recently … It would have cost more to repair the gun than it cost Jim King to buy it."

The defense lawyer conceded that King "was troubled by the fact that he really didn't have a strong alibi" and had shared his concerns with his friend, Mike McKown. He described the scene at King's Golden, Colorado home the evening of July 3, with the fireworks display occurring across the road while his client "was handcuffed and had to stand on his porch for hours while his home was exhaustively searched."

"What led the police to arrest and charge this man with this brutal crime?" Robinson asked. To answer that question, he began developing the timeline—a very different timeline from the one jurors had heard from the chief deputy DA.

"This was not a normal night," he said. "At 5:04 a.m., some

four hours before these guards were going to be murdered, somebody opened a door—a door that shouldn't have been opened"—in a storage tunnel behind the security vault. Ordinarily, Robinson said, a guard would have been dispatched to figure out what happened. But on this occasion, someone in the monitor room simply pushed a button to turn it off. "Why? We don't know."

When the imposter posing as Bob Bardwell sought an escort at the freight elevator at 9:14 a.m., he added, "Jim King is about to start driving to the Capitol Hill Community Center."

After describing the murders in the monitor room, Robinson focused on the confounding event that occurred at 9:33 a.m. "What happened was that the murderer—the robbers—the men or man covered up his tracks … by going over to the console and re-alarming that room that had been accessed at 5:04." He intimated that someone had been lurking in that room for four-and-a-half hours.

The monitor room contained all kinds of clues: a palm print on the entryway to the battery room, fingerprints near the VCR equipment, and a footprint on the plexiglass window. "The men or man who left those palm prints," he revealed, "the men or man that left the footprints, the men or man that left the fingerprints, have never been identified."

Of all the guards, former guards, armored car tellers, and bank employees the police and FBI interviewed, the defense attorney said, "*No one* mentioned Jim King as even a possible suspect." Nobody felt he fit the description of the robber.

If not Jim King, then who? Robinson segued to Paul Yocum—an immediate suspect because he'd been tried for a prior theft at the very same bank. When officers visited Yocum on June 24, he told the jury, they saw an arsenal of .38- and .357-caliber ammunition and speed loaders.

"The police come back with the first of four warrants," he continued, "that Detective Jon Priest swore under oath that there was probable cause to believe that Paul Yocum committed these murders." And when they arrived to execute the warrants, Yocum was attempting to destroy the evidence at his lawyer's instruction. He read verbatim quotations from the former guard's highly incriminating diary, in which Yocum had spewed his venom at bank officials for what they'd put him through, vowing his revenge.

But as of July 2, Robinson noted, the police and FBI were again focusing on Jim King, in part because he'd shaved off his mustache. Yet he'd only done so *after* first speaking with the FBI. "Contrary to what you've heard today, Jim King did on occasion shave his mustache."

As for former guard Dana Pappas's anticipated testimony about King having a plan to rob the bank, he said, the evidence would establish that "almost all of the guards routinely talked about … how they would rob the bank if they could do it … Other guards talked about murdering guards, some of them in very brutal form." Tellingly, Dana Pappas had told the police "he was absolutely certain" Paul Yocum was the man responsible for the massacre.

Though Buckley hadn't mentioned James and Carolyn King's 1987 bankruptcy filing, Robinson freely acknowledged their financial difficulties, telling jurors that "was another reason the police were suspicious of them." It was because of their bankruptcy, he said, that they'd stopped using credit cards, and had $800 in cash in their possession the evening of July 3. "That money had nothing to do with this robbery," he asserted, noting how the fingerprint lifted from one of the bills didn't match David Barranco's prints.

The defense attorney emphasized what *wasn't* found during the July 3 search: "videotapes, walkie-talkies, sunglasses," clothes fitting the robber's description, "the gun, ammunition consistent with the murder ammunition, shoes, blood. Blood. No blood on any shoes or any clothing. And they didn't find any keys … They checked over 100 banks, including numerous branches … No secret accounts."

Robinson revealed that another viable suspect existed in addition to Paul Yocum—a man named Dewey Baker, who was currently incarcerated in California, charged with four separate bank robberies. A Michigan woman named Linda Johnson had been corresponding with Baker, he told jurors. When he was released from prison on a prior occasion, Johnson had been there to meet him. Baker had come to Denver in May of 1991. He'd written Johnson "and told her about a big job he had planned in Denver." Following Father's Day, he "told her about a bank job he didn't want pinned on him in which four guards *were dusted*."

As he neared the finish line, Robinson tried to humanize his client, the man the government was trying to portray as a diabolical monster. "He's a law enforcer, not a law breaker," the defense lawyer said earnestly. "This is a non-violent person, who relied on his badge, not his gun. On quiet authority, not a baton.

"When he was done as a police officer, he was done with his gun. It was a tool. If it hadn't been broken, he would have kept it. He threw away his gun. He shaved his mustache. And he increased the size of his safe deposit box. And here he is. The people who know Jim King will tell you that he is the *last person* that they would believe could possibly have committed these brutal, brutal killings."

His opening statement now complete, Robinson paced back to the defense table, filling the seat between Walter Gerash and his client. He'd planted plenty of seeds all three hoped would germinate, over the coming weeks, into sufficient reasonable doubt to motivate jurors to vote "not guilty."

Battle lines now drawn, Judge Spriggs recessed court for the day, the People's case set to begin the following morning.

26

WHO WAS THAT MASKED MAN?

The prosecution began its case with David Barranco, the lanky 25-year-old vault manager who'd filled the disguised gunman's black satchel with nearly $200,000 in cash. Buckley assumed his position behind the podium—less than three feet from where the defendant sat—as the Arizona native, visibly nervous, stood before Judge Spriggs to take his oath. The People's star witness, adorned in a light gray suit and paisley tie, spoke in a barely audible voice, the bearded jurist reminding him on several occasions to speak up.

Though the 14 Denverites in the jury box would hang on his every word, they'd need to memorize his answers because they weren't permitted to take notes. More than 100 witnesses would be paraded before them over the next three weeks. Without the aid of notes, however, there was precious little chance jurors would be able to accurately recall their testimony—in any detail at least—when it finally came time for them to deliberate on their verdict.

The deputy DA walked Barranco through the activity in the cash vault on Father's Day morning. All deliveries had been completed by 8:30 a.m., the witness said. He remembered seeing two guards come through the vault at about nine o'clock, one of whom wasn't wearing a uniform—presumably Scott McCarthy. A little while later, he told jurors, while standing near David Twist and Maria Christian, he saw a "flash" out of the corner of his eye. Twist told him a man wearing a suit had walked by, which Barranco found strange because bank employees typically dressed casually on Sundays.

When the three employees tried to follow the intruder, the man spun around, pulled out a gun, and cocked the hammer before ordering them onto the floor. Seconds later, Barranco testified, they were joined by Kenetha Whisler and Chong Choe.

The gunman asked who the "cashier" was. Barranco eventually spoke up, indicating that he was the manager. He was forced to his feet and told to fetch a black bag around the corner. With the gun pointed at him, the robber made him fill the bag with money while the other tellers were locked in the mantrap. He told the jury the gunman seemed "very calm and collected" as well as "very acclimated to the area."

Barranco described spotting Nina McGinty crouching beneath the counter in her booth and how he redirected the robber to Chong Choe's station instead. When the gunman asked him what was in the Saturday vault, he lied, telling him it only contained paperwork, rather than money. At that point, he was ordered to join the others in the mantrap. He recounted how the group eventually escaped and sought help in the main lobby of the Cash Register Building.

With that background out of the way, Buckley focused the remainder of his direct examination on Barranco's description of the gunman and subsequent identification of James King. The prosecution witness repeated, essentially verbatim, how he'd described the intruder to detectives and FBI agents immediately following the robbery. When the prosecutor asked him to review the McKown and Yocum lineups, he confirmed that neither of their photos matched his recollection of the gunman—particularly Yocum with his floppy ears.

Buckley handed him the red and blue binders he'd reviewed with Agent Kirk on June 20. Barranco confirmed that he'd paused on Photo 8 in the red book—a current guard named John Perpetua—and Photo 16 in the blue book, who he now knew to be James King. Regarding the latter, he recalled telling Kirk that the mustache and hair were very similar to the robber's, but that the robber's face was a little fuller.

The veteran prosecutor next handed him the six-pack he'd been shown on July 5, the day after King's arrest. "When you looked at that lineup, did you positively identify anyone?"

Barranco told the jury he'd identified the second photo.

"Is that person present in court today?"

"Yes, he is." He pointed at the defendant, clad in the same brown suit he'd worn the prior day.

Buckley ended his examination by handing the witness a .38-caliber Colt Trooper—which had been marked as a prosecution exhibit—asking him if it resembled the weapon the gunman had pointed at him on Father's Day. Barranco confirmed that it did.

•••

Robinson slid by Buckley on his way to the podium—loaded for bear—diving head-first into his two-hour cross-examination. "Now, you're convinced that Jim King committed the crime?" he asked.

"Yes, I am," Barranco said, nodding confidently.

"And part of that is that you've read in the newspaper, and seen on TV, a number of things, including evidence that the police say they have against Jim King?"

Barranco acknowledged consuming such information, but disagreed with the defense lawyer's unstated premise. "That hasn't changed my mind or attitude," he insisted. "To this day, I remember extreme details."

"At least that's your belief today," Robinson interjected. "That despite this very fearful, stressful incident, you have a solid memory of all the details?"

"Exactly," the vault manager said, still very sure of himself. "I mean, it's something that's never going to go away, probably."

King's defense counsel began chipping away at his professed certainty—boring in on Barranco methodically—ultimately getting him to concede that the robber's mirrored sunglasses and gun were both distracting, and that he'd taken "only a couple of quick glances" at the man. He also agreed with Robinson that the intruder had been wearing a "pretty good disguise" and he'd told Detective Priest on June 21 that he believed his mustache was fake.

"It didn't seem real natural," he testified. Before long, the People's first witness was wringing his hands and chewing on his nails—his discomfort escalating as the defense lawyer drilled down on details.

"Let me ask you a simple question," Robinson said. "On June 20, 1991, with John Kirk sitting across from you or next to you, did you identify Jim King as the United Bank robber?"

"No, I didn't," Barranco admitted, noting he'd pointed to similar features between Photo 16 and the robber. He blamed the poor quality of the black-and-white images for his failure to make a positive identification.

"When you first saw Jim King's photograph for the first time … number 16, did you react to it emotionally?"

"Um, I did look at the picture for an extremely long time."

Unwilling to accept his non-responsive answer, Robinson pressed him. "Did it cause any emotional reaction in you?"

"Not in an immediate flashback or anything, but …" His answer trailed off.

"During the rest of that day, did you think about that photograph *at all*?"

Now pushed into a corner, Barranco summoned conviction. "*Yes, I did.*"

"You did?" Robinson said, his tone signaling disbelief. "Did you have second thoughts about that photograph—that day?"

The Arizona native shifted uncomfortably in his seat, before telling jurors he'd actually been certain as to who the robber was as far back as June 20.

"I really haven't said this before," Barranco said, "but at that time it was my gut feeling that that was the man"—his reference to King's photo in the blue binder—"and I don't know to this day what held me back from saying that. But for some reason, I was hoping this FBI agent could read me well enough to investigate the matter further. I didn't want to make a false arrest. But my gut feeling was—and I never said, 'This is your man, go get him,' but—I don't know what held me back."

Clearly frustrated with his soliloquy—which he considered fabricated from whole cloth—Robinson showed Barranco the transcript of his testimony at a prior hearing at which he'd testified that he didn't recall having *any* second thoughts about King's photo after seeing it in the blue book.

"I feel I answered that incorrectly," the witness said. Yet he freely admitted that he never told Detective Priest and FBI agents—with whom he met for 90 minutes the very next day—that he harbored any second thoughts whatsoever.

"Today, in this courtroom, for the very first time, you're revealing to all the people here, that you had second thoughts all along and *just never told anyone*?" Robinson did all he could to avoid sneering as he asked the question.

"That's correct."

His point having been made, the defense attorney moved on to his next subject: moles. He strode over to the defense table and stood beside his client, pointing to two flesh-colored bumps near his left cheek. Barranco confirmed that he could see the moles all the way from the witness stand. He conceded he never reported seeing any moles to the police or the FBI.

Robinson was now ready to move in for the kill, his final questions—and use of props—carefully choreographed in the weeks leading up to the trial. The bold gambit he was about to undertake held at least some potential to backfire. But it didn't. Instead, it became the signature moment of the entire trial.

"Wouldn't you agree with me that wearing a hat, a false mustache, and sunglasses is a pretty good disguise?" The key set-up question.

"Yeah, it's fairly good." Barranco was already taking the bait.

Robinson picked up a posterboard exhibit from the defense table—Defendant's Exhibit E—and sauntered to the witness stand to present it to Barranco. At the center of the exhibit was the face of a man on which a fedora-style hat, sunglasses, and bushy mustache had been drawn on a transparent, plastic overlay. He held it up so the judge and jury could see it too, asking Barranco if he could identify the man behind the disguise.

"Take as much time as you want," Robinson said, barely able to contain his glee as he soaked in the witness's puzzled expression. Seven seconds ticked by with no answer. "Nobody you know?"

When Barranco finally answered in the negative—in a muffled tone—the defense lawyer handed the exhibit to his bald-headed law partner, who stood beside him holding the posterboard like a human easel.

"Have you ever seen the movie *Presumed Innocent?*"

Again, a negative response. Robinson asked the witness if he'd ever seen *Raiders of the Lost Ark* or *Indiana Jones and the Temple of Doom*. To those questions, Barranco nodded affirmatively—finally a glint of recognition—agreeing that he had.

Robinson reclaimed the exhibit from Gerash, now unveiling the black-and-white picture beneath the disguise.

"Would it surprise you to see Harrison Ford under the photograph you could not identify with sunglasses and a hat?"

At the time, Ford was the hottest leading man in Hollywood. And now, here he was in a Denver courtroom—his image at least—playing a crucial role in a real-life murder trial. It was as close to a "Perry Mason" moment as this trial would get, Barranco outwardly embarrassed he'd failed to recognize the megastar.

Judge Spriggs couldn't resist the temptation to jump into the fray. "Looks not at all unlike Mr. Gerash in his youth," he blurted out. "I'd never noticed the resemblance before." His quip precipitated raucous laugher throughout the courtroom.

As the giggling subsided, Robinson put a bow on his perfectly executed plan. "Suffice it to say that you didn't have a clue that it was Harrison Ford behind the sunglasses, mustache, and hat in Exhibit E, correct?"

"Correct," Barranco said dejectedly, almost under his breath. In essence, what he was now conceding was that the strategic placement of a fedora, shades, and mustache on even one of the most recognizable faces on the planet was sufficient to conceal his identity. The logical consequence of his admission was that the United Bank gunman's choice of that very disguise—stache real or not—rendered it impossible for him and his co-workers to accurately identify the face they'd seen in the cash vault.

Having made his point in dramatic fashion, but concerned a juror or two might be thinking he was beating up unfairly on the People's witness—who after all, was a victim too—Robinson approached the stand with a second overlay exhibit. He felt reasonably certain that, this time, Barranco would succeed in guessing the identity of the man behind the sunglasses, hat, and mustache—allowing him to depart the witness stand with some semblance of his dignity intact.

"George Bush," Barranco answered confidently, referring to the sitting president.

"Good for you!" Robinson said with a toothy smile, peeling off the plastic overlay to reveal the most photographed man in the world.

"Your honor, that's all I have," he announced, closing out one of the most effective cross-examinations in the 90-year history of the City & County Building. As he reclaimed his seat between Gerash and King, he patted his client on the shoulder and smiled—immensely pleased with how he'd fared with the prosecution's most important witness.

Robinson's victory lap, however, was short-lived. Judge Spriggs sensed that some type of foul play had been involved in the theatrical flourish the entire courtroom had just witnessed. He asked Buckley whether, prior to trial, the defense lawyers had shared the Ford and Bush overlay exhibits with his team. The lead prosecutor told the judge they hadn't.

Gerash jumped to his feet. "They had no surprises," he said in a booming voice. "We showed them our exhibits."

But the judge wasn't buying it—now royally pissed—telling Gerash and Robinson he wasn't going to permit a "trial by ambush." In full view of the jury, live TV audience, and jam-packed gallery, he wagged his finger at the lead defense attorney, elevating his voice. "I'm telling you, Mr. Gerash. You know that you were supposed to do this a long time ago … and I view your neglect to be something less than accidental… I don't want any more surprises."

• • • •

Lamar Sims took to the podium to walk Maria Christian, the government's second witness, through her testimony. Christian provided a description of the bank robber quite similar to Barranco's, confirming that the gunman had used several terms of art well-recognized by bank employees: "mantrap," "bait money," and "loose money." He had a "soft-spoken" voice, she said. "Monotone, soft, calm."

Christian told jurors that the well-dressed man looked familiar to her, as if she'd possibly seen him before in a guard uniform. Her start date, she noted, had been May 22, 1990—nearly three months before James King quit. When asked whether the person who robbed her was present in the courtroom, she didn't hesitate to point her finger directly at the defendant.

As Buckley had done with the first witness, Sims handed her the red and blue photo books of current and former guards. Christian shared with jurors the facial features she'd picked out in three different photos—none of which were of James King. Shown the Yocum lineup, she testified that she was sure his face didn't match the robber's.

During his cross-examination, Gerash ushered his client to within three feet of the witness stand, employing him as a human exhibit. King stood like a statue, his face devoid of any expression, as his lawyer pointed to a mole just above his right eyebrow, three on his forehead, and four more on or near his left cheek—eight in all—each blemish a flesh-colored bump raised ever so slightly from his skin.

"You didn't see any mole on the robber, did you?" he asked in a harsh tone.

"I didn't really notice any moles," Christian acknowledged. The defense attorney also got her to concede that she'd seen television coverage of King walking to and from various court appearances, which had reinforced her view that he was the bank robber.

To Lamar Sims, the fuss Gerash was making about his client's moles was much ado about nothing—considering the gunman's use of a hat and band-aid, likely to conceal those very features.

"The man that counsel brought into your face this morning," he asked Christian, "is that the man who robbed you?"

"Yes," the bank teller confirmed.

••••

Later that same day, a small color TV atop a rolling cart was wheeled in front of the jury box to permit jurors to watch video footage of the three separate crime scenes—including the gruesome images of McCullom, Mankoff, McCarthy, and Wilson lying in pools of their own blood. The prosecution also introduced still photos of the deceased guards. Warned ahead of time how disturbing the images would be, most of their relatives had left the courtroom—the two women who remained in the front row unable to suppress their tears.

The next day would prove even more difficult for the slain guards' families, with Drs. Thomas Henry and Alan Stormo taking the stand to discuss their autopsies. The pathologists described for the jury—in excruciating detail—the precise locations where bullets had entered the victims' bodies and the internal damage each had caused.

Buckley handed Dr. Henry two bone-white, Styrofoam mannequin heads, one labeled "Phillip Mankoff" and the other "Todd Wilson." He asked the medical examiner to insert yellow and gray knitting needles where bullets had penetrated each man's head. Though Gerash objected vehemently to the graphic demonstration, Judge Spriggs sided with the prosecution, allowing it to proceed.

As Dr. Henry simulated the trajectory of each bullet, he had to exert significant force to push the needles through the sturdy foam material. High-pitched squeaking noises echoed throughout the courtroom as each needle dug deeper and deeper into the faux heads.

Dr. Stormo repeated the same exercise with mannequin heads representing Bill McCullom and Scott McCarthy. After he simulated the entry of the final bullet, all four Styrofoam heads—16″ needles sticking out in every direction—were deposited on the evidence table in a chilling display of the carnage. The forensic pathologists also shared with jurors how they'd extracted the actual bullets from the victims' flesh and bones, pulling the lead slugs and fragments out of small morgue envelopes marked as exhibits.

Their testimony was certainly not for the faint of heart, leaving even those with strong constitutions feeling a bit queasy. A reminder, however, of what the case was truly all about: four flesh-and-blood human beings whose time on Earth had been abruptly terminated by those very bullets.

27

LOCKED AND LOADED

Detective Frank Kerber was accepted as an expert witness on firearms and ballistics. With Bill Buckley behind the podium, he testified that the murder weapon had most likely been a .38-caliber Colt revolver and that three different types of ammunition had been pumped into the victims' bodies: Remington-Peters 110-grain, semi-jacketed hollow-points, Winchester-Western or Federal 110-grain, semi-jacketed hollow-points, and Winchester-Western 158-grain lead Lubaloy bullets. Each of the slugs recovered, he told jurors, was associated with types of ammunition that at one time or another had been issued to members of the DPD.

"Did you find any bullets or fragments that were inconsistent with being fired from the same firearm?" the silver-haired prosecutor asked.

"No, I did not," Kerber replied. He told jurors he was able to exclude a .38-caliber Smith & Wesson as the type of weapon that fired the slugs he'd examined.

Buckley had the detective step down from the witness stand to demonstrate with the Colt Trooper exhibit how empty shell casings can be emptied into the shooter's hand with the gun's ejector rod. As he began showing jurors how the cylinder can then be reloaded with a speed loader, Gerash jumped to his feet to object. There was no evidence, he asserted, of speed loaders having been involved in the commission of the crime. "I mean it's just speculation."

Judge Spriggs swiveled to face Buckley. "Is there any evidence of any kind to indicate that speed loaders were used in this matter?" Their colloquy was taking place in full view of the jury.

As Buckley responded, he held the gun above his head, pointed at the ceiling. "Judge, it is our position that there were 18 rounds taken to the scene," he said. "That the first rounds were emptied out … the next six rounds were deposited with the speed loader, that is our—"

Spriggs interrupted him. "How many rounds were fired altogether that you can account for?"

"Eighteen," the prosecutor said confidently.

"That's not true!" Gerash protested. "I object. That's not true."

"Seventeen rounds in the victims and one in the door," Buckley continued. "A total of 18. It is our position that there were six in the gun to start with and two speed loaders with six rounds each."

The judge overruled the objection. But Gerash didn't relent. "It's also consistent with being fired by two or three people—" he got out before Spriggs stopped him in his tracks, overruling his objection a second time. Finally allowed to speak, Kerber resumed his demonstration, showing the jury how a speed loader can easily reload six bullet cartridges into a Colt Trooper.

••••

The defense team knew that Detective Kerber posed an existential threat to their case. If jurors accepted his testimony at face value, it wasn't much of a leap for them to conclude that the killer had probably been a cop—just like James King. Consequently, when Gerash stepped up to the podium, he was well aware that his client's ability to walk out of the courtroom a free man depended in significant part on his poking as many holes in the expert witness's testimony as he possibly could.

He racked up several points right off the bat. Kerber

admitted that he couldn't positively determine whether the bullets recovered from McCullom's body were pressurized +P ammunition, and that the DPD supplied its officers only with pressurized ammo. He readily conceded that each of the slugs he analyzed could have been .357 Magnum—rather than .38 caliber—a type of ammo the DPD didn't issue. The detective also acknowledged that 110-grain semi-jacketed hollow-points—including those with a special, ring-shaped base like those retrieved from McCullom's corpse—were generally available in stores.

"You found three types of bullets in the bodies of the deceased guards," Gerash said. "Isn't that correct?"

"Yes, sir," Kerber answered.

"And all of these bullets, the Remington-Peters, the Western, and the other brand, they were all commercially available to the public?"

"Yes, sir." The detective further admitted that all three manufacturers made .357 Magnum bullets the DPD didn't keep in stock.

Gerash referred the firearms expert to the section of his written report in which he'd listed the types of Colt revolvers that could have fired the bullets extracted from the victims. Only four Colts were included on his list: the Cobra, Detective Special, Police Positive, and .357 Python.

"You never mentioned the Trooper, did you?" he asked, confident he was about to land a significant blow.

"No, sir," Kerber agreed. "I cut myself off after three or four models so I didn't ramble on." He also conceded that other "cheaper and lesser brands" of revolvers fired .38-caliber bullets with a left-hand twist and that, since 1961, thousands of Colt-brand revolvers had been sold all across the Denver community. The prosecution witness further acknowledged that he couldn't state positively that the two lead Lubaloy bullets removed from Wilson's body had been fired from the same gun used to kill his fellow guards.

Shifting to the total number of rounds discharged by the killer, Kerber admitted that he was unaware of how many bullets had missed their target. And also unsure of whether all of the projectiles fired from the killer's weapon had been re-covered. He agreed with Gerash that many of the fragments retrieved couldn't be matched with larger portions of the slugs from which they'd split off. In other words, the detective couldn't say with any confidence how many shots had actually been fired.

As Kerber departed the witness stand, Gerash felt confident he'd achieved his mission. At best, the firearm expert's testimony supported the notion that the same Colt-type revolver had fired each and every bullet recovered from the victim's bodies. But as to the critical question of whether the DPD had been the source of those bullets, Kerber's testimony fell far short of the mark.

• • • •

Lieutenant Patrick Mulhern had served as the chief range officer at the DPD firing range during the final decade of James King's career. The uniformed officer told jurors that every police officer had to qualify with his firearm on a quarterly basis by shooting a minimum score. During the summer shooting session, he noted, a safety inspection was performed on each weapon fired at the range.

Buckley walked the lieutenant through written requisitions for the different types of ammunition the DPD had purchased at various points in time, starting with 35,000 rounds of .38 Special Winchester-Western 110-grain, +P semi-jacketed hollow-points in April 1977. From April 1984 through September 1986, the department had ordered the identical ammo from Remington-Peters—72,000 additional rounds.

Mulhern explained that at officers' annual qualifying shoot in the summer, they'd be required to expend all department-issued ammo. After the session, they'd be issued 18 fresh rounds.

"Was there a close control of the return of the old ammunition?" the career prosecutor asked, fully expecting Mulhern to answer in the negative. To his surprise, however, the uniformed witness told jurors that there *was* "fairly close" control over officers' return of unused ammo.

Buckley took a second swing. "Were there some instances when the ammunition was not actually returned by the officers?"

"Not to my knowledge," Mulhern said—again, defying the prosecutor's expectation. "No, sir."

His testimony was backfiring badly. If what he was saying was true, a police officer like the defendant could never have possessed more than one type of ammunition at a time—certainly not the three different types extracted from the slain guards' bodies. Buckley therefore tried another approach.

"Were there sources available to the officers to get extra ammunition out at the various substations?"

"Yes, sir," Mulhern said. "We did have emergency stores at all of the substations available for the officers in the event there was an emergency." He testified that the emergency stores would have been available to command officers like sergeants.

Buckley asked if those emergency supplies were closely controlled. Mulhern finally supplied the answer he'd been seeking, indicating they weren't.

During his cross-examination, Gerash got the chief range officer to confirm that when King had qualified at the range in the summer of 1986—his last session as a police officer—he would have been required to expend all rounds he'd previously been issued. A huge point for sure. Yet he missed the opportunity to make an even bigger one: that Mulhern's testimony failed to establish that the DPD *ever* supplied highly pressurized +P+ ammunition.

Lamar Sims called Officer Robert Crago, one of Mulhern's subordinates, to address that very issue. Crago had worked at the range from 1984 to 1992—which included King's final three years on the force.

Crago told jurors that +P+ ammo was special ordered for law enforcement agencies. He confirmed that he'd seen boxes of +P+ bullets at the DPD's firing ranges. And though officers would typically receive only 18 rounds of ammo when their shooting session was complete, if they asked for more, Crago said, they'd receive it. In fact, boxes of ammo sat out in the open for them to take whatever they wanted.

As for the service revolver owned by the defendant, Crago told the jury he personally inspected it in September 1989 when King fired it at the range to obtain his security guard license—and it passed. He testified that in all his years inspecting firearms at the range, he'd never seen a cracked cylinder on a Colt Trooper.

During his cross, Gerash tried valiantly to get Crago to concede that +P+ ammo was available commercially in stores—not just to police departments. "You're sure of that?" he pressed the witness.

"Well, to the best of my knowledge, it was on the box of the ammo we got. It said 'law-enforcement-issue only.'"

Gerash walked up to the evidence table and grabbed three green-and-yellow boxes of Remmington-Peters semi-jacketed hollow-points and handed them to Crago, challenging him to find such a designation.

"This one doesn't," Crago said. "Because it's just a +P round."

"That's the round that was issued in '86," Gerash said in a snippy tone. "Where does it say it's just for officers?"

Crago reiterated that the reason the box didn't say that was "because it's not the +P+ ammo."

In case there was any doubt in a single juror's mind, Sims had Crago clarify the difference between +P and +P+ ammo during his redirect. The prosecution witness testified that the Remmington-Peters +P bullets Gerash had placed before him were manufactured by a different company altogether than the +P+ bullets made by Winchester-Western and Federal— confirming for a third time that +P+ ammo was "law-enforcement-issue only."

$$\bullet\ \bullet\ \bullet\ \bullet$$

The People's final witness on the subject of guns and ammo was a retired police officer named Thomas Butler. Like King, Butler had devoted a quarter century to the DPD, his last ten years as a firearms examiner in the crime lab. Since retiring in 1982, he'd opened up a gun shop and worked as a gunsmith—performing repairs on a wide variety of firearms, which had also been his side hustle during his last 15 years on the force. Butler was particularly well acquainted with Colt Trooper revolvers, having carried one throughout his police career just like the defendant, whom he knew well.

Significantly, King had come to Butler's gun shop during his employment with United Bank of Denver to seek a repair of his Colt Trooper. Buckley showed the retired officer the $20 receipt dated October 12, 1989, about three months into King's stint as a security guard. Butler explained that the ex-cop's gun was "slightly out of time," meaning that the cylinder didn't lock into place when the hammer was pulled back. The repair required the replacement of a small part connected to the cylinder.

"Other than the timing problem," the prosecutor asked, "did you examine the weapon in detail to make sure there was nothing else that needed to be repaired?" Butler testified that he did, particularly the cylinder.

"In what condition was the cylinder of that Colt revolver in October of 1989?"

"Just fine," the gunsmith told the jury.

Buckley asked him if he'd ever seen a cracked cylinder on a Colt revolver.

"I've seen several that they were more than cracked," Butler replied. "Sections of the cylinder would be missing." He explained that in every instance he'd seen such a problem, it had been caused by an explosion resulting from the gun being fired with homemade bullet cartridges containing excess gunpowder.

"The cylinder will usually come apart in two or three fragments," he added, the area above the cylinder sometimes bowing. Using the Colt Trooper exhibit, he stepped down from the witness stand to demonstrate what that would look like.

When Butler resumed his seat, Buckley drove the point home with an additional question. "So did you say when that happens, it doesn't merely just get a crack, *it blows apart*?"

"Yes, sir," the gunsmith agreed. "The ones I've seen." He testified that of the 100 to 200 Colt Troopers on which he'd performed repairs, he'd never seen a cylinder that was merely cracked—only ones that had exploded.

Buckley ended his direct examination by asking the expert witness if he recalled, during his time as a cop, being issued Winchester-Western 158-grain lead Lubaloy ammunition—which Lieutenant Mulhern hadn't mentioned during his testimony. Butler told jurors he did, noting that type of ammo wasn't particularly efficient.

With that answer, the silver-haired prosecutor resumed his seat at counsel table, content he'd scored several major points—finally.

This time around, Gerash's cross proved most unhelpful. "What do you do when you see a cracked cylinder?" he asked.

Buckley rose to his feet, pointing out that Butler had testified he'd never seen one.

"That's not true at all," Gerash retorted, his voice thundering across the courtroom. "He had examples of—"

"Just a moment," Judge Spriggs interceded. "First of all, let's find out if he has."

"Have you seen cracked cylinders on pistols?" Gerash asked.

"I really can't recall one," Butler answered, repeating his earlier testimony. "They're fragmented, usually."

Inexplicably, the seasoned defense attorney then unearthed a fact far more helpful to the prosecution than the defense. "Mr. King brought in a Winchester 94 pump shotgun on June 18, 1990, didn't he?"

Butler confirmed that he had, and that the ex-cop had paid him for repairing the shotgun. Yet that was the very same month the accused killer told detectives and FBI agents he'd discovered a crack in the cylinder of his Colt Trooper. Why would he seek repairs on a shotgun he used for pleasure and ignore a dangerous defect in the gun he was carrying for protection as a security guard?

Gerash made matters even worse with his next series of questions, starting by asking the gunsmith if he knew what a hairline crack was. Butler confirmed that he did.

"Did you look for a hairline crack at that time—in October of '89?"

"I examined the gun," Butler replied. "I didn't see a hairline crack."

"And you were examining it for cracked cylinders?" Gerash asked, his tone conveying disbelief.

"I was examining the cylinders," Butler said, "because the part that needed repairing had to do with the cylinder."

Thomas Butler's 30 minutes on the witness stand couldn't have gone much better for the People's case. James King's entire defense hinged on the jury believing that he'd discovered a dangerous crack in the cylinder of his Colt Trooper too significant to repair, causing him to discard it altogether. If the gunsmith was to be believed—and his depth of experience and demeanor made him a very credible witness—that scenario seemed highly implausible.

28

EAR WITNESS

Since the first moments following the initial report of the bank robbery—before the murdered guards' bullet-ravaged bodies had even been discovered—police detectives and FBI agents had placed enormous emphasis on the six armored tellers' descriptions of the gunman's physical appearance, particularly his face. By stark contrast, those tasked with investigating the crime had paid precious little attention to the only feature of his body he hadn't been able to disguise: his voice.

Though voice lineups are not nearly as common as in-person or photo lineups, it is puzzling that in their zeal to identify the killer, detectives and FBI agents seemingly gave little consideration to undertaking such a process. After all, the tellers had heard the gunman's voice for much of the eight minutes he'd been in their presence—even while face-down on the floor—as he articulated his commands in a calm, albeit stern, tone. The phrases he employed were so seared in their memories, several of the tellers could still recite them verbatim by the time of trial.

Following James King's arrest and arraignment—based in significant part on the identification of his face from a photo lineup—the DPD had a golden opportunity to take the next step to solidify its case. While held captive in his jail cell, the accused killer could have been ordered to provide samples of his voice for the tellers to compare with other random voices.

And since many in the DPD were familiar with King's voice from having worked alongside him for years, any attempt he might have made to disguise it would have been futile. Yet despite all that, a voice lineup wasn't pursued.

The issue of whether any of the tellers might recognize King's voice first cropped up at his preliminary hearing in October. After Kenetha Whisler testified that she vividly recalled the gunman telling her, "Get out and go lie with the others," she confidently asserted that she'd be able to recognize his voice again.

At that point, Lamar Sims asked King to stand up at the defense table and repeat the phrase, "Get out and go lie with the others." But Walter Gerash immediately objected, angrily telling Sims and the presiding judge—who wasn't Dick Spriggs—"Mr. King will do no such thing." When the judge asked Sims for his response, the deputy DA withdrew his request, suggesting that a voice lineup would be conducted at a later date.

A similar issue arose at a hearing before Judge Spriggs in early March, with Whisler on the stand a second time. On that occasion, the 35-year-old bank employee stated that while she was testifying at the October preliminary hearing—when Sims had asked King to stand up and repeat the phrase, "Get out and go lie with the others"—she actually overheard him say to his attorneys, "Where did that come from?" Whisler told Judge Spriggs she was certain, based upon what she'd been able to hear, that King's voice was identical to the voice of the man who robbed her and her fellow tellers.

Fearing that the government would have her repeat that same testimony at trial—with their client's life hanging in the balance—the defense fired a preemptive strike days before jury selection commenced, requesting that Spriggs order a formal voice lineup. The defense lawyers felt reasonably confident that, if performed the proper way, none of the tellers would select King's voice from an assortment of different voices.

Unbeknownst to the prosecution team, Scott Robinson had visited with his client in jail to capture his voice on audiotape, having him read phrases spoken by the gunman: "Get down on the floor and cover your eyes," "Who is the cashier?," and "Don't look at me." He'd gotten five other men to record the same phrases. The defense proposed that Whisler and any other tellers who believed they could identify the robber's voice be required to listen to each of the six recordings prior to testifying at trial.

After holding a brief hearing to consider the motion, Judge Spriggs ruled that he *would* permit a voice lineup, but only if conducted by the DPD. Frustrated with his decision, Gerash told a reporter from the *Rocky*, "I don't want the police to do it, because so far they have violated my client's rights." He therefore withdrew the motion.

The judge's ruling, however, left open the possibility Gerash and Robinson could still use their lineup—including the recording of their client's voice—during cross-examination of the tellers. It remained to be seen whether they possessed gonads large enough to actually take that gamble.

• • • •

On Tuesday, May 26, the start of the second week of trial, Whisler was sworn in as a witness—this time with 14 jurors who'd be hanging on her every word. She testified in a soft, docile voice how she'd been working in a booth isolated from the other tellers when everything suddenly became quiet. She recalled hearing a clicking noise that drew her attention away from her work—presumably the robber cocking the hammer of his gun. When she turned to her left, she saw a well-dressed gentleman walking in her direction.

Whisler told jurors that because she hadn't yet seen the man's weapon, she stepped outside her booth to greet him, finally noticing the gun when he came within a foot of her. "Get out and go lie with the others," he ordered her. She provided the same physical description of the gunman she'd given on several prior occasions: late 30s to early 40s, 6'1" to 6'2", 240 to 250 pounds, a perfectly groomed, thick salt-and-pepper mustache, and a band-aid on his left cheek. At his command, she dropped to the floor next to the other tellers.

The bank employee described how she used a metal spoon to break out of the mantrap and how she and the others had raced across the parking deck to the building lobby to seek help. Buckley walked her through her meeting with Agent Kirk to review the photo binders of past and present guards, her meeting with Agent Gedney at which she identified the .38-caliber Colt revolver, and her selection of James King from a photo lineup on July 5.

He asked her if the person sitting at the end of the defense table was the "man who robbed you on Father's Day, June 16, 1991?"

"Yes," Whisler said without hesitation.

Buckley shifted his focus to the October 1991 preliminary hearing. Whisler repeated her testimony from March that she'd overhead King say, from the defense table, "Where did that come from?"

"When you heard him say, 'Where did that come from?,' what went through your mind?"

"The same sound that I heard that day from the robber," she told the jury. "The same voice."

Seeking to put an exclamation point on her voice identification, the prosecutor asked how the voice she heard from the defense table compared with the robber's voice.

"It was him," Whisler declared, her answer direct and assertive. She pointed out how she'd even told her victim advocate, upon leaving the courtroom, what she heard the accused killer say.

"Your witness," Buckley told the defense lawyers, approaching his counsel table with a noticeable bounce in his step.

• • • •

Walter Gerash was peeved. Precisely what he feared would happen without a formal voice lineup had just occurred before his very eyes. Though he had the defense voice lineup at the ready, he and Robinson ultimately decided it would be too risky—perhaps downright foolish—to use it. What if Whisler picked their client's voice? They might not be able to recover from such a blow. The voice lineup Robinson had labored to put together would never see the light of day.

Instead, Gerash tried his best to shake Whisler from her testimony. He insisted she'd made a different statement at the March hearing—telling him then that the voice she'd heard from the defense table in October had actually been deeper than the robber's. He showed her a passage from the hearing transcript, in which the stenographer had typed the words "a deeper, lower voice." Whisler told him she didn't recall making any such statement, and that she stood by what she'd just explained to the jury.

Having failed to make any dent in her voice identification, Gerash quickly transitioned to Whisler's descriptions of the robber. He had her confirm that she'd been as close as one to four feet from the gunman during the robbery.

He used his client as a human exhibit, walking him to within three feet of the witness, pointing out the moles all over his face. Whisler cringed with trepidation as King approached—adorned in a camel-hair sport coat, white shirt, and tan tie—her intensely visceral reaction another dramatic moment in the trial.

"You didn't see any moles on the robber's face at the time of the robbery?" Gerash asked. "Isn't that correct?" She agreed she didn't.

"Now isn't it true that, when you saw the robber, your eyes were on the gun more so than anything?" Whisler gave another affirmative response. But she denied the photo she'd selected from the six-person lineup on July 5 was the same one she'd passed over in the blue binder on June 20. His "picture was not in there," she insisted—even though that wasn't accurate.

In response to Gerash's questioning, Whisler acknowledged—with mild embarrassment—that in an effort to learn more about who might have been involved in the crime, she'd consulted a man who identified himself as a "cowboy psychic."

As for her July 5 photo identification, Gerash asked her to

confirm she'd been told—prior to being shown the six-pack—that a man named James King had been arrested. Whisler told the jury that wasn't true. But the defense lawyer had the receipts, showing her the March hearing transcript—pointing out the passage in which she'd testified that she had indeed learned of King's arrest prior to seeing the photo lineup.

"You were under oath at that time?" Gerash bellowed. Rather than treating her gingerly—a victim of the crime herself—his questions conveyed anger and contempt.

"Yes," Whisler sheepishly agreed.

During his redirect examination, Buckley noted that Whisler had seemed upset when the defense lawyer walked his client up to the witness stand. "Did that upset you when he came close to you?"

She confirmed that it did. As for the moles King's attorney had pointed to, Whisler told jurors that the robber's hat had covered almost his entire forehead.

One final time, the lead prosecutor asked, "As you sit here today, is the defendant the person who robbed you?" But Whisler didn't get to answer, Gerash's furious objection to the repeat question quickly sustained by the judge.

The accused killer's attorney was still seething as he reached the podium to conduct his recross, this time shouting his questions at the frightened witness.

"Now that hat didn't come down over his chin, where he had a mole, did it?" Whisler conceded the obvious point, her tone almost apologetic.

"And that hat didn't come down over his eyebrow where he had a mole, did it?" Gerash stood beside his client, pointing at the blemish.

"No," Whisler agreed, slumping in her seat.

"And when you saw the gun in his hand, you swore under oath that he had no gloves, is that correct?"

"Correct," she said, her voice weary. With that final answer, Kenetha Whisler was finally permitted to step down, more than a bit shaken from the back and forth over two solid hours.

•   •   •   •

Next into the lion's den was Nina McGinty. From the moment she claimed the hot seat, her palpable anguish was on full display as she repeatedly choked back tears. She dabbed her eyes and blew her nose with a tissue she fidgeted with nervously while fielding Sims' questions. In a deep, halting voice, the 34-year-old described the terrifying ordeal she'd endured Father's Day morning, telling jurors she'd tried to stay hidden under the counter, "because if he saw me, I'd probably be shot."

Like Whisler, McGinty recalled the sound of the robber's voice, describing it as very calm, but also "very, very authoritative." She distinctly remembered him telling the group, "I want you to crawl into the mantrap. Yes, I want you to crawl on your bellies into that little room."

Sims asked if the person who had her cowering in fear was in the courtroom.

"Yes, he is," McGinty said, identifying King at the defense table.

The prosecutor showed her the six-pack she'd reviewed on July 5, asking if she'd been able to make a positive identification.

"It was sitting in my lap," McGinty recounted—her hands beginning to tremble—"and I got terrified all over again."

"What was it that terrified you?"

"Picture number two was that of the robber," she said, her voice wobbly.

Less than half an hour into his direct, Sims passed the witness to the defense. This time, it was Robinson who made his way to the podium, his soft, gentle approach with the bank employee in sharp contrast to his partner's aggressive interrogation of Kenetha Whisler. Yet despite his measured tone and demeanor, Robinson succeeded in chipping away at McGinty's identification, peppering her with more than 200 questions over the next hour.

He had her reveal that the voice she heard that morning sounded familiar—like she'd heard it before. Yet she'd only begun working at the bank in February 1991, six months after King had quit. She described the gunman's sideburns as being unusual—long, narrow, silver, neatly manicured, and running down to the bottom of the earlobe. Yet as the jury had already seen in photos—and could visualize every day—the defendant wore his salt-and-pepper sideburns short and wide.

McGinty agreed she could see bumps on King's face all the way from the witness stand, but hadn't noticed any bumps or unusual markings on the gunman's face during the robbery. Rather than accompanying his client to the stand—as his partner had done—Robinson walked over to the defense table and had King turn his head so McGinty could visualize his left cheek—where he had a collection of moles. She suddenly became overwhelmed, sobbing and sucking in giant breaths, apologizing when she finally regained her composure.

Robinson pivoted to her review of the photo binders—gently placing them on the witness stand—a subject on which he remained focused for nearly 20 minutes. McGinty agreed with him that the only photos in either book that "were similar in any way to the mental image" she had of the bank robber were the three she pointed out to Agent Kirk—none of whom were of James King.

"Nine days after the robbery," Robinson asked, "Jim King's photograph did not fit the mental picture you had of the robber in any way, did it?"

"Not from that photograph," McGinty admitted, referring to Photo 16 in the blue binder. "All I saw when I looked at that picture was a forehead." Her voice tinged with resignation, she agreed with defense counsel that nothing about King's nose, mustache, sideburns, or even the shape of his face as depicted in that photo fit the mental image she had of the robber.

She also agreed that when she woke up the morning of July 4, she learned from the radio that someone had been arrested. Fifteen minutes later, she received a call from the police. "They had told me that someone was in custody and that I was not to listen to the radio, read the paper, or watch any TV."

"How was the rest of your fourth of July?"

"Terrible!" she lamented.

"Nervous all day?"

"Yeah." She told the jury she believed she'd be required to do an in-person lineup at police headquarters "and come face to face with the man who robbed the bank at gunpoint."

"When you sit here today, and you bring up a mental picture of the robber," Robinson asked, "what you see now is Jim King?"

The prosecution witness pushed back. "I see the same man that was in the vault on that day."

"But on June 26 of last year, when you had that mental picture, you didn't see Jim King, did you?" It was the third time the defense attorney had asked the same question. For that reason, Judge Spriggs sustained Sims' objection.

Despite Robinson's effective cross-examination, Sims elected not to ask a single additional question on redirect. Nina McGinty was left to slink off the witness stand, having been forced by attorneys on both sides to relive—in excruciating detail—the most horrifying experience of her entire life.

• • • •

The final eyewitness to testify was David Twist. The slender 25-year-old told Buckley that he recalled the robber being about 45 to 50, 6' tall, 180 to 200 pounds, with gray hair, a rounded face, and a well-trimmed gray mustache. Twist told jurors he couldn't see the gunman's forehead at all because it was covered by a Bogart-style hat. He remembered his voice being "calm and steady. He seemed to know what he wanted… and took control right away." Twist confirmed picking King out of a photo lineup on July 3 and identified him sitting at the defense table.

Buckley asked him to describe the difference between the way King's photo appeared in the blue binder and how it had been presented in the six-person lineup. The bank employee explained that the cropped photo in the six-pack was a better representation of what he'd actually seen on Father's Day "due to the hat he was wearing."

During his cross, Gerash bore into Twist as fiercely as he had with Kenetha Whisler. Standing beside his client and pointing at his head, the defense lawyer asked, in an incredulous tone, "Is Mr. King's hair gray?"

"Uh, on the sides," the soft-spoken witness said. "A little bit, yes." Not satisfied with that answer, Gerash rose to his tiptoes to wave his hand over the top of the defendant's head, getting Twist to concede his hair wasn't gray on top.

The prosecution witness confirmed he'd been standing less than five feet from the gunman in excellent lighting. Gerash asked whether he'd seen a mole on his chin, two above his eyebrows, or five on the side of his face from his cheekbone down to his lip. To each question, Twist gave the same answer: "No, I did not." He admitted telling detectives that the robber's complexion was "clear" and "normal."

When Gerash focused him on his review of the King lineup on July 3, Twist acknowledged that the only one of the photos he'd previously seen was King's. And also that, even though he'd selected the ex-cop's photo based on the "seriousness of his expression," the robber's sunglasses had prevented him from seeing his eyes.

On redirect, Buckley decided he too could employ the defendant as a human exhibit, standing behind him and pointing at his left cheek. "Can you tell whether any one mole on the left side of his face is more visible than the rest," he asked. "Is one more prominent than the others?"

"Yes," Twist said. "The one on the lower cheek."

"Is that the side of the face where he had a band-aid?" Buckley was implying that King had used a band-aid to conceal his most prominent mole.

"Yes, it is," Twist agreed.

But Gerash got last licks, escorting his client all the way to the witness stand once again, almost close enough for Twist to touch him. As screaming sirens from nearby fire engines invaded the courtroom, the Bronx native pointed at the mole on his client's lower left cheek. "It wasn't covering *this mole*, was it?" His voice thundered across the courtroom, even louder than the blaring sirens.

"No, it was not," Twist conceded. Judge Spriggs thanked him for his time and let him go.

Taken as a whole, the eyewitness testimony proved to be a mixed bag. That Whisler, McGinty, and Twist had each ignored King's photo in the blue binder before subsequently selecting him from a photo lineup weakened their identification considerably. Each had to make significant concessions during cross-examination—particularly about the moles clearly visible on his face. Though Whisler projected certainty that King's voice and the robber's were one and the same, she and the others seemed equally certain about their visual identification—the same one they'd failed to make when first given the chance.

What the jury would ultimately make of this mish-mash, only time would tell.

29

ALL IN THE FAMILY

The rules by which criminal cases are tried generally prohibit witnesses from observing the trial until after they've been questioned—to prevent them from tailoring their own testimony to fit what others before them have said. The prosecution team, however, had agreed to make an exception for James King's family members, who'd been watching the trial from the first row of the gallery since its inception.

His wife, Carolyn, hadn't missed a single minute, the most she'd gotten to see her husband since his arrest, their 30th anniversary "celebration" on April 28 relegated to a not-so-conjugal visit across opposite sides of a glass partition at the county jail.

As the court day neared its end that Tuesday, to the surprise of many in attendance, Bill Buckley informed the judge the 48-year-old mother of three would be the People's next witness.

"Step forward, Mrs. King," Judge Spriggs instructed her.

The dark-and-curly-haired, slender woman rose from her seat between sons James Jr. and David and cautiously approached the witness stand. As she stood to take her oath—adorned in a loose-fitting turquoise sweater and dark gray slacks—Walter Gerash announced the defense would waive the marital privilege protecting the confidentiality of her communications with her husband. "We want her to testify," he said, eager to signal to the jury she had nothing to hide.

Though she had every reason to be angry with the prosecution for charging her husband with murder and forcing him to stand trial for a crime she believed he knew nothing about—not to mention locking him up like a caged animal for nearly a year—as Carolyn answered Buckley's questions, she didn't display the slightest hint of hostility or irritation. In fact, her demeanor was warm, pleasant, and engaging. She smiled frequently, testifying in a straightforward, unfailingly polite manner.

The chief deputy DA began with questions about the defendant's service revolver. His wife told jurors he'd carried the weapon in the holster of his gun belt during his employment with United Bank, which he hung in his closet upon the completion of each workday. The leather belt, she recalled, also contained speed loaders and handcuffs. After he quit working at the bank, she said, he stored the gun and belt in a gray metal box in the den.

"Did you ever tell him to get rid of that gun?" Buckley asked.

"I don't remember telling him that," she replied.

"Did you ever tell your husband to get rid of any gun that he had?"

"No," she said, shaking her head. "Not that I remember."

The veteran prosecutor approached the witness stand with an enlarged photo displaying a brown-framed shadow box filled with King's police memorabilia. The frame included his badges, shoulder patches, handcuffs, whistle, and police ID cards—ones that had actually been issued rather than the fake ones discovered in their safe deposit box. Because the judge had ruled the latter irrelevant in response to a pretrial motion, the jury would never learn of their existence. The ex-cop had built the shadow box himself, his wife testified, its contents included to convey pride in his career as a police officer.

As for his mustache, Carolyn testified her husband had worn it off and on for about ten years, confirming the stache had adorned his face on Father's Day. He'd shaven it off near the end of June, she said, because "he had pimples and sores underneath the mustache." She told jurors she distinctly re-membered seeing the blemishes once the facial hair was re-moved.

Finding that testimony difficult to believe, Buckley whipped out a blowup of the driver's license photo of the de-fendant taken on June 28, which depicted him without a mus-tache. Standing beside his wife, he asked her to point out the pimples and sores, telling her he couldn't see any. Carolyn pointed to an area just beneath the ex-cop's nostrils—actually a bit above where his mustache had been—claiming she could see them "because I know where they were."

The silver-haired prosecutor eventually turned to the timeline of events on Father's Day. Carolyn testified that her husband awoke between 8:00 and 8:30 a.m. After they ate breakfast together, she said, he left at approximately 9:15 a.m. to play chess. She told the jury she was mowing the lawn when he returned around 10:00 a.m. They finished working on the lawn together and then went to the cemetery, stopping at Dairy Queen for ice cream on the way back.

She testified that their son, David, had been home all morning. Their middle child, Greg, arrived with his girlfriend at about 2:30 p.m. and their eldest, James Jr., appeared a little later. Though they all participated in Father's Day dinner, she recounted, they ate in shifts—in multiple locations—rather than enjoying a formal meal together.

Buckley ended his questioning by showing Carolyn her husband's mugshot. Regarding that picture—taken more than a week after he'd shaved off his mustache—she agreed there were no pimples or sores to be seen.

• • • •

Walter Gerash couldn't believe his good fortune. The govern-ment had taken a huge gamble in calling his client's wife as an adverse witness—a gamble he felt certain had backfired. Caro-lyn, he believed, had been the most sincere, authentic witness to have taken the stand thus far. If jurors were as enamored of her as he considered likely, how could they possibly conclude she'd willingly share a bed with the murderous thug responsible for the bank massacre?

To add icing to that cake, he'd now have *two* opportunities to question her, once during the People's case and a second time during the defense's. Better still, this time he'd get to lead the witness in order to elicit the most helpful testimony possible.

In response to his questions, Carolyn explained that the larger safety deposit box—which they'd been talking about getting for months—hadn't been intended merely for her and her husband, but also for their sons. Jimmy, she said, was about to be sent to Mexico on a work trip. They decided to store his birth certificate in the box so he could retrieve it when he went to apply for a passport. She'd actually accompanied her husband to First Bank of Westland the morning after Father's Day, she recounted, remaining in the car to smoke a cigarette while he went inside.

Gerash stood beside her, holding up the exhibit of the defendant's police memorabilia. "Out of the three photographs of his police identification," he asked, "how many was with a mustache and how many without a mustache?"

"Two without and one with," she replied.

"So it's not unusual that he shaved his mustache off and later on grew it, was it?" His booming voice was tinged with indignation and umbrage. Carolyn told jurors it wasn't unusual at all.

The defense lawyer asked how the idea arose for King to play chess on Father's Day. His wife told the jury that a week or so before, she approached him and said, "It's your day. What would you like to do?" He responded by saying he'd like to start playing chess again. They next spoke about it when he awoke on Father's Day morning, she said, sharing with jurors that he used to play at the community center fairly regularly on Sunday mornings.

Carolyn testified she distinctly recalled him returning from his trip to play chess. She was surprised he'd come home so early, explaining he was typically gone for hours when he played. As he exited his car, he informed her that he'd gone to the community center, but no one was there. After waiting a few minutes, he said, he decided to come home. He changed into shorts and the two of them worked on their yard together.

Gerash asked Carolyn whether her husband owned any clothing similar to how the bank tellers had described the gunman's attire. She told jurors that the only hat he owned was made of straw, which he used to protect himself from the sun. He didn't own mirrored sunglasses, a dark sport coat, or a black and blue tie with diagonal stripes, she said. Rather, he was a "casual dresser."

As for his courtroom attire, she testified that the only time her husband had ever owned a suit—present circumstances excluded—was when they were first married. The loose-fitting, camel-hair jacket he was wearing at counsel table was a Christmas present she'd gotten for him years earlier. She couldn't remember when he'd last worn a tie. As for the black shoes seized from their kitchen during the police search, she said, they belonged to David, not her husband.

During his redirect, Buckley had Carolyn confirm that, for many years, the defendant had been assigned to desk jobs that required him to wear civilian clothes, rather than a police uniform. Though she agreed he'd worn a sport coat while working in the ID Bureau, she told jurors he put on the same one every day.

After nearly two hours of testimony, the accused killer's wife was permitted to resume her seat in the gallery. Though Buckley had touched on many subjects, the Texas native hadn't asked a single question about the financial turmoil that had led her and her husband to declare bankruptcy. Or how cash strapped they'd been prior to the bank heist. The jury would be left to decide the case without ever learning those seemingly important details.

••••

As Gerash inched his way to the starting blocks to take a mental victory lap over Carolyn's stellar performance, the People called their next witness—yet another surprise: King's youngest son, David. From the moment he took the hot seat, something about the mustachioed 25-year-old's body language appeared off. Unlike his mom, he seemed defensive and evasive—as if he *did* have something to hide.

Buckley had been itching to question King's youngest child since reviewing the report of his July 3 FBI interview. He was optimistic his examination would chisel at least a crack—if not a few—into the foundation of the defendant's alibi.

David, an auto mechanic, testified that the first thing he recalled doing after waking up on Father's Day—somewhere between 9:00 and 11:00 a.m.—was working on his car. After about ten or 15 minutes, he told jurors, he went to an auto parts store to purchase a part.

"Do you recall telling the FBI agent and the police that when you got home from the auto parts store," Buckley asked, "your mother was home, but you did not see your dad?"

David denied ever having made such a statement. "They asked me who I saw *before* I left," he answered, "and I said I saw my mother."

The lead prosecutor handed him the written FBI report, which stated that when he returned from his errand, "his mother was home but he did not see his dad."

"Did you or did you not tell them that?" Buckley pressed him. David denied he had. He testified that he was unsure of whether his father's Ford Fiesta was home when he left for his errand, but was certain it was gone by the time he got back. When his mother and father returned later that afternoon, he said, they parked in the driveway. He recalled telling the officers questioning him that his dad was carrying a chess board as he got out of the car.

David told the jury that he worked on multiple vehicles all afternoon and into the evening, taking a break only for dinner—which he ate in the kitchen with his mom while his dad was in the living room. He couldn't remember if his brothers had come by, agreeing with Buckley they didn't share a formal Father's Day meal as a family.

The deputy DA next began a line of questioning about the defendant's police revolver. Though David was familiar with the gun, he told jurors he didn't even know it was a Colt Trooper. He'd used it for target practice and was hoping to inherit the firearm once his dad no longer had any use for it.

"When was the last time you saw the gun?" Buckley asked.

For some reason, it took David five full seconds to answer that seemingly innocuous question. "When he worked at the bank," he finally said.

Eleven minutes into his direct exam, the veteran prosecutor yielded the podium, having scored few, if any, points for the People's case. Had Gerash resisted the temptation to follow up with questions of his own, David's testimony would have amounted to an utterly forgettable blip in the weeks-long trial. But the bald-headed defense lawyer couldn't beat back the urge.

He asked the surprise prosecution witness if he'd noticed anything wrong with the revolver when he used it for target practice, which David told jurors had occurred before his dad started working for United Bank.

"When you pulled the trigger back," he testified, "the cylinder that rotates had a little bit of movement." His father had actually asked him to check with someone at the range to see if it could be fixed. Because he shot at night, however, the gunsmith shop was closed.

"Did your dad approach you concerning the gun and some equipment with the gun?" By "equipment," Gerash was referring to the retired cop's Sam Browne police belt.

"Not really the gun," David replied. "I was working in the garage one day, and he brought out the belt he had when he was a policeman, and asked me if I wanted it. And I asked him if it came with the gun."

"And what did your dad say?"

"He said 'no,' he got rid of it, because it wasn't safe. It would blow up in your face." That conversation in the garage, David recounted, had occurred in September or October of 1990—a month or two after his dad had ceased working for United Bank.

• • • •

The moment Gerash announced he had no further questions, Buckley shot out of his chair like a cannon ball.

"Show me in that report of July 3, 1991, where you told anybody that your father came out in the garage and told you that he was going to get rid of the gun because it was defective?" Apparently, Buckley believed David had testified his father told him he was *planning* to get rid of the gun, rather than what he'd actually said—that he'd *already done so*.

Gerash momentarily interrupted the flow with an objection, which was overruled. When the prosecutor re-asked the question, it came out differently: "Did you think it was important to tell the FBI agent or the detectives that your father had come to talk to you and said he was *going to* get rid of the gun because it would blow up?" This question too exposed his misunderstanding of David's earlier testimony.

Rather than correcting him, the defendant's son noted that during their discussion about the gun, the detective asking him questions had received a page and excused himself to make a call. When he returned, David said, the detective steered their conversation in an entirely different direction.

"Did you ever tell them that your father said he was *going to* get rid of the gun?" Buckley persisted. "Yes or no."

"No," David replied, still not correcting the prosecutor's mistaken understanding about his earlier testimony.

Buckley asked whether his dad told him what was wrong with the gun when they'd spoken in the garage. David responded in the negative, noting he didn't ask.

"Were you interested?"

The witness shook his head. "Not if he already got rid of it. It wouldn't make a difference."

Buckley's misunderstanding was now out in the open, David finally having corrected the premise of his last several questions. The gun *no longer existed* when he and his father spoke in the garage, he was now saying—under oath—for the second time.

The chief deputy DA articulated his confusion. "Didn't I

hear you say that he had *not yet* gotten rid of it, but told you you couldn't have the gun because it might be dangerous, and he was *going to* get rid of it?"

For 13 solid seconds, David didn't say a word, his eyes darting side to side as he struggled—in front of the jury, packed courtroom, and national TV audience—to formulate an answer. After what seemed like an eternity, his lips finally parted. "I don't remember if that's what I said or not." He shrugged his shoulders for emphasis.

Why would he have been confused over what he'd told the jury his father had said? Was it because he'd fabricated the entire garage conversation and couldn't recall the fictional details he'd made up? If he'd been telling the truth, how difficult would it have been for him to accurately recall what he'd testified to just minutes earlier?

"Did you ask him whether or not he could get it repaired so he could keep it?" Buckley asked, once again expressing his mistaken belief. When David responded that he didn't, the prosecutor followed up, asking, "Why not?"

Had he been telling the truth about the supposed garage conversation, there was only one way he could have answered the question—by repeating, for the third time, that his father had told him he'd already thrown the gun away, rendering it impossible to fix it. But that's not what David King said.

Instead, he suddenly accepted Buckley's premise that the gun still existed when he and his dad spoke about it in the garage—a complete 180—explaining he hadn't asked about a possible repair because he figured it would be too expensive.

"To repair a cylinder?" the deputy DA scoffed.

"I did not know what was wrong with it," David said, adding that he also hadn't asked his father to repair the gun because he preferred semi-automatic weapons over revolvers. Yet this answer made even less sense because he'd already testified that he wanted to inherit the gun when his dad no longer needed it.

"Well, this was the gun he carried for 25 years, right?" David agreed with that incontrovertible fact.

"Did it have some sentimental value to you as his son?"

Once again, David's eyes darted side to side before he answered, almost under his breath, that it didn't.

"Why did you want it then?" Buckley inquired, jamming David's earlier testimony right down his throat.

"Because I like target practicing," he said. Another nonsensical answer.

The veteran prosecutor's final question again assumed the gun still existed during the father-son exchange in the garage. He asked whether David knew "how much it would cost to fix it as opposed to throwing it in the trash?"

David responded that he had no idea what was wrong with it—shrugging his shoulders again—and therefore couldn't answer.

With that response, David King's 25 minutes on the witness stand came to a dramatic close. It was unclear, however, whether Bill Buckley and his team recognized the sudden about-face in his testimony—and its potential import—arguably the most significant development in the entire trial.

Had David invented the entire garage conversation in an effort to convince jurors the gun's disposal had long predated the bloodshed on Father's Day? If his dad had nothing to do with the crime, why would he concoct such a story in an effort to protect him? And if his testimony about their supposed father-son conversation—either version—was actually fiction, had the narrative been authored by him, or by the accused killer (and author) himself?

All highly important questions, the answers to which held the potential to land David King's father on death row.

30

DEWEY BELIEVE HIM?

Through their next three witnesses, the People hoped to establish that the alibi James King had supplied law enforcement—that he'd been trying to find a chess game at the Capitol Hill Community Center on Father's Day morning—was demonstrably false.

Ed Huntington, a middle-aged African American man, had been employed as a maintenance worker at the community center since 1984, residing in a camper at the edge of the property. With Lamar Sims behind the podium, Huntington told jurors about a wedding that occurred the Saturday before Father's Day—which lasted late into the evening. He and a buddy named Gary Hendry had arrived early Sunday morning to move the tables and chairs used for the wedding from a detached meeting hall back into the "mansion." They used the building's rear door to return the smaller tables and its front entrance—which had a wheelchair ramp—for the larger ones.

Before he and Hendry began working, Huntington testified, they had a cup of coffee downstairs in the basement, in the exact same location where the Denver Chess Club had met until the mid-1980s. During the time the club was still active, he explained, members had used a basement door at the rear of the facility to gain entrance with a key stored in a lockbox. During the time they were having coffee from 8:30 to 9:15 a.m., he told jurors, no one had knocked on the basement door or tried to gain entry.

He and Hendry moved tables and chairs for the next 60 to 90 minutes, Huntington said, going back and forth between the two buildings several times. At no point did he notice any vehicles in the rear parking area—where chess club members used to park. If a car had pulled up to the building, he testified, he'd have heard it. He also never saw anyone standing on the front stairs or porch.

Having played chess at the community center on countless occasions himself, Walter Gerash knew its layout nearly as well as the People's witness. He got Huntington to concede that the process of loading tables and chairs onto racks in the meeting hall was time consuming, and that he couldn't see outside while engaged in that task. And also, that while he was rolling tables to the mansion's front porch, he wouldn't have been able to see anyone at the rear of the building.

When Gerash tried to get him to admit that a car could have been at the building for five to ten minutes without him seeing it, Huntington agreed, but told the defense attorney he would have *heard* it. And on redirect examination, Sims got him to say that if anyone had knocked on the front door while he was inside the mansion, he would have heard that too. The prosecutor elicited similar testimony from Gary Hendry.

Josephine Vaughan, the community center's building manager, made an ultra-brief appearance to share what she'd learned from reviewing the nonprofit's records. Based on her analysis, the chess club had last paid fees to use the facility in 1984. As for when the club had actually stopped using the building, however, she had no idea.

••••

During his opening statement, Scott Robinson had forecast that jurors would hear about a man named Dewey Baker, who'd planned a "big job" in Denver he didn't want pinned on him. A serial bank robber whose checkered past made him a much more logical suspect than a retired police officer.

But the defense could only put those facts before the jury

if Judge Spriggs allowed such "alternative suspect" evidence. During a lunch break on Friday, May 29—outside the presence of the jury—Robinson made an "offer of proof" so the judge could determine whether the jury would get to hear anything at all about Dewey Baker.

He began his soliloquy by noting that Baker had been paroled in Michigan on May 2, 1991, after serving time for four different bank robberies. A woman from Ann Arbor he'd befriended through correspondence, Linda Johnson, had gone to meet him upon his release. He promised her he'd come back to get her in a brand-new RV as soon as he completed a "big job in Denver."

Robinson asserted that Baker "matched the description" of the United Bank gunman as well as the person trying to rent a car at Stapleton Airport Father's Day afternoon. He handed the judge photos of the convicted robber, which depicted a man in his forties with a dark cowboy-type mustache and prominent brown mole on his left cheek—consistent with where the bank tellers had seen a band-aid on the gunman's face.

According to Robinson, when the parolee left Michigan, he took Johnson's phone card to enable him to pay for long-distance calls. The defense had obtained records listing each call he made in May and June. Baker had phoned the Colorado State Prison and visited a former inmate he knew in Pueblo, Robinson said. He'd tried to enlist the ex-con's help with a bank job in Denver before stealing his .22-caliber gun. On May 13, Baker had flown from Denver to San Francisco, where he spent the next several weeks.

Johnson's phone card established a pattern of calls throughout June, all emanating from California. Robinson highlighted a 25-hour gap between 4:46 p.m. on June 15 and 6:10 p.m. on Father's Day—enough time, he claimed, for the convicted bank robber to have flown from San Francisco to Denver, committed the crime, and flown back.

Baker was supposed to return to Michigan on June 21 for the wedding of Johnson's son, the defense lawyer recounted, but told her he couldn't make it because something had gone wrong with the "big job." He hinted to her on several occasions that he was involved in the United Bank robbery, describing it as "an incident where four guards had been dusted." He told Johnson he was hoping the crime couldn't be pinned on him due to a lack of physical evidence.

Where was Dewey Baker now? In the Santa Clara County Jail, charged with yet another bank robbery in San Jose, where he'd been held by the feds since October. His court-appointed lawyer had informed Robinson that his client would take the Fifth Amendment if called as a witness in the King case. For that reason, the defense intended to have Linda Johnson testify to all the facts Robinson had just outlined. She was planning to board a train to Denver at about five o'clock that afternoon, he told the judge.

"I want to hear a little more about these statements he allegedly made, and who did he make them to and when," Judge Spriggs interjected. "I want to know exactly what he's supposed to have said."

"He has never out and out said, 'I committed the crime,'" Robinson acknowledged. Rather, he'd "implied he was involved."

"Well what did he say?" the judge pressed him. "You say he implied he was involved. I want to know what he said."

"He said, 'I hope they don't pin this one on me,' the one where four guards got dusted in Denver."

"That's not an implication he did it," the bearded jurist retorted. "That's an implication he *didn't* do it."

Bill Buckley jumped into the fray, handing the judge a letter Baker had written to a fellow inmate in which he'd called his so-called confession to the United Bank murders "a crock," noting he "never even knew about the job" until Gerash's investigator contacted him.

Judge Spriggs had heard enough, ruling that the evidence of Baker's purported involvement in the crime was far too flimsy to allow his Michigan-based girlfriend to testify about it.

Yet just as it appeared the matter was resolved, Gerash's longtime secretary, Annette Calvert, came barging into the courtroom to whisper into her boss's ear. She told him she'd just received a call from a man who'd been watching the proceedings on Court TV—from the Santa Clara County Jail. When the collect call connected, Dewey Baker—the serial bank robber himself—was on the other end of the line.

At the next break in the proceedings, Calvert found herself on the witness stand fielding questions from her boss. She'd taken excellent notes, sharing with Judge Spriggs precisely what the California inmate told her.

Baker had begun their conversation by asking if a letter he'd written approximately a month earlier had arrived at Gerash's office. His secretary told him it hadn't. He revealed he'd been discussing with his public defender what he should do. And that though he'd be willing to testify in the King case, his attorney was advising him to take the Fifth. Calvert testified he then said, "But maybe I would be willing to implicate myself."

Baker told her he'd been in prison for 14 years and had "no love for police officers." "But he says he knows 'our guy is innocent as the day is long,'" she testified, reading from her notes. He also stated that James King was "a poor, innocent son of a bitch."

After marinating over Calvert's riveting testimony, Judge Spriggs informed the lawyers he was open to reconsidering his ruling. First thing Monday morning, he said, he wanted to speak directly with the serial bank robber himself, telling Buckley he was in charge of making the arrangements.

The call ultimately occurred in the judge's chambers on Monday at noon—with prosecutors and defense lawyers huddled around his desk. Though Dewey Baker was on the line, he told Spriggs he wouldn't talk to him over the telephone. His court-appointed lawyer quickly interceded, making clear his client would plead the Fifth if compelled to testify.

As the short call ended, Judge Spriggs shook his head in exasperation. The entire exercise had been a colossal waste of time. "My ruling stands," he told the assembled group. The jury wouldn't be hearing a single word about Dewey Calvin Baker's "big job" in Denver—real or imagined.

31

BANK SECURITY 101

Over the course of the lengthy trial, Detective Jon Priest made the short journey from the prosecution table to the witness stand on nine separate occasions. He testified about the evidence discovered at the bank as well as items found during the search of the defendant's home and safety deposit box. Significantly, he confirmed that Carolyn King had expressed her belief during the July 3 search—directly to him—that her husband's longtime service revolver *did* still exist, and was being stored in a metal box in the den, even though the box was found empty that evening.

During the search, investigators had discovered a receipt for the repair of a .22-caliber North American Arms mini revolver. The ex-cop had apparently seen fit to replace the cylinder of *that* gun in November 1989—though he claimed to have thrown away his trusted service revolver less than a year later due to a faulty cylinder.

Though the prosecution wanted Priest to inform jurors about the 21 passages in King's police manual describing officers being shot in the back and back of the head, Gerash's vehement objection was sustained. Not a word of the 350-page tome would be admitted into evidence.

The homicide detective told jurors he'd made several test drives between the downtown bank and the accused killer's home, noting that nearly the entire 11.4-mile drive was in a 55-mile-per-hour zone. On a quiet Sunday morning, he'd been able to complete the trip in just ten to 13 minutes—leading Gerash to begin referring to him as "Speedy Priest" and "Race-car Driver Priest."

During cross-examination, the detective was forced to admit that, in all the searches undertaken at the defendant's home, yard, vehicle, safe deposit box, and Mount Olivet Cemetery, not a single shred of evidence had been found connecting him to the crime: no money, gun, speed loaders, sunglasses, hat, clothing, doctor's satchel, guard logbook pages, VHS tapes, keys, two-way radios, or Markey card. And unlike the size-8 shoes initially believed to match the prints at the bank, the footwear seized from James King's bedroom—that actually belonged to him, rather than his son—was size 10.5.

Both sides had asked Judge Spriggs to allow jurors to be transported to the bank for a jury view—a request the bearded jurist accommodated near the end of the trial's second week. Just before the anointed hour arrived, Priest stood beside enlarged floorplans mounted on an easel, pointing out various areas of interest jurors would get to see.

The 14 decision-makers then piled into a light-blue prison bus for the short ride—the judge, court officials, prosecutors, Detective Priest, defense lawyers, and bank security personnel joining them at the downtown complex. Despite the statement made by Norwest's chairman in March 1991 that "United is a great name"—that Norwest had no plans to change—the signage greeting jurors upon their arrival read "Norwest Bank."

In an eerie experience for all in attendance, the group retraced each of the killer's steps. They began by descending the freight elevator in which he'd held Bill McCullom at gunpoint before marching him to his own execution. They zig-zagged their way through the concourse level, exploring both the guard monitor room—where Phil Mankoff, Scott McCarthy, and Todd Wilson had been pumped full of lead—and the cash vault, where the terrified vault employees had been robbed at gunpoint.

During their foray through the bowels of the bank, jurors were required to remain silent, no matter what questions they had. Even Buckley and Robinson—acting as their tour guides—had to use gestures and pantomimes to point out each door, hallway, or room they considered significant. Jurors were then herded downstairs to the lower concourse level, finally making their way to the incinerator room, where a flurry of bullets had extinguished McCullom's life.

••••

As the witness most knowledgeable about the bank's security systems and procedures, Jim Prado occupied the witness stand for five solid hours, fielding a myriad of questions from Buckley and then Robinson. The 35-year-old with Coke-bottle glasses and shock of wavy brown hair no longer worked for the bank, having been unceremoniously canned by Norwest over the Christmas holidays for a minor disciplinary infraction. Prior to his abrupt termination, he'd spent nearly his entire adult life in the bank's security operation, beginning as a guard himself at the age of 20.

Prado told jurors that only two guards were typically on duty at a time, a third if one was being trained. He couldn't recall a single instance besides Father's Day in which four had been assigned at the same time. From his review of the Markey card access report, he was able to confirm that Mankoff had been showing McCarthy around the bank that morning—Mankoff's card preceding McCarthy's at numerous readers throughout the complex, including in the cash vault, where guards weren't supposed to be when money was being counted.

An hour into his direct exam, Buckley asked the prosecution witness if James King was present in the courtroom. Prado nodded. His face lit up with a huge smile as his eyes met the defendant's—as if he'd spotted a long-lost childhood friend rather than the killer who'd murdered four members of his team. An unscripted moment conveying a subliminal message to jurors that King's boss held genuine affection for the man they were supposed to believe was a ruthless assassin.

Prado confirmed the ex-cop had been aware of a make-shift camera installed in the monitor room to catch guards eating or drinking, and that its footage was delivered to a VCR in the locked supervisor's office. In April 1991, he said, Norwest replaced the makeshift camera with a permanent one, which remained aimed at the U-shaped security console. But when he entered the monitor room on Father's Day, he told the jury, the camera had been turned in the opposite direction—presumably by the killer.

The defendant also knew about an incident in which another guard, Doug Bagley, had been fired for propping open the monitor room's entry door—so he could fetch a snack without being detected—which had locked him out upon his return. Prado told jurors King had been trained to ensure nothing like that ever happened on his watch.

The former guard supervisor testified that on Sundays, only Elevator #3 was available to the guards, providing them access to the concourse level, first floor, Lincoln Street level, and all nine levels of the parking garage. Though Elevator #3 was discovered keyed off on garage's seventh floor, to Buckley's surprise, Prado testified that weekend guards never parked there.

The lead prosecutor segued to the sensor that had gone off in the records tunnel at 5:04 a.m. Father's Day morning, asking Prado to confirm that it was unreliable. That particular alarm—a microwave sensor—had been installed in the early 1980s, the witness said. He agreed it had problems, sometimes going off in the middle of the night for no particular reason, noting that moving objects like mice or something falling off a shelf could trigger it.

●●●●

Robinson had even more questions for Prado than his adversary, hoping the former bank employee would lend credence to several defense theories. In response to his questions, the bespectacled witness testified that guards generally parked at Motor Bank #1—under the parking garage, near the freight elevator—not on the seventh floor.

The defense lawyer asked a series of questions about how

guards began accessing the cash vault shortly after the defendant quit working for the bank. Prado told jurors that, prior to late August 1990, guards had opened the outer and inner mantrap doors with an MK1 key. As of August 29, 1990, however, "in-out" readers had been activated at each door, requiring guards to insert their Markey cards to enter both—their MK1 keys no longer an option.

Shifting topics, Robinson placed a clear plastic bag on the witness stand that contained a 7-Up can and a disposable coffee cup. Upon inspecting those items, Prado told the jury he'd discovered them Father's Day afternoon inside the entrance to the records tunnel—along with several cigarette butts—not far from the microwave sensor that had activated at 5:04 a.m. He decided to leave them in place for the police to gather as evidence. When he discovered them still there four weeks later, he mentioned the items to an off-duty cop, who finally bagged them as potential evidence.

All of which led Robinson to the subject he considered central to his client's defense: the 5:04 a.m. alarm. Prado testified that whoever had been in the monitor room at that time—one of the soon-to-be-murdered guards—had pushed one button to signal his awareness of the alarm and another to turn it off. But that wasn't standard protocol, he said. Rather, a guard should have been dispatched to the records tunnel to investigate its cause.

The microwave sensor remained disengaged for four-and-a-half hours, he told jurors. During that time, the security system wouldn't have been able to detect or document anyone's presence in the tunnel. And then, at 9:33 a.m., the alarm had been reactivated by the push of another button in the monitor room—by someone who was still alive—perhaps the spookiest fact in the entire case.

Prado confirmed that the 5:04 a.m. alarm puzzled him when he first became aware it. And that he had several discussions with investigators trying to figure out what it meant.

He agreed with the defense attorney that the tunnel's microwave sensor had repeatedly been set off by a fluorescent light years earlier—a problem that had been fixed by Mosler, the security company that installed it. As for whether a renegade mouse had set off the alarm Father's Day morning, Prado confirmed that several traps had been set in the tunnel and that "there were no furry perpetrators found." Indeed, a history report he ran listed no false alarms in the 30 days preceding Father's Day.

Prado testified that at 7:54 a.m. that morning, Mankoff and McCarthy had gotten stuck in the cash vault's mantrap when the first-day trainee had tried to use his Markey card on the inner door after Mankoff had used his card to enter the outer door. That created an "out of sequence" error, he explained, making the inner door inoperable. Having carefully studied the Markey card usage records, he said, the robber hadn't experienced that same problem.

"So that robber, that person, apparently knew—or managed to figure out—how to use the Markey card correctly?" Robinson asked.

"Or in-out reader," Prado said. "Yeah." He confirmed the robber would have gotten stuck in the mantrap if he'd hurriedly tried to exit without waiting for the inner door to close before using a Markey card on the outer door.

Prado agreed with King's lawyer that his client ordinarily worked the 12:30 p.m. to 12:30 a.m. shift, such that he wouldn't have had the chance to develop a solid working knowledge of the Sunday morning cash vault operation. And also, that the floorplans to the bank discovered during the search of his home were supplied to every guard to assist with their training—without any expectation they'd be returned. He also agreed that by June 16, 1991, the diagram of the concourse level—which he'd drawn by hand—had become obsolete due to several changes in the layout.

Prado described King as a "thorough" guard who acquired "competent knowledge" of bank security, but agreed with Robinson that he wasn't "some sort of superstar guard that knew everything." The ex-cop had made suggestions on several occasions, Prado recounted, as to how security could be improved. He told jurors King took his job seriously, unlike some other guards.

He agreed with the defense attorney that most of the guards "war gamed" how a robber might try to rob the bank. But he wasn't concerned by that chatter, he said, explaining, "To me it looked that they were concerned about their own protection, and the protection of the bank, so if they could figure out a way to survive or for the bank to survive through something, that was good."

"Did you in fact encourage the guards to anticipate ways in which someone might try and commit a robbery?" Robinson asked.

"Yes." Prado agreed guards even discussed scenarios as to how a robber might try to kill them. Yet when he was involved in such discussions, "the guards always lived."

"For good reason, right?" Robinson asked as laughter cascaded across the courtroom.

"Jim King did not want the guards to be unarmed, did he?"

"No," the prosecution witness agreed.

"He was quite vocal while he was there," Robinson asserted, "that in order to safeguard the personnel and the bank's money, that the security guards should be armed."

Again, Prado concurred. He also agreed that King wasn't a "gun nut," telling jurors, "He didn't appear to be aggressive." In fact, that was one of the reasons he and Tom Tatalaski had decided to hire the retired police sergeant in the first place—because he didn't fit that "macho role."

• • • •

Tatalaski, the security section manager, replaced his former subordinate on the witness stand. He told jurors it had been his decision to hire the accused killer. When Buckley asked if King was present in the courtroom, Tatalaski hesitated as he peered at the defense table, noting, "I knew Mr. King with a mustache and sideburns when he was employed at the bank."

The high-level manager had an entirely different take from Prado about the seventh floor of the parking garage, telling jurors it was "mainly for employees who work at night and on the weekend." He testified that he was the one who placed the order for the "in-and-out" Markey card readers to be installed at the cash vault, which had arrived in August 1990. Prior to them being installed, he said, every guard—including King—had been briefed about their impending installation.

"Were the readers for the cash vault any different," Buckley asked, "in terms of the way they operated from the readers at the entryway to the guard monitor room?"

"They were both the same," the prosecution witness answered.

During his cross-examination, Tatalaski acknowledged that when the FBI first interviewed him, he'd pointed to Mike McKown and Paul Yocum as potential suspects—not James King. And that, to him, the FBI composite drawing "appeared to be Mr. McKown." He also agreed with Robinson that his review of security records established that Bob Bardwell had never entered the bank on any Sunday during the 13 months King had been on the payroll—implying the ex-cop wouldn't have even known his name.

•••

Buckley brought Detective Priest back to the stand in an effort to rebut points Robinson had made through his questioning of Jim Prado. For starters, Priest testified he'd actually observed the 7-Up can, coffee cup, and cigarette butts in the records tunnel on Father's Day. Because the coffee cup had dry residue at the bottom and the soda can was dry, he said, they appeared to have been there for quite some time—which is why he didn't ensure they were bagged as potential evidence.

He shared with jurors that he'd conducted a number of experiments with the microwave sensor in the records tunnel, noting he had to get within ten to 15 feet before it would go off. The 7-Up can and coffee cup by the entrance were much further away than that, he said. He noted that the sensor was in close proximity to a fan and two different lights that would sway like a pendulum due to the air current the fan created—implying that such swaying could have caused the 5:04 a.m.

alarm.

Despite Buckley's efforts to clean things up with Jon Priest, the defense had scored numerous points through Jim Prado's testimony—apart from the message conveyed by his obvious affection for the defendant. King's thoroughness had been appreciated, not the source of concern. Any war-gaming in which he'd engaged had been encouraged, not a precursor to him going rogue. The bank plans discovered at his home were completely innocuous.

Changes had been made to the cash vault entry procedure after King's departure, yet the killer/robber had flown through that mantrap without any difficulty. And the 5:04 a.m. alarm in the records tunnel—coupled with the soda can, coffee cup, and cigarette butts—were at a minimum difficult to explain, if not signs that there had been much more to the Father's Day massacre than the scenario laid out by the prosecution.

In short, to the extent Buckley and Sims believed Prado and Tatalaski's testimony would move the needle in the direction of a conviction, they had to be disappointed with how that evidence actually panned out.

<h1 style="text-align:center">32</h1>

PARADE OF GUARDS

As the People's case raced toward the finish line, the prosecution called a series of witnesses whose employment at United Bank of Denver had overlapped with the defendant's. First up was Mike McKown, the weekend guard who'd befriended King and had himself briefly been considered a suspect.

As he took the witness stand—sporting a tan, three-piece suit and striped tie—anyone with a good set of eyes would have immediately noticed the dissimilarities between his appearance and King's. McKown's mop of hair was dark brown—obviously dyed that color—as were his closely trimmed mustache and unkempt sideburns. At only 45, he was ten years King's junior.

McKown told jurors he'd lived in Arvada, Colorado, working both as a substitute teacher and a weekend security guard from February 1988 until June 1990. Over the course of his two-and-a-half years at United Bank, he trained 32 fellow guards.

Sims had the witness identify King at counsel table, and confirm that the retired cop had been one of his trainees—eventually becoming his partner. McKown told the jury the ex-cop was very knowledgeable about the bank's layout and security systems, and that a friendly "bone of contention" existed between them as to who knew more.

Flashing a playful smile, he recounted a time King had

challenged him to locate a poster of actress Morgan Fairchild he'd discovered during one of his guard tours, which he found buried in a janitorial closet. McKown had accepted the challenge, acknowledging it had taken him months to locate the poster.

"How well did you come to know the defendant?" Sims asked.

"Quite well," the prosecution witness said. "I'd have to say he's one of my best friends." His answer was tinged with emotion, revealing his warm feelings toward King despite the heinous crimes he'd been accused of committing.

"Difficult to be here today?" the prosecutor asked.

McKown nodded. "Yes," he said meekly.

He testified that he and his partner shared an interest in chess, telling jurors King was far better at the game—playing with half of his pieces and still beating him like a drum. "Let's say I never won," he added with a chuckle, locking eyes with the defendant as a smile crept across his lips.

Sims asked him about guards war-gaming scenarios in which the bank might be robbed. It was a subject that routinely came up "with almost every guard whoever worked there," McKown said. "Just by the nature of the job, we would role-play or game play, if we were going to hold this place up, how would we do it? Mainly as a way of finding deficiencies in the system so we could take care of them." Asked to recall King's contributions to such scenarios, however, he came up empty.

McKown testified that although he hadn't carried a weapon while working at the bank, King had believed it necessary to be armed, carrying an old, well-worn revolver in the holster of his Sam Browne belt.

Twenty minutes into his questioning, Sims transitioned to Father's Day, when McKown was living with his sister near Seattle. The prosecutor approached the witness stand holding the letter the defendant had mailed to McKown on June 21. "I thought you might want to hear about the United Bank murders and robbery," the handwritten note had begun, continuing on to state how the guards and ex-guards were "of course" being blamed. The letter also mentioned a vacation King had been planning to take in August to visit Las Vegas and Arizona.

McKown told the jury that, after receiving the letter, he decided to play a practical joke on his former partner. He called him on June 24, pretending the FBI had been with him when he'd opened the letter and had reviewed its contents. He said to his friend, "They wanted me to call you and ask you where you got the money to take this wild trip to Vegas." Though he thought he was being funny, King wasn't finding their conversation the least bit humorous—"the classic example," McKown said, "of a joke gone flat." He told jurors his friend seemed concerned.

"What did he say?" Sims inquired.

"Well, why do they want to know?" McKown recalled him saying. "Why are they asking you about it?"

McKown testified that he continued to play along, telling his former partner the FBI was "just curious."

But King didn't appear the slightest bit amused. He started to ramble nervously, saying, "I was getting kind of worried because ... I was downtown by myself around the time it happened." He told McKown he'd gone to play chess at the Denver Chess Club, dropping his wife off at work on the way. When he arrived, he said, "it was closed ... or they had moved." He stumbled into another person who was also looking for the chess club and talked with him. "The guy evidently left," McKown testified, "and Jim came home."

As he neared the end of his direct examination, Sims approached the witness stand with the FBI composite sketch. "In terms of the numerous guards that you trained and knew," he asked, "who does that composite most resemble?"

McKown took a few seconds to study the drawing. "It probably looks like Jim the most," he finally said. "It looks a lot like Jim."

Robinson drew the assignment of cross-examining the former bank guard. He got McKown to confirm he had no idea at the time of his June 24 conversation with King that the FBI had just interviewed him in his Golden, Colorado home— which might have explained why he wasn't seeing the humor in his friend's practical joke.

In response to the defense lawyer's questions, McKown told jurors he considered security at the bank "abysmal. There was none." And that he "didn't feel safe. I had made suggestions on how to improve the system and they were ignored. And I thought, 'Well if you don't want help, if you don't want information, then why should I be here?'" The woeful security, he said, was the primary reason he quit.

"Do you feel that Jim King was a violent, aggressive person?" Robinson asked.

McKown shook his head. "No."

On redirect examination, Sims used the report of McKown's July 9 FBI interview to refresh his recollection as to the specific words King had used during their telephone conversation.

"He said he was a little concerned because he didn't have an ironclad alibi, or a good alibi," McKown testified. "He said that he was kind of stuck."

When the questioning ended, as the ex-guard was stepping down from the stand, he glanced over at the defense table. The defendant nodded at him, as if to signal his affection. McKown left little doubt the feeling was mutual, gently squeezing King's shoulder as he passed by on his way to the courtroom exit.

••••

Next to take the stand was Harry Glass, the young guard with shoulder-length hair who'd been relieved by McCullom and Mankoff at 12:30 a.m. Father's Day morning. It was Glass's fingerprint that had been lifted from the Mountain Dew can found propping open the monitor room's entry door.

The former weekend guard shared with jurors the chaotic scene that greeted him when he arrived at the bank for his next shift 12 hours later, a slew of police cars lining the street. Buckley showed him a picture of the Mountain Dew can, having Glass confirm he'd tossed it in the trash bin in the monitor room before heading home for the night.

The deputy DA wanted to make absolutely sure jurors knew — despite the fingerprint evidence — that Glass had nothing to do with the crime. "Mr. Glass, on Father's Day, around 9:15 in the morning," he asked, "did you come back into the bank, with your hair hanging to your shoulders, and kill four guards?"

The 26-year-old recoiled in his seat. "No, I didn't."

He was so shaken by the experience and "the loss of my friends," he said, he quit the very next day. He found security at the bank "really lax and unprofessional" and told the jury it was "ridiculous" for guards not to be armed — himself carrying a .357 Mangum revolver "before they took our guns away."

As Glass departed the witness stand, Warren Webber entered the courtroom. He'd worked as a weekend guard from February to June 1990, overlapping with the defendant the entire four months.

Webber told jurors he'd see King every weekend, either partnering with him during the graveyard shift or overlapping with him when he worked the 6:00 a.m. swing shift. He had a distinct memory, he said, of the ex-cop carrying a gun in a police belt that also included two speed loaders. Of all the guards Webber had worked with, he testified, King and McKown were the two who knew the layout the best.

On cross-examination, he acknowledged receiving a set of floor plans from Jim Prado, which he kept at home. "It took a long time to find your way around in the place," he explained. As a whole, he found the guards generally dissatisfied about the bank's security. Indeed, King had told him he was "disgusted" by it. Webber agreed with Gerash that guards would routinely war-game how the bank might be robbed.

Neil Tubbs, a young guard supervisor, was next to testify. Answering Buckley's questions, he told jurors that the rule prohibiting food, drinks, and smoking in the monitor room wasn't well enforced. Guards would even leave the complex while on duty, he said, to fetch food from nearby convenience stores and fast-food restaurants.

Tubbs recalled King carrying an old Colt Trooper, the blue coloring of which had been wearing off. His gun belt, Tubbs said, included pouches for two speed loaders. He testified that guard rounds on Sunday mornings included visiting the room directly across from the incinerator room.

Buckley asked if there were ever false alarms on the motion detectors in the records tunnel. Tubbs recounted how the air vent by the fluorescent light fixture would cause the light to sway, sometimes triggering the alarm.

During Robinson's cross, he acknowledged that King "was a solid performer." And also, that the ex-cop had told him about a malfunction in his revolver that needed to be fixed. Tubbs confirmed the "in-out" card readers installed beside the cash vault in September 1990 were different from the readers outside in the monitor room, because the new readers required the same Markey card to be used going in and going out.

George Anders, a much older guard, replaced Tubbs on the witness stand. He'd been working at the bank since April 1990, overlapping with King during his final four months. Anders recalled the defendant making a remark that he wouldn't work at the bank unless he was armed. He also remembered him reading military and police magazines.

Anders testified that King had given him two reasons for taking the weekend job. First, though he had enough income to live on, he said he had plenty of spare time and wanted some extra spending money to take his wife out to dinner. Second, he mentioned writing a police manual for officers and security guards. Anders noted how helpful King had been while he was learning the ropes, staying in touch with him over the radio to make sure he could find his way around.

Roger Gottschalk had been employed as a guard from September 1989 to March 1991, working weekends at first, then shifting to full time six months later. He told jurors he and King had worked together on several weekend shifts. The retired cop had actually shown him the hollow-point bullets he carried, telling him they had more stopping power than regular bullets, and that he'd been able to retain his police-issued ammo after he retired. Gottschalk also recalled King wearing a pedometer, to make sure he knew how far he was walking while on his rounds.

Though Gerash tried to get him to admit that all of the guards war-gamed the bank being robbed, Gottschalk told him the only guards he recalled doing so were McKown and King.

Reclaiming the podium, Buckley asked, "Did James King show a curiosity about learning the bank different from other guards?"

"It seemed to me he did," Gottschalk replied. "It seemed like he wanted to get to know where every door and every hallway led to."

The final guard to testify in the People's case was Dana Pappas, whose testimony Buckley had previewed during his opening statement. The clean-cut, curly-haired 29-year-old had worked as a weekend guard for three to four months starting in June 1990, receiving his training from the defendant himself.

Pappas described King as "very knowledgeable" about the "entire labyrinth of the bank," telling jurors he would frequent areas that weren't part of routine guard tours—areas he had no business being—taking notes in a notepad. He testified that he observed King measuring and timing distances from point to point.

Pappas also recalled the ex-cop describing how he'd rob the bank: by calling into the monitor room from either the parking garage or loading dock to gain entry, shooting the guards in the monitor room, robbing the cash vault, and exiting through an elevator.

Gerash tried his best to take the sting out of the former guard's seemingly damning testimony. "Isn't it true, when you were interviewed two days after the homicide," he asked, "you positively stated that you felt Yocum had committed the homicide and bank robbery?"

"I didn't positively state that," Pappas answered as he rocked in his chair. "I said those were my feelings."

"And then you began to give all the reasons—is that correct?"

"There was some discussion about why," he reluctantly agreed. "Yes."

In response to another question, the ex-guard testified he'd observed Bill McCullom greeting King in the monitor room during a shift change—which was impossible, since Mc-Cullom hadn't begun working at the bank until 30 days after King quit. Pappas also agreed that his discussion with King about how to rob the bank had been so brief and innocuous, he'd already forgotten about it the next day.

With Gerash's help, he recalled an instance in which King had placed a newspaper clipping on the bulletin board about a bank guard having been shot and killed. "He stressed the point," Pappas said, "that all the guards should be armed."

As for the camera recording activity in the monitor room, he told jurors Jim Prado had let both him and King know it wasn't actually hooked up.

Gerash asked the witness whether he'd been fired from his job due to attendance problems.

"No, I quit," Pappas retorted. "I had taken the part-time position at the bank hoping to upgrade to a full-time position." But the impending Norwest takeover was causing downsizing in personnel, he said, which led him to change his mind about seeking a full-time job.

••••

The government's final three witnesses were intended to establish that King had been well aware—long before Father's Day—that the Denver Chess Club had moved from the Capitol Hill Community Center to a new location. Proving that single fact held the potential to eviscerate the defendant's alibi—exposing it as a complete fabrication. But the evidence didn't come together as the prosecution team had hoped.

A chess club member named Larry Duke told jurors the club had met at the community center until the mid-1980s, and that it took some time to find a new location. They finally obtained space at the VFW post on Ninth and Bannock, he said, before moving to their present location, the VFW on Colfax and Tennison. Duke recalled seeing King at the chess club on two occasions: first at the community center and, more recently, at the Colfax and Tennison location. But he told jurors he couldn't recall with any precision when that second time had occurred.

During cross-examination, Gerash asked if the second occasion had been on July 2, when he—Walter Gerash—had been King's opponent across the chess board.

"Well, I don't know about that date," Duke said. "All's I'm saying is that I did see him down there approximately about a year ago. Whether it was more than a year, less than a year, I'm not sure." He agreed, however, that Gerash had been present that same evening.

A postal worker named Al Skarie—clad in his government-issued uniform—testified that he'd been a member of the chess club for about four years. Buckley asked if he'd played chess against King at the VFW post on Ninth and Bannock—fully expecting him to say he had. But Skarie told the prosecutor he had no such recollection, stating he'd last played against King at the community center.

"Did you ever tell FBI Agent Gedney that you played with him at the VFW post at Ninth and Bannock on two or three separate occasions?" Buckley asked, quickly growing frustrated with his own witness' answers.

"I said that I probably had," Skarie said, "but I wasn't sure on the Ninth and Bannock location."

Gerash made even clearer during his cross that Al Skarie had nothing helpful to offer the prosecution, asking, "You do remember when you did play him, it was at the Capitol Hill Community Center on Thirteenth and Williams?"

"Absolutely correct, sir," Skarie agreed.

Buckley next brought Agent Gedney to the stand to impeach Skarie's unhelpful testimony. Gedney testified that the postal worker had mentioned playing chess with King at the VFW on Ninth and Bannock on two occasions in the Fall of 1989 and that he never said anything at all about playing with him at the community center.

And on that murky note, after presenting 59 different witnesses and 248 exhibits, Bill Buckley announced to Judge Spriggs, "Your honor, at this time, we'd rest our case." The baton was officially being passed to Gerash and Robinson to present whatever evidence they believed would help their client beat the rap and march out of the City & County Building a free man.

33

SMORGASBORD OF DOUBT

As is true for the defense of any criminal defendant, Gerash and Robinson's primary mission was to convince jurors that reasonable doubt existed as to whether their client had committed the crimes for which he was standing trial. Their goal was to provide jurors an assortment of discrete facts that didn't fit the tidy picture Buckley and Sims had attempted to paint during their two weeks in control of the evidence.

The defense team began with a young police officer, Sue Scott, who'd moonlighted as a security guard at United Bank during the summer of 1991. It was Officer Scott whom Jim Prado had told about the 7-Up can, coffee cup, and cigarette butts he stumbled across in the records tunnel on Father's Day. Scott told jurors that when she went to investigate with Prado on July 14, those items were still there.

Not only had she bagged them up and taken the items to the DPD's property bureau, she wrote Detective Priest a letter to make him aware of what she'd found, even calling him a couple of days later. In contrast to Priest's testimony, she revealed that the detective made no mention at all of having ever seen those items before.

The defense team then shifted to the mysterious traveler at Stapleton Airport who attempted to rent a car for cash on Father's Day afternoon. Three rental car agents and the airport's customer service representative provided the jury detailed descriptions of the man, which closely approximated how the eyewitnesses described the robber who invaded the cash vault. Yet when asked if the traveler they'd observed was the man seated at the end of the defense table—the defendant, James King—all four defense witnesses answered in the negative.

At that point, Scott Robinson began focusing like a laser on the alternative suspect even Detective Priest had at one point believed was responsible for the crime: Paul Yocum, who stood trial just a year earlier for the May 1990 ATM theft. Jodine Lang, the co-chair of the neighborhood crime-watch program, was the first of several witnesses to testify about the floppy-eared former guard. Yocum's neighbor testified about her sightings of him as he headed toward downtown between 8:30 and 9:00 a.m. on Father's Day morning.

Gerash's partner next called FBI Agent William McMath, to probe him about his June 24 interview in the ex-guard's living room. The special agent told jurors that Yocum claimed he'd never left his apartment until 11 o'clock that morning, which was squarely at odds with the testimony they'd just heard from Lang. Robinson had McMath describe in great detail the arsenal of weapons and ammunition discovered in Yocum's closet.

Another FBI agent, Charles Evans, was called to testify about the second arsenal unearthed at the former guard's childhood home in Flagler. Robinson had Evans step down from the witness stand to inventory the massive collection of speed loaders, shell casings, and .38-caliber bullets found during that search. The defense attorney also had the agent read from Yocum's highly incriminating diary, to demonstrate his animosity toward his superiors at the bank and his thirst for revenge.

But not everything in the diary was incriminating. Buckley had Evans read entries in which Yocum had proclaimed his innocence as to the ATM theft, and which revealed his nightmares "about being found guilty of a crime I did not do." The lead prosecutor also had Evans confirm that all of the ammunition discovered during the various searches was intended for Smith & Wesson firearms, not a Colt-type revolver like the murder weapon.

However, to the extent Buckley was trying to convince jurors that a Colt Trooper couldn't have fired Yocum's ammo—or that speed loaders designed for a Smith & Wesson revolver wouldn't have fit one—Robinson had the perfect rebuttal witness at the ready. Tony DiVirgilio, a private investigator hired by Gerash, had been seated next to the defense table the entire trial, whispering into the defense attorneys' ears several times a day. DiVirgilio knew a thing or two about speed loaders and ammo, having worked for many years as a police officer himself.

Robinson had the former cop perform a simple demonstration, taking one of Yocum's speed loaders—clearly marked "Not for Colt"—and inserting its six .38-caliber bullets into the cylinder of the Colt Trooper marked as a prosecution exhibit. It took DiVirgilio all of two seconds to slip the cartridges from the speed loader into the Trooper's cylinder.

Robinson also called Jon Priest to the stand to hash through details of Yocum's incriminating behavior on June 24—including his attempt to discard a bag full of evidence purportedly at the direction of his lawyer. The lead detective admitted they'd even pulled the boots off Yocum's feet because the sole pattern appeared similar to the shoeprints discovered at the bank. And further conceded they'd seized semi-jacketed hollow-points and lead Lubaloy bullets from the ex-guard's closet—all consistent with the "death bullets" removed from the victims' bodies.

••••

Some of the evidence the defense team presented to the jury was designed to rebut theories at the heart of the People's case. One such theory was that a retired police officer like James King would never voluntarily part with a treasured memento of his service like the weapon he'd carried for 25 years. Robinson had Officer Tony Pierson take the stand to dispel any such notion.

Pierson had been with the DPD for nearly two decades. From 1984 to 1986, he'd worked alongside King at Stapleton Airport, getting to know him as a meticulous professional who took his job seriously. Robinson asked whether, during those two years, the defendant had expressed "affection or an attachment to his firearm."

"No," Pierson said. "I would say quite the contrary."

Robinson asked the longtime cop what he intended to do with his own service weapon when he eventually retired.

Pierson's answer stood in stark contrast to the prosecution's theory. He told the jury, "My personal feeling is, I was going to take a torch, cut the thing up, and throw it in the river."

••••

One of the few highlights of the prosecution's case was Kenetha Whisler's testimony that, during the October preliminary hearing, she'd heard the defendant say, "Where did that come from?" and believed his voice to be identical to the robber's. Robinson called three witnesses to rebut the notion his client had made any such statement. First up was the presiding judge himself, Brian Campbell.

"Judge Campbell, did you hear Jim King say, 'Where did that come from?' during the preliminary hearing?"

"I did not hear that statement," the jurist said. "I have no recollection of Mr. King making any statement at any time during the preliminary hearing."

But that testimony went only so far. Under Buckley's questioning, Campbell explained that at the time of King's alleged statement, his attention had been focused solely on the attorneys—who at that juncture were in the midst of spirited arguments over Gerash's objection to Sims' request that King stand up and speak.

The defendant's sister, Myra Church, took the stand next. Not only had she been present throughout the entire trial, she told jurors she'd also attended the preliminary hearing, occupying a seat in the first row of the gallery—directly behind her brother. Not once, she testified, did she hear him say a single word while a witness was on the stand.

Tony DiVirgilio made a brief encore appearance to provide his input on the subject. He told the jury he'd been seated at the defense table during Whisler's testimony, three seats to King's left. Asked by Robinson if he'd heard the defendant say, "Where did that come from?," DiVirgilio responded, "I did not."

But Sims made clear through his cross that the defense investigator wouldn't necessarily have heard the remark due to the heated exchange taking place between Gerash and Sims over whether King would be forced to speak. DiVirgilio conceded that, like Judge Campbell's, his attention had been focused on Gerash's vehement objection, not on the defendant.

• • • •

Though Buckley had been largely unsuccessful in his attempt to establish the defendant knew full well that the Denver Chess Club had moved locations long before Father's Day, Gerash wasn't taking any chances. He paraded five additional chess club members before the jury to rebut the lead prosecutor's contention. Michael Presutti, a member of the club since 1978, testified he'd never seen the defendant at either of the two VFW posts where club members played after moving from the Capitol Hill Community Center.

Richard Buchanan, president of the Colorado State Chess Association, reviewed records of the rated games in which King had played. He confirmed that the only time the retired cop had played a rated game at either VFW post was on July 2, 1991, the day he played against Gerash—more than two weeks following the bank massacre. The records also revealed that King had played 244 rated postal games, the last of which had been in September 1989.

Rodney Cruz, the current club president, had become a member in December 1989, when its venue was on Ninth and Bannock. He testified he'd never seen King at that location. After the club moved to the West Colfax VFW in September 1990, he told jurors, he'd only seen him there once—when he was seated across the chess board from Walter Gerash.

Steven Jared testified that he met the defendant at the community center in the late 1970s and had played chess with him one random Sunday morning in either 1984 or 1985. What stuck in his memory was King mentioning that he was a police officer. Jared testified he'd never seen the ex-cop at the club's next location on Ninth and Bannock, where it had moved to in either late 1987 or early 1988.

Richard Garcia testified that he'd served as president of the chess club from 1985 to 1990. He echoed Jared's testimony that the club moved to the VFW on Ninth and Bannock in late 1987 or early 1988. The big difference between the community center and the VFW, he noted, was that the former was accessible to club members 24 hours a day. At the new location on Ninth and Bannock, however, games were restricted to Tuesday evenings.

• • • •

Because much of the eyewitness testimony had dwelled on the robber's hair and mustache, the defense decided to call someone who knew an awful lot about those particular subjects: James King's longtime barber. Neilus Rome told jurors he'd cut the defendant's flat top every three to four weeks—always on Tuesday or Wednesday mornings at 10:30 or 11:00 a.m.— for 20 to 25 years, the former cop one of his most reliable customers.

Rome testified that King had straight hair with no curls and a light-brown mustache with a few gray whiskers—not, in his opinion, salt-and-pepper. When he trimmed the defendant's hair, he said, he always cut the sideburns off just above the middle of his ears. He noted that King would sometimes shave off his mustache, mostly during the summer months. When he wore his stache, he kept it neatly trimmed himself, never allowing Rome to touch it.

The old-school barber had a distinct recollection of King's mustache being gone the first time he came in for a haircut following Father's Day. He couldn't recall if that was the very next Tuesday or the Tuesday of the following week. Asked by Robinson if King ever had "long, silver, manicured sideburns down to the bottom of his ear"—Nina McGinty's description—Rome answered, "No, never."

During his cross-examination, Buckley showed the barber King's most recent DMV photo, taken shortly after Father's Day. Rome agreed that his sideburns, by that time, contained a good bit of gray.

• • • •

Robinson and Gerash had gotten off to a solid start, poking what they believed were significant holes in the People's case. Yet they knew their biggest obstacle would be their client's alibi. Fortunately, they had a pair of witnesses waiting outside the courtroom eager to tell jurors what they'd observed 11 miles away from the bank on Father's Day morning.

34

WON'T YOU BE MY NEIGHBOR?

Roberta Trujillo resided in a 900-square-foot rental home directly across the street from the bungalow owned by James and Carolyn King. The married, 30-year-old Coors brewery worker was young enough to be their daughter.

Though the defendant told the FBI he couldn't think of anyone who might be able to support his alibi, on July 5—the day after his arrest—that's precisely what Trujillo had done. She recounted to a pair of FBI agents that she'd spotted King working in his front yard at 9:00 a.m. on Father's Day, as she was departing in her car to visit her mother. In view of the 11 miles between their neighborhood and the United Bank of Denver, if her recollection proved accurate, the ex-cop and former weekend guard couldn't have been at the downtown complex at 9:14 a.m.—even by Speedy Priest's calculations.

Walter Gerash hoped the bespectacled, brown-haired alibi witness would deliver a knockout punch to the People's case. But as she took the witness stand in a simple white dress—an elaborate pink bow clipped to the bottom of her braided pony tail—James King's soft-spoken neighbor appeared extremely nervous, momentarily even forgetting her own address.

As she settled down, Gerash began walking her through her personal timeline on Father's Day morning. Trujillo told the jury she'd been awakened at 7:30 a.m. by Chewy, her pet Vietnamese pig.

"What time did you go to your mother's?" the defense lawyer asked, referring to her parents' home four blocks away.

Trujillo's eyes rolled upward, as did her eyebrows, as she tried to recollect. "Approximately nine," she finally said.

"How do you know it was nine?"

"Because my mother used to always go on Sundays for the coffee klatch with a bunch of women that get together and drink coffee."

"Every Sunday?" Gerash asked.

"Yes, sir," Trujillo said, nodding vigorously.

"What happened when you drove by the Kings' residence, in relation to Mr. King and his wife?"

"I said, 'Happy Father's Day, you old fart'" —her term of endearment for her 54-year-old neighbor. "I always used to tell him that." Yet she expressed uncertainty as to precisely what time on Father's Day she'd made that remark.

Gerash approached to show her the report of her FBI interview. "Did you or did you not at that time tell them that … 'as she drove past King's residence at approximately 9:00 a.m., she waved to both King and his wife.' Did you tell them that?"

"Yes, sir," she said. She testified that the ex-cop had been operating a weed-eater at the time, wearing a straw hat, T-shirt, and shorts. She also eyed another neighbor as she drove away, David Bell—who lived next-door to the Kings—atop a riding mower cutting his grass.

Trujillo recounted staying at her parents' home long enough to wish her dad a happy Father's Day and then heading off to Safeway, returning home about an hour after she'd left. She didn't notice what was going on at the Kings' residence upon her return because "I was too busy doing my own thing."

Concerned the jury might think Trujillo would fabricate a story to help her neighbor out of a jam, Gerash asked, "Are you testifying here because you like Jim King?"

To his surprise, Trujillo answered in the affirmative.

He tried again. "But your testimony under oath here is not colored because you like him, is it?"

"No," Trujillo said, finally catching his drift.

During his cross, Buckley hoped to blur Trujillo's time-line as much as he possibly could. He and Sims had actually visited her home prior to the commencement of the trial to better understand what she might say. The prosecutor got her to agree that because her mother had been scheduled to meet with friends at nine o'clock, she had to leave her own home before then. Trujillo pointed out, however, that it only took about 30 seconds to make the four-block drive.

"When you talked to the FBI," Buckley asked, "you told them you didn't know what time it was, you didn't have a watch—that these were approximate times?"

"Yes, sir," she conceded. She also agreed she'd made several trips from her home that day, including multiple forays to Safeway and the 7-Eleven.

"In fact, didn't you tell us that at the point in time when you said, 'Happy Father's Day' to the defendant," Buckley asked, "it was closer to noontime when you made that comment to him—when we visited you?"

"I told you I did not know what time it was," Trujillo replied.

The deputy DA pressed her. "Was it later in the morning when you said that to him?"

The accused killer's neighbor looked upwards with a puzzled expression, then shook her head, finally saying, "I do not know." As for when she'd left for her parents' home, she told Buckley it had been "around nine o'clock. It could be three minutes till, three minutes after."

The silver-haired prosecutor also got her to agree she saw King in his yard "all the time," leaving the impression she might have been confusing Father's Day with another day altogether.

When Judge Spriggs informed her she was excused, Trujillo flashed a giant smile, relief washing across her entire body as if she'd just been released from a torture chamber. Halfway to the defense table, she embraced Gerash warmly, in full view of the jury. And upon reaching the defendant's seat, she patted him on the left shoulder, her affectionate gesture raising anew how much of her testimony had been born of their friendship.

• • • •

David Bell's residence at 675 Juniper Street sat due north of James and Carolyn King's property, on a large corner lot adjacent to Seventh Avenue. The mustachioed 39-year-old seemed straight out of central casting for a John Wayne western—clad in a short-sleeved button-down, jeans, and well-worn cowboy boots—his ultra-deep voice rivaling that of another western star, Sam Elliott. He testified that he owned his own business, supplying light-duty cranes to construction sites.

Bell described his parcel as having two large swaths of grass, one to the north of his house by Seventh Avenue and the other—next to King's property—to the south. During the five or six years he'd lived there, he said, he developed a system for cutting both sections with his riding mower, always tackling the north side first.

When Gerash asked what time he'd begun mowing the northern patch on Father's Day, Bell told jurors it had been about 8:00 a.m. Yet that's not what King's lawyer expected him to say. He approached the witness stand with the report of Bell's FBI interview—which included a starting time of 9:00 a.m.

His memory now refreshed, Gerash asked him a second time when he'd started mowing the grass. Inexplicably, Bell supplied the exact same answer. "It's basically, you know, what I've said all along ... That [I] started mowing the lawn like eight o'clock."

For some reason, Buckley decided to jump to his feet. "That's not what it says," he told the judge. Gerash fully agreed, pointing Bell to the section of the report reciting that he'd cut his grass from 9:00 to 10:00 a.m.

The defense witness shrugged his shoulders. "That's what that says," he agreed. Yet Gerash didn't inquire which of the two versions was actually correct, moving on to another topic altogether.

"How long does it take you to do the north side before

you do the south side?" he asked.

Bell told jurors it took 60 to 90 minutes to complete each patch, and that he typically moved from the north side to the south side through his front yard.

"Tell the jury what you saw concerning Mr. King at approximately ten o'clock."

"I saw Mr. King in his front yard working on his lawn or trees or whatever," Bell said. "He was working on his yard." Asked if he noticed the defendant getting out of his car, he replied, "I did see him drive up, but I'm not sure ..." He shrugged his shoulders without completing his thought. When he first saw him, King was wearing a T-shirt and shorts. He recalled his own dog running over to the Kings' pooch and them "chasing each other up and down the fence."

Gerash asked how he knew all those events had occurred on Father's Day. Bell explained that he had his six-year-old nephew staying with him, "and I made sure that he called his father on Father's Day." They made that call, he said, just before going outside to work on the grass.

"Did you see him take anything out of his car at ten o'clock?" Gerash asked, even though Bell hadn't said he actually saw King get out of his car or that he observed him at ten o'clock. Yet Buckley didn't object. "No," Bell responded.

Having gotten away with it once, Gerash pressed his luck a second time. "When Mr. King got out of the car and you saw him, was there any exchange between you and Mr. King?" Again, the lead prosecutor didn't object. This time, the defense witness said, "No, other than just" —he hesitated, waving his arms without speaking—"eye contact, probably."

Gerash then did it a third time, on this occasion while Buckley was fumbling with papers at the prosecution table. "When you saw Mr. King get out of the car, did you think it was a big deal?"

"No, it's just life as usual," Bell said.

Buckley used his time on cross to make the alibi witness's testimony even more convoluted than it had been on direct. "Do you remember telling Mr. Gerash, under oath," he asked, "that you started cutting your grass around eight o'clock when you first were asked the time?"

Bell agreed he did. He also agreed it was only after the defense lawyer showed him his prior statement that he changed his testimony.

"You do not have any way to know exactly what time you started cutting the lawn, do you?" the deputy DA pressed him.

"No, sir," Bell acknowledged. He agreed he hadn't been wearing a watch.

"The words that you used with the FBI on July 5 were, you were 'pretty sure'—not positive, but 'pretty sure'—that you saw James King sometime *after* 10:00 a.m.?" Bell confirmed that was true.

"Sometime after 10:00 a.m. means you don't know exactly what time you saw him after 10:00 a.m. Is that true?" Again, the defense witness agreed.

"Where in the statement do you say anything about seeing him in or around his car?" Buckley asked, finally getting to the improper premise Gerash had inserted into three separate questions.

"Um, I don't believe that it's in there," Bell admitted.

During his redirect, Gerash asked, "How soon, when you moved over to the south side, do you see Mr. King drive up in the car?"

"It was basically while we were moving over there," Bell replied. Asked what he meant by "we," he told jurors that his nephew had been sitting between his legs on the riding mower. It was his nephew's presence, he said, that gave him a clear memory of these events having occurred on Father's Day.

Buckley had one final chance to poke holes in Bell's testimony and leave a lasting impression. "When you told the FBI you cut your grass around 9:00 to 10:00 a.m.," he asked, "you're not telling them that's the time it took you to cut the grass. You're telling them that's the time you *started* cutting your grass. Isn't that correct?"

Bell nodded. "Correct." He testified that he wasn't sure when he began doing so. Comfortable he'd gotten all he could from the supposed alibi witness, Buckley resumed his seat. As he did, Gerash sprang up from his, trying to get in the last word. "But you—"

The hard-nosed judge cut him off at the pass. "No, that's it, Mr. Gerash." He told the defense witness he was excused. Unlike Roberta Trujillo, as Bell paced toward the courtroom exit, he didn't pause to embrace the defense lawyer or pat his client on the shoulder. Indeed, he made no eye contact with either, seemingly eager to put the entire experience behind him, whether his testimony had helped his next-door neighbor or not.

35

EXPERTS OF THEIR OWN

The defense team marched their own expert witnesses before the jury in an effort to inject doubt about three critical subject areas: (1) whether the bullets extracted from the victims matched ammunition issued by the DPD, (2) the likelihood of a Colt Trooper's cylinder developing a crack, and (3) the reliability of the vault tellers' eyewitness identifications.

Special Agent John Riley had been assigned to the elemental and metals analysis unit of the FBI crime lab in Washington, D.C. for 25 years. His job focused on using a highly sophisticated spectrometer to determine the elemental composition of various types of metals, including lead bullets.

Shortly after King's arrest, the DPD had flown Agent Riley to Denver to gather samples of lead from the semi-jacketed hollow-point bullets recovered from Bill McCullom's corpse. He was also provided four boxes of the Remington-Peters ammunition the DPD had issued during the 1985-1986 time period. Upon his return to the nation's capital, he used the FBI's spectrometer to determine if the elemental composition of the lead in each set of bullets was the same.

The entire exercise had been arranged to substantiate detectives' working theory that the bullets fired into the slain guards' bodies had come from the DPD, thereby increasing the odds the killer had served as a cop. But if Agent Riley had actually confirmed a match between the McCullom bullets and the DPD ammo, he surely would have taken the stand to share those findings during the People's case. That it was Walter Gerash now calling him as a defense witness left little doubt Riley's testing hadn't gone as Bill Buckley, Jon Priest, and their colleagues had anticipated.

The FBI lab analyst explained that one of the key chemical additives in the lead portion of a bullet is antimony, which is used to make the lead harder—the more antimony, the harder the bullet. In bullets manufactured with a copper jacket, however, the copper acts as the hardener, making the addition of antimony unnecessary. Riley therefore found it surprising that antimony was present in the copper-jacketed hollow-points recovered from McCullom's body—two having an antimony content of .65% and the other two .85%.

Gerash placed the four boxes of Remington-Peters ammo the DPD supplied Agent Riley on the witness stand. Knowing full well what his answer would be, the defense lawyer asked whether the bullets in the green-and-yellow boxes contained antimony.

Of the 40 bullets he randomly sampled, Riley testified, none contained even a trace amount of antimony. He wasn't the least bit surprised by that result, because bullets with copper jackets—as he'd already explained—typically don't contain antimony. He agreed with Gerash that his written report labeled the DPD's ammo "significantly different" from the slugs recovered from McCullom's body due to the presence of antimony in the latter.

When King's attorney yielded the podium, Buckley did his best to neutralize the lab analyst's testimony. In response to his questions, Riley noted that a single box of 50 bullets could contain several different elemental compositions of lead, though "most of the time, these differences will be quite small." He explained that such differences occur because the lead used to manufacture bullets isn't completely homogenous.

Through his redirect, however, Gerash got Riley to admit that an antimony level of .65% or .85% signaled the additive's purposeful introduction by the bullet manufacturer—

something Remington-Peters obviously hadn't done with the semi-jacketed hollow-points acquired by the DPD. Thus, as the FBI analyst stepped down from the stand, the import of his testimony couldn't have been more clear: the bullets used to execute Bill McCullom hadn't come from the defendant's longtime employer.

• • • •

Gunsmith Tom Butler had been one of the prosecution's most effective witnesses, leaving jurors with the distinct impression that the cylinder on a Colt Trooper revolver wouldn't just crack, but would rather explode and splinter into pieces. To counter that testimony, Gerash called Ikey Starks, a gunsmith for the past 25 years and the owner of the Sports West gun shop, located five blocks from DPD headquarters.

Starks testified that cylinders can and do crack because the wall thickness of the outer edges of each chamber is very thin. Over time, he explained, a crack can form due to excessive use or excessive pressure. The experienced gunsmith noted he'd seen both cracked and ruptured cylinders over the course of his career. He opined that a cracked cylinder is dangerous, telling jurors he'd had customers junk their guns at his shop due to that very condition.

Starks agreed with Gerash that a revolver being out of time—as Butler had testified King's Colt Trooper was—can contribute to the formation of a cracked cylinder. In his opinion, a gunsmith repairing a timing problem wouldn't necessarily notice a hairline crack. Asked how much he would have charged to replace the cylinder of a Colt revolver in 1990, he provided a range of $200 to $250.

Buckley began his cross-examination focused on ammunition, rather than cracked cylinders, asking Starks to confirm that Winchester +P+ ammo was "police-issue-only."

The defense witness stared at him with a blank expression, clearly stumped. He finally shook his head, stating he didn't know, confessing he'd never seen a box of "police-issue-only" ammo.

"Because you can't get it," Buckley declared.

"That's pretty obvious," Starks agreed.

"Do you know the difference between +P and +P+?"

"One plus," Starks answered smugly. He contended, incorrectly, that +P and +P+ ammo were actually one and the same.

Finally turning to the subject of cracked cylinders, Buckley took a gamble. "Have you ever seen a cracked cylinder in a Colt Trooper?"

To his good fortune, the defense expert admitted he never had.

••••

It had been more than two weeks since Scott Robinson sprang the Harrison Ford overlay exhibit on David Barranco during the first day of trial—a huge moment for the defense. At the time, Robinson had been virtually certain the People's star witness would fail miserably in his attempt to identify the face lurking behind the hat, sunglasses, and mustache. Why had he been so confident? Because the Ford overlay had been part of a research study conducted by the next defense expert to take the stand.

Dr. Edie Greene, a faculty member at the University of Colorado at Colorado Springs, was an experimental psychologist who specialized in the growing body of knowledge regarding eyewitness identification. After receiving Gerash's call seeking her assistance, she'd cajoled 44 of her undergraduate students to take part in a study to test how a disguise might affect an eyewitness's ability to make an accurate identification.

The students were shown six black-and-white photos of famous men whose faces were obscured by a clear plastic overlay on which an artist had drawn a fedora-style hat, dark sunglasses, and bushy mustache—similar to what FBI artist George Noble had drawn in his composite sketch.

One by one, Robinson showed the overlay exhibits to the

jury as if the group of 14 was participating in the same study—the guessing game far more entertaining than testimony about antimony and cracked cylinders. Even Judge Spriggs joined in the fun, making snarky quips each time the defense lawyer unveiled a new face. As each famous man was revealed, Dr. Greene jotted down on a flip chart the percentage of her students who'd accurately identified him, both with and without the disguise.

The reason why Robinson had elected to use the Harrison Ford overlay was because not a single one of Dr. Greene's students had been able to recognize him beneath the disguise—though 89% of them had accurately identified the *Raiders of the Lost Ark* star sans hat, dark glasses, and stache.

The same disguise had also prevented nearly all of her students from identifying auto executive Lee Iacocca, whom 81% recognized with no disguise versus just 6% with the disguise. Similarly, whereas 73% recognized actor Jack Nicholson sans disguise, only 11% had with the disguise. Though photos of Marlon Brando and Robert Duvall had also been used, the overwhelming majority of students couldn't identify either even without the disguise. As for George Bush, all of Dr. Greene's students had successfully identified the incumbent president with no disguise, as compared to only 28% who recognized him with the disguise.

The psychology professor testified that more than 20 studies apart from hers documented the impact of a disguise on eyewitness identification. One she found particularly compelling had been conducted at the University of Wisconsin.

In that study, the student-subjects had watched a videotaped reenactment of a robbery in which the robber had worn a knit cap pulled over his hair, without obscuring his face. Half of the subjects observed the robber with the knit cap and half without it. Both groups were then shown an eight-person photo lineup that included the robber. Only 27% of the students who'd seen the robber in the knit cap were able to identify him versus 45% who'd seen him without the cap.

Another well-studied problem with eyewitness identification, Dr. Greene told the jury, is "weapon focus." When a weapon is involved in the commission of the crime, she explained, that is naturally where a witness's eyes will be drawn. She pointed to seven different studies that documented the negative effect weapon focus has on eyewitness identification.

The defense expert also testified about problems inherent in an eyewitness being exposed to a picture of the suspect before being asked to make an identification from a six-pack containing the same photo. Familiarity of the alleged perpetrator's features from the prior picture, she explained, often leads to erroneous identification.

She described a 1980 study conducted at Yale in which students had observed someone enter their classroom searching for a wallet he claimed to have lost during a prior class. Twenty-five minutes later, half of the students were shown a dozen photos and asked to pick out the wallet-seeker—who wasn't actually included among the photos. The other half weren't shown any photos at all. About a week later, the entire class was shown a six-pack that included both the wallet-seeker and the most frequently selected image from the 12-person array only half the students had seen.

A whopping 44% of the students who'd seen the prior image selected that same photo from the six-pack, rather than the photo of the actual wallet-seeker. By stark contrast, only 22% of that cohort correctly identified the man who disrupted their class to search for his wallet. The Yale study was one of several Dr. Greene cited that illuminated the problems inherent in "photo-biased" identifications.

Yet another concern with eyewitness identification, she testified, is that once witnesses make an identification, they are privately and publicly committed to that choice. It is very difficult, she said, the eleventh time they're telling the same story, to alter it due to the external pressure they feel to be consistent.

"To what extent, if any," Robinson asked, "does the level of confidence expressed by a witness about an eyewitness identification relate to the accuracy of the identification?"

"The level of confidence is only a very modest indicator of how accurate a person is," Dr. Greene explained. That reality had been borne out by more than 30 separate studies. Yet unfortunately, she said, the most important consideration jurors typically apply in evaluating eyewitness testimony is how confident witnesses appear in their identification.

Lamar Sims drew the unenviable assignment of cross-examining the psychology professor, who, by any objective assessment, was making a very favorable impression on the jury. He got her to concede that none of the studies she'd testified about involved real-life situations, though she wouldn't agree with him that substantial differences existed between experiments and real life. She readily acknowledged that she'd never interviewed any crime victims to corroborate her research and that there are things that happen in the real world "you can't duplicate in the laboratory."

Fascinated by her testimony, Judge Spriggs had a question of his own that neither of the lawyers had asked. "Doctor, isn't it just simply a good deal easier to recognize somebody in person than it is from a black and white photograph?"

"There's no doubt about that," she agreed.

Reclaiming the podium, Robinson seized on the opening to underscore a key defense position. "Is that why live lineups might be more conducive to an accurate identification than a photo lineup?"

"That's exactly why," the defense expert said. "Because you've seen somebody live. The best way to try to recognize them is to see them live again." Photographs, she explained, "can be deceiving, and so it's very difficult to make an identification of somebody from a photograph that you've seen live."

Concerned jurors might find fault with the DPD's decision not to conduct a live lineup, Sims asked if a suspect's change of appearance following the crime might impair an eyewitness's ability to make an accurate identification in a live confrontation. Dr. Greene agreed that a change in appearance could make an in-person lineup more problematic.

All in all, however, the University of Colorado professor's testimony proved nothing short of a home run for the defense, making a major dent in the identifications offered by Barranco, Christian, Whisler, McGinty, and Twist. If a hat, dark sunglasses, and bushy mustache could conceal the identity of the most famous men in America, the same disguise on a complete stranger—wielding a gun no less—was surely enough to cast significant doubt on the cash vault tellers' identifications.

By the time Dr. Greene exited the courtroom, Gerash and Robinson couldn't have been more pleased with how their presentation of evidence was unfolding. If they could maintain that momentum with their final three witnesses, they believed, the odds of their client being released back into society—and being spared a life in prison or the death penalty—were very good indeed.

36

ALL IN THE FAMILY: PART 2

James King, Jr. had sat beside his mom, aunt, and brother David in the gallery's front row through much of the trial—well aware his turn on the witness stand would eventually arrive. He was sworn in just before 5:00 p.m. on Thursday, June 4 as the third week of trial neared its end.

Like his namesake, the stick-figured, clean-shaven 29-year-old was soft-spoken and even-keeled. His wispy brown hair fell to the top of his shoulders and a pair of wire-rimmed glasses sat perched on the bridge of his nose. Unlike his younger brother, Jimmy seemed completely at ease on the hot seat, his affect calm and pleasant during both Gerash's direct and Buckley's cross.

He told the jury he worked for Air Sciences, an air-monitoring company, designing computerized equipment to detect pollutants in the ambient air. He'd lived in his own condo for about five years, typically visiting his folks on Sunday afternoons. After only one semester of college, he decided formal education wasn't for him, quickly developing a passion for computers. He formed his own computer consulting company barely past his twentieth birthday.

As he outgrew and replaced his own computers, Jimmy testified, he gave his hand-me-downs to his dad, first an early-market machine with limited functionality beyond video games, followed by a more dexterous IBM-compatible PC in

1989 or 1990. Because he knew his old man had been trying to write a book—and revered chess—he'd furnished him with word processing and chess software.

Sometime in June 1991, he learned his employer would soon be sending him off to Mexico. Since he didn't already have a passport, he needed to apply for one. He asked his dad to fetch his birth certificate from his safety deposit box at the bank, testifying he'd received it the following Sunday. Though Jimmy wasn't very clear about which Sunday that was, Gerash's questions implied it was after his father had obtained a larger box on June 17.

The defense lawyer abruptly shifted to the subject of backup storage disks. Because his dad was working on a book, Jimmy recounted, he encouraged him to create backups on 5 ¼-inch floppy disks and store them "off-site." His father asked him if the safety deposit box would be a good location, to which Jimmy had replied, "That would be the safest place to put it." He recalled having similar conversations with his dad many times in the two to three months preceding June 1991.

Gerash placed a red-and-white cardboard box on the witness stand. Jimmy picked it up, using it to demonstrate that was how floppy disks were both sold and stored. His father had several similar cardboard and plastic boxes, he told jurors, in which he stored "hundreds of floppies."

"Do you know if your dad made any journey to the safety deposit box to see if it would fit," Gerash asked, "or what box would be appropriate?"

"I remember him telling me that the disks wouldn't fit in the box he had," Jimmy answered. He recalled that when his father had given him his birth certificate, he'd also mentioned his plan to supply him with a key for the new box and "thought it would be a good idea if I kept … my house papers, title, and the like in the box."

When Buckley replaced Gerash at the podium, he cut straight to the chase. "What dramatic information was on your father's computer that needed to be locked in a safety deposit box?" His tone conveyed disbelief.

"Well, when you consider the words in a book," Jimmy

said, "maybe a thousand hours' worth of work?"

"Did you stress quite often to him that he should put these floppy disks into a safety deposit box?"

"I didn't specifically say a safety deposit box," Jimmy said, his answer contradicting his earlier testimony.

The deputy DA asked if he was aware that, when detectives accessed his dad's safety deposit box following his arrest, it didn't contain a single floppy disk.

Jimmy's eyes rolled upward as he racked his brain to retrieve an answer. After five seconds, he finally nodded. "Yeah, I was aware of that. There was also quite a bit of other stuff in the box."

"I'm asking you about floppy disks," Buckley pressed him. "You're aware there were no floppy disks in that safety deposit box?"

Jimmy shrugged his shoulders, conceding—a second time—that he was aware.

Asked where he kept his own floppy disks, the accused killer's son agreed he didn't store them at a bank. He told jurors he kept them in a fireproof box at his home and in a media safe at his office.

"Your dad kept his in a plastic box right by his computer," Buckley declared. "Didn't he?"

"Mmhmm," King's son agreed. "That's why we had discussed getting an off-site backup for him."

The silver-haired prosecutor had made his point. To the extent Gerash was trying to imply that his client had secured the larger box the day after the bank massacre in order to store his backup disks—rather than the stolen loot—it made little sense that, 18 days later, not a single floppy disk was there to be found.

• • • •

Carolyn King found herself back on the witness stand the next morning. This time around, she wore a V-neck magenta blouse, white patterned jacket, and white skirt. A simple gold necklace encircled her neck.

Gerash quickly turned to what she and her husband had been doing on Father's Day. Carolyn testified that they ate breakfast together between 8:30 and 8:45 a.m. and her husband had gone outside for approximately 15 minutes before leaving to play chess. She said he was wearing a T-shirt and shorts both when he departed and when he returned. Yet that was different from what she'd said her first time on the stand— which was that he'd changed into shorts after returning home.

She testified she was mowing the lawn when her husband returned and that he helped her finish the job before they went to the cemetery—precisely what she'd told Buckley when she testified the first time.

Carolyn told jurors her husband had been diagnosed with high cholesterol in 1976. His doctor had advised him to get more exercise, including walking. She bought him a pedometer as a Christmas present—after he started working at the bank—to see how far he walked during his 12-hour weekend shifts. On weekdays, she said, they walked together at the park or in shopping centers when it rained.

Trying to garner sympathy from the jury, Gerash had her describe the ordeal she endured as officers were ransacking her home on July 3—how she'd been rousted from bed and forced to sit outside on the porch for hours as neighbors gawked at the massive police presence at their home. Carolyn recounted that officers had instructed her she couldn't speak to her husband and that she was shaking, leading to his request that they bring her a blanket.

When the defense lawyer yielded the podium, Buckley walked up to the witness stand to hand the defendant's wife the report of her FBI interview. "Did the FBI agent and Denver detective who interviewed you on July 3 ask you to recount your activities for that morning, Father's Day?" Carolyn agreed they had.

"And would you look at the statement before you," the prosecutor asked, "and tell the jury where in the statement you ever mentioned anything about you or your husband doing any kind of yardwork that day?"

Buckley leaned back against the mahogany partition separating the main part of the courtroom from the gallery, his arms crossed, certain he'd caught the defendant's wife in an outright fabrication. Fifteen seconds ticked by as she scanned the document. "There's nothing," she finally conceded.

"In that same statement, did you tell the FBI agent and the detective that your husband was a loner and had no friends at the bank?"

"Yes, I did," she acknowledged. Content with that answer, the prosecutor announced he had no further questions.

Gerash strode to the witness stand, attempting to repair the damage Buckley had just inflicted. "Did they ever ask you in these two statements," he inquired in his booming voice, "whether or not you helped with the lawn as the two witnesses said?"

"No, they didn't," Carolyn responded.

"But they interviewed your two neighbors, didn't they?"

"Yes."

"And they told them about the lawn, didn't they?"

"Yes," she agreed. She also agreed that, despite what she told the FBI agent and detective, her husband did have a friend at the bank: Mike McKown.

Buckley rose to ask one final question. "Mrs. King, when the FBI agent and the detective interviewed you, did they ask you to recount your activities on Father's Day? Yes or no?" Nodding her head, she agreed they did.

Excused by Judge Spriggs, Carolyn flashed a huge smile as she neared her husband's seat, their eyes meeting as he mouthed the words, "I love you." Yet as pleased as the defendant was, this time around, the prosecution had pierced his wife's seemingly invincible credibility, exposing inconsistencies between the story she told lawmen—and earlier in the trial—and what she was now claiming to be the truth. As is often the case, the sequel failed to capture the oomph of the original performance.

The prosecution had finally blunted the defense team's momentum. Everything would come down to their last witness—the most significant witness of all.

37

SAVAGE KILLER?

The final witness to take the stand for the defense was the accused killer himself, James W. King. That the retired Denver police officer and former security guard would ultimately testify in his own defense was never much in doubt. After all, he was the only person on the planet who could vouch for his whereabouts during the 42-minute murderous rampage at the heart of the case—or who could explain the mysterious disappearance of his longtime revolver.

For the 14 jurors, this was without question the most consequential moment of the entire three-week trial. A crescendo. How they assessed the defendant's testimony and demeanor—whether his words rung true or hollow, whether the depravity of a beast could be detected lurking beneath his mild-mannered façade—would likely eclipse everything they'd heard and seen from the 94 men and women who preceded him to the witness stand.

Was James King the cold-blooded assassin who'd fled the bank on Father's Day leaving a trail of bloodshed, and unrelenting misery, in his wake? Over the next few hours, the ordinary citizens tasked with answering that question would likely be making up their minds, the defendant's life literally hanging in the balance.

Walter Gerash settled in behind the podium as his client—adorned in the camel-hair sport coat, white shirt, and brown slacks and tie he'd worn for the majority of the trial—stepped forward to take the oath. In a hushed voice most unnatural to him, Gerash began by asking, "Mr. King, did you commit these crimes?"

The ex-cop wheeled with a purpose to face the jury. "No, I did not," he said, his tone strident, facial expression conveying indignance. He shifted his gaze back to his lawyer.

"Were you involved in any way with these crimes?"

For the second time, the defendant pivoted in his chair to look jurors square in their eyes. "No," he replied, his pent-up emotion bubbling to the surface. "I have *never* killed anyone or robbed anyone."

With his client's full-throated denial now out of the way, the seasoned defense attorney took a step back, having King share with jurors highlights from his unique biography.

As the words spilled out of his mouth, anyone with a working set of ears would have noticed something most peculiar about his voice. Its pitch was unusually high for a man, as if someone was squeezing his vocal cords. In contrast to his lawyer's rich baritone voice, King's was more of a husky alto—like that of a cartoon character in a kid's show. He also had a unique way of speaking, his words delivered softly with a lumbering cadence, his sentences occasionally ending in an upward intonation.

The retired Denver cop testified that he'd discharged his weapon only once in the line of duty, during his rookie year, when he fired a warning shot in the air while chasing a suspect. Asked what had happened next, King deadpanned, "he ran faster." Though his witty remark precipitated a cascade of laughter, the defendant's expression remained stern for several seconds, until a faint smile slowly meandered across his lips. During his entire police career, he told jurors—again, with an ultra-serious expression—"I never fired my pistol at any human being."

For about half of his 25 years on the force, he revealed— while working in the radio room and ID Bureau—he carried a .38-caliber Colt Cobra with a two-inch barrel, rather than his larger Colt Trooper. He considered each weapon merely "a tool of the trade," holding no more significance to him than that.

Gerash had him explain how the DPD's annual qualifying shoots worked. During his last few years on the force, the ex-cop testified, "we were required to shoot up our ammunition that we had carried the prior year as the first 18 rounds that we shot at the target." They would then use department-issued "wadcutters" for the remainder of the session before leaving with 18 fresh rounds.

The defendant confirmed that upon his retirement in September 1986, he kept the ammo issued to him at his final shoot that summer—110-grain Remmington-Peters semi-jacketed hollow-points. Those 18 bullets, he told jurors, represented the totality of ammunition he had left from his police career.

When he learned about his high cholesterol, he testified, he had to diet and began taking Lopid pills. His doctor told him he should exercise at least three times a week for 30 minutes to get his pulse rate up to 140, which he accomplished by walking. During his tenure at United Bank, he used his patrols "to get some good exercise in." He employed a pedometer "to get some idea of how many miles I walked each day walking the floors of the bank," averaging five to seven miles per shift.

He testified that Jim Prado had provided him floor plans for each of the three buildings comprising the bank complex. Gerash showed him the prosecution exhibit of the plans discovered at his home during the July 3 search. The defendant pulled out his glasses to examine them, explaining he received the plans from his supervisor, who told him they were his to keep.

King told the jury the bank required him to shoot at a firing range every six months. In December 1989, he qualified at the Federal Reserve Bank's indoor range, where he fired bank-supplied ammunition rather than his leftover police ammo. He continued carrying the latter, he said, the entire time he worked as a weekend guard.

An hour into his questioning, Gerash asked his client if he discovered "something wrong" with his Colt Trooper during his employment at United Bank.

"Yes, after I shot in June of '90," King explained, "I was

cleaning the weapon … shortly after I had shot. I discovered the crack in the cylinder."

"Did that present a danger to you or anyone else in your opinion?"

"Oh sure," he replied. After quitting in August 1990, he testified, "I took the gun apart and put it in the trash"—initially just the cylinder and the remaining parts the following week.

The defense attorney asked what he recalled about his conversation with his son David in the garage.

Once again, the ex-cop swiveled to face the jury. "Dave has kind of always liked my police stuff," he said, noting he'd given him old police jackets and hats in the past. "I had promised him the gun, but it was unsafe." So he offered him his Sam Browne police belt instead.

"Do you remember what he said?"

"Well, I think he wanted the gun, too." He confirmed that David's testimony accurately captured their dialogue. Yet at no point did Gerash have him clarify which of his son's two competing versions of their conversation was actually correct—whether he trashed his gun before, or after, they spoke.

The diminutive defense attorney spent considerable time on the subject of chess. King testified that he started playing rated games at the Denver Chess Club while working in the DPD's ID Bureau in 1977—before the Capitol Hill Community Center became its venue. He told jurors he played 20 to 30 times at the community center over several years—mostly formal, rated games—guessing he last played there around 1984. From that point until 1989, he noted, he abandoned over-the-board games altogether in favor of correspondence chess.

"Now, did there come a time when you decided that you wanted to go back to the Denver Chess Club?" Gerash asked.

The defendant testified he made that decision during the spring of 1991, telling his wife—prior to Father's Day—"I'd like to go back and play some chess at the chess club."

He recounted rising from bed around 8:00 a.m. on Father's Day, having breakfast with Carolyn at about 8:30 a.m., then going outside, where he "puttered around in the yard" in his T-shirt and shorts. He told jurors that at about 9:00 a.m., his neighbor, Roberta Trujillo, yelled out of her car window, "Happy Father's Day, you old fart!" He waved to her and continued working in the yard.

"And what happened then?" Gerash asked.

"I decided to go play chess." He testified that he parked in the driveway directly behind the community center, then walked 20 feet to the stairwell leading down to the basement. But he didn't descend the steps, he explained, because the lockbox that contained the keys to the basement door was gone.

Asked if he still recalled the combination, King replied, "When I was there, it was rook-king-rook, which would be R-K-R. It would have changed, but I figured that I could figure something out."

Yet that testimony made no sense. On the one hand, he was telling jurors he didn't bother to descend the steps to the basement door because he didn't have a key to unlock it. Yet on the other, he was saying that even had the lockbox still been there, he felt certain the R-K-R combination wouldn't have worked, in which case *he still wouldn't have had a key*. What was he going to "figure out" to gain entry into the building with an inaccessible lockbox he couldn't "figure out" without the lockbox?

All of which begged the bigger question. Why would he even have assumed the chess club was still meeting at the community center—where he'd last played seven years earlier? Robinson told jurors during his opening statement his client had made a phone call a few days before Father's Day in an attempt to determine the club's current location. But the subject of a pre-Father's Day phone call didn't work its way into Gerash's questions or his client's answers.

"After I saw the lockbox was gone," King continued, "I knew the chess club wasn't there anymore. But I wanted to see if I could find anybody that might know, so I walked around to the front." He spotted "an individual standing there"—at the bottom of the main staircase—"and I asked him if he knew where the chess club was. And he didn't know anything about the chess club."

He testified that he climbed the stairs to the front door and looked inside, but didn't see anything. "I tried the door, and it was locked. So I left."

If he'd actually ascended the front stairs to determine whether anyone was inside, why did he refuse to descend the staircase at the back—the one chess club members had actually used to enter the building—to determine whether anyone was in the basement? Or if *that* door was locked? King didn't provide an answer to those questions. Nor were they asked.

He estimated that it took him two minutes from the time he exited his car to explore the community center until he got back in and began his drive home. When he pulled into his driveway, he said, he saw his next-door neighbor, David Bell, mowing his grass.

His testimony about what happened next differed markedly from what his wife told jurors both times she'd taken the stand. Whereas Carolyn recounted that she was mowing the lawn when her husband returned, the defendant felt certain his wife was inside the house, pushing a button in the dining room to open the garage door for him. Since he wasn't wearing a watch and Carolyn was inside near a clock, he testified, her recollection of when he returned would be better than his.

After he and his wife visited the cemetery and stopped at the Dairy Queen, he told jurors, he dropped her off at home before leaving again at about 1:00 p.m. to get his Ford Fiesta washed. Gerash didn't ask him where he went to do that—or why he felt the need to wash his car.

Later that afternoon, King recounted, his wife informed him about the bank robbery. He switched channels and started watching the news, seeing the crime scene displayed on his TV.

"What was your feeling?" Gerash asked.

The ex-cop turned to face the jury yet again. "Well, when I heard that the guards had been killed, it was sorrow." He testified that he didn't know any of them.

The defense lawyer shifted gears, asking, "Did there come

a time that you decided to get a larger safety deposit box?" King told jurors he did so the very next day.

"When you first went in to change the box, did you bring anything in or take anything out—if you remember?"

King said he didn't recall. He testified that he did remember, at some point, putting a notary seal and an empty floppy-disk storage box in the larger container.

It was during one of his trips to the new box, he said, that he realized he'd lost his driver's license—which he needed to show to gain access to his box. It was the only time in his life, he noted, he'd sought a duplicate license.

"Why did you shave your mustache off?"

"Well, I'd like to say I felt like it, and really, that's what happened," the defendant said, his voice tinged with defiance. "I had a sore on there and it was an irritant and sometimes I can correct them and sometimes I'm willing to put up with the sores that I get. This time I didn't. And so I shaved my mustache."

Gerash showed him the letter he wrote to Mike McKown five days after the massacre. King told jurors he didn't consider his friend's subsequent phone call a joke because "I knew that they were investigating everybody they could and I figured that they would get to me—and they'd already come by."

His lawyer had him clear up some confusion from McKown's testimony. King explained that he'd taken Carolyn to work the same day he and McKown spoke—not on Father's Day—noting his wife didn't even work on Sundays.

Gerash asked whether he made a phone call in *July* to determine the current location of the chess club.

"I called you," King said. "You invited me to go play there… Until I called you, I couldn't find an address or a phone number for a chess club."

"Pursuant to your desires of getting back into chess, did you show up at 4747 West Colfax on July 2, 1991?" The defendant confirmed he did.

"Did you know anyone there other than me?" Gerash inquired.

King stated that he recognized "a couple of guys that I'd seen before." He told jurors he and his lawyer played a rated game, chuckling when Gerash announced they wouldn't divulge who won. "I'd prefer that," King said, flashing a wide smile.

Asked if anything unusual occurred the following day, the defendant's light-hearted demeanor evaporated. "I was arrested and charged with this crime."

"When you were arrested … how did you feel?"

King swung his head to face the jury as more emotion swept across his face. "It was a feeling that you're having a nightmare," he said, "except I knew it wasn't a nightmare." In case it wasn't already clear, Gerash had him confirm he'd been in jail ever since.

••••

For Bill Buckley, the cross-examination of James King would arguably be the most consequential of his entire career. For more than two hours, jurors had soaked in the retired sergeant's gentle, even-keeled demeanor as he answered his lawyer's questions. It was now up to the veteran prosecutor to demonstrate that, despite the persona he'd projected from the witness stand, the defendant was actually a ruthless killer and sociopathic liar—equal parts Dr. Jekyll and Mr. Hyde.

In answer to Buckley's questions, King admitted that when he was first questioned, he'd volunteered his opinion that the perpetrator was someone "with a thorough knowledge of the bank security system."

The prosecutor wanted jurors to know about an incident of cowardice the defendant displayed early in his police career, just before being reassigned from the patrol division to the radio room. "Do you remember a specific incident familiar to other officers," he asked, "where you left your partner alone, left a bar fight, and went to the car, locked yourself in the car and called for help, but did not go back to assist your partner?" King claimed not to recall any such incident.

"Do you recall being placed in the radio room because

other officers didn't want to work with you after that incident?"

"I don't remember that," the ex-cop said. "I turned in a transfer request to go to the radio room."

Buckley approached the witness stand with a two-page outline for King's autobiography, *A Life! What For?*, asking him to share the title with the jury.

"In that autobiography, you mention getting married to your wife, but there's no mention of your sons in there anywhere, is there?" King confirmed that was the case.

"We've heard from your son, David, and your son, James," Buckley said. "Your third son is Greg?"

"Yes, sir," the defendant agreed. Not only was Greg not seated with his mom and brothers in the gallery, he hadn't set foot inside the courthouse a single time during the trial.

"What are your feelings about Greg?" the deputy DA asked. "Have you ever referred to him as the 'tattooed one' in a derogatory way?"

"Not in a derogatory way," King said. "But I have referred to him that way." Though Buckley didn't ask, the defendant's middle child worked as a tattoo artist, his own arms filled with colorful ink. King testified that he loved all of his sons, and that he'd last seen Greg when he visited him in jail two weeks earlier.

Thirty minutes into his cross-examination, Buckley hadn't scored a single significant point. King appeared calm and composed as he answered each question, not showing the slightest outward indication of discomfort.

Just after the clock tower bells chimed at 3:00 p.m., however, the career prosecutor shifted into a higher gear, beginning to ask questions that finally forced the defendant into a defensive posture.

He had the ex-cop and wannabe author read aloud from a section of his police manual that stated, "The poor condition of an officer's weapon is a major concern when the officer is involved in a shooting. Failure to take proper care and maintenance of your weapon is a real danger to yours and others' life." With that foundation laid, Buckley finally dove into the subject of cracked cylinders.

King repeated that he discovered the crack in the cylinder of his Colt Trooper after shooting at the firing range in June 1990. "I don't remember exactly when I cleaned it after that," he said. "But within a week or two." He estimated it had likely been toward the end of June.

"And you continued to carry that gun—with a cracked cylinder, and bullets in it—until you quit the job in the middle of August of 1990?" Buckley asked, his tone signaling disbelief. Without hesitation, the defendant answered in the affirmative.

The prosecutor then asked the obvious follow-up question. "Weren't you afraid of hurting yourself or some other innocent bystander if you might have to pull it and shoot it at the bank?"

Yet King didn't flinch. Rather, the highly trained former cop—hundreds of pages into a dissertation on proper police procedures—offered an explanation that would have left even a young police cadet scratching his head.

"If I ever had to use the gun," he began, "my life would be in danger and it wouldn't matter whether the person was shooting at me or I blew myself up. It wouldn't be much different." In other words, there's no point in an officer pulling a properly functioning weapon on an armed assailant since bad guys always prevail in such gun battles. Somehow, King was able to maintain a straight face—speaking in his lumbering monotone—as he provided this nonsensical explanation.

Buckley grilled him further, for the first time injecting passion into his questions. "So you continued to carry a gun that you are telling us you knew to be defective?"

Again, without even the slightest pause, King leaned into the mic and said, "That's right."

Sensing he had the defendant on the ropes, Buckley continued to pummel him. "Now the bank had a number of Smith & Wesson revolvers right there for you to use if you wanted to?" King agreed.

"And you chose instead of taking one of their guns temporarily, to carry a gun that you're telling us you knew was dangerous."

"Yes, sir," King acknowledged.

Though the deputy DA moved on to other subjects, he'd just scored the biggest point of the entire trial, substantively at least. For his part, though, judging by his body language, the defendant didn't appear the slightest bit rattled—cool as a glass of lemonade on a steamy summer afternoon.

Buckley next focused on the ammo the ex-cop carried with him while working at the bank. King agreed six of his 18 bullets had been loaded in his revolver, the other 12 in two speed loaders he carried in pouches on his Sam Browne belt.

"Where were the speed loaders when the police searched your house on July 3?" the silver-haired prosecutor asked.

For the first time, King displayed a confused expression. Ater five seconds, he finally leaned into the mic. "I don't know."

"Did you throw those away?"

"Yes, sir," the defendant responded.

"Well then you do know where they were," Buckley asserted in an accusatory tone. "You threw 'em away."

King backpedaled, claiming to have been confused by the prosecutor's initial question. "Oh, I thought you meant a location, sir."

Buckley asked why he'd discarded the speed loaders instead of giving them to someone who could use them. Digging the hole deeper still, the defendant replied, "They were department-issue. I'm not sure they were worth giving to somebody else." Yet he readily conceded he had friends still working for the DPD and that the official policy of the department was for all police-issued equipment to be returned.

The deputy DA asked what he'd done with the police belt and holster he'd worn while working for United Bank.

"Well, finally I threw it out also," King answered. "I offered it to David first and then I threw it away."

"What did you do with the 18 rounds of 110-grain ammunition?"

"I threw them away also," he claimed, telling Buckley he'd thrown the bullets in the trash.

"You threw live ammunition in the trash?" the prosecutor

asked, his words laced with incredulity.

In perhaps his most fanciful testimony yet, King testified that he extracted the cartridges out of the gun and speed loaders—all 18—emptied the gunpowder out of each, and then threw them in the trash. Asked if he'd mentioned anything like that to the investigators questioning him, he agreed he hadn't.

Though his withering cross was now racking up significant points, Buckley was still hoping to land a decisive, knockout blow. He set the table by getting the former bank guard to reiterate that he noticed the supposed crack in his Colt Trooper's cylinder in late June 1990.

"Do you recall that your gun was checked pursuant to a requirement by the United Bank of Denver, by the Federal Reserve range," Buckley asked, "and that it was found to be in good working order on June 20th of 1990?" He glared at the defendant, adrenaline coursing through his veins as if he were an actual prizefighter.

After a brief pause, King leaned into the mic, his eyes darting side to side. "I don't remember the man inspecting my firearm." Because Buckley didn't have a written document memorializing the inspection, his punch didn't land squarely, allowing the defendant to stagger back to his proverbial corner without falling to the canvas.

The lead prosecutor transitioned to the defendant's June 24 FBI interview. "Did you say anything in that statement about doing any yardwork of any kind?"

"I don't think so," King acknowledged. He told Buckley he thought the agents were merely interested in places he'd gone, not the activities he'd been engaged in at home. He agreed Mike McKown called him about a half an hour after the agents departed.

"Do you recall telling Mr. McKown, 'I'm kind of stuck because I don't have an alibi for the time of the bank robbery?'"

"I don't remember using the term 'stuck,' but I probably did say that."

"If you didn't do anything wrong, you don't need an alibi, do you?" The defendant readily agreed.

As for his July 2 interview with Detective Hemphill, he

denied telling him that his wife wanted him to get rid of his Colt Trooper—even though that information was recorded in the detective's report. What he told Hemphill, he said, was that "my wife was uncomfortable with the gun around the house." He agreed he didn't mention to Hemphill anything about doing yardwork that morning.

The deputy DA moved on to King's phone call with Sergeant Hildebrant on July 3. He directed the defendant's attention to his testimony that he and his wife left for the cemetery at 10:30 a.m. Surprisingly, King volunteered that he was "just guessing at the times." Asked about Hildebrant's visit later that same day, the ex-cop agreed that he told his former DPD colleague he hadn't seen or talked to any of his neighbors on Father's Day morning.

"When you got on the stand today, you said you remember seeing Roberto Trujillo and you remember seeing Mr. Bell?" Now it was Buckley's voice thundering across the courtroom. King agreed, admitting he made a different statement when Hildebrant asked that very question on July 3.

When the prosecutor asked whether he made any calls prior to Father's Day to determine the current venue of the Denver Chess Club, in stark contrast to what his own attorney told jurors during his opening statement, King conceded he hadn't made any such call.

Buckley asked a flurry of questions designed to highlight the defendant's deep knowledge of the bank's layout and security systems.

The former security guard testified that he used the freight elevator several times each day. He also knew that the street-level camera aimed at the freight elevator produced poor-quality images. He told the jury someone had called into the monitor room from the phone beside the freight elevator—to seek an escort inside the bank—several times each shift.

King admitted he'd been in the incinerator room several times, and was aware the light switch was located on the wall on the left side of the room. He also knew that opening the incinerator room door wouldn't set off an alarm and that there was a VCR in the locked supervisor's office that sometimes recorded what guards were doing in the monitor room.

As for the Sunday morning cash vault operation, the defendant testified that he rarely worked on Sunday mornings and didn't know what time the tellers began their shift. But he admitted to being aware the armored car couriers would normally arrive with their bags filled with cash around 7:30 a.m.

The Texas-reared prosecutor pivoted to King's new safety deposit box, asking him if he needed the expandable green folder to pick up his son James Jr.'s birth certificate or his son David's car title—drawing a negative response to each question. The defendant further agreed he didn't need a privacy booth to deal with either document.

Buckley quizzed him as to why getting Jimmy's birth certificate had been so urgent. King admitted he had no idea when he'd actually gone to retrieve the birth certificate or when his son obtained his passport.

"Would it surprise you that the records from the Passport Service show that it was issued January 2, 1992?"

"Then he must have just gotten it," King said, undercutting one of the key aspects of his eldest son's testimony.

"You said you put an empty computer disk box in the safety deposit box?"

"I checked to see if it would fit," the defendant said. "I didn't leave it there." Yet that is the opposite of what he told his own lawyer during his direct examination.

Buckley asked where the floppy disks were when the DPD seized the box on July 5. "They weren't in the safety deposit box, were they?" King agreed they weren't.

"Then why, when you came into the bank on the morning of Monday, June 17, did you tell Mrs. Peralez you were in a big hurry and that you didn't care if you had to pay an extra $10 fee?"

"I don't remember telling her that I was in a big hurry," King answered defensively. "I do remember saying that the fee was no big deal."

Nearing the end of his cross, the chief deputy DA pointed to the litany of occurrences King was asking the jury to believe were mere coincidences: (1) carrying the same number of bullets used in the commission of the crime, (2) shaving off his mustache at the same time he lost his driver's license, and (3) disposing of his gun. "And it's also a coincidence that you just happened to be in downtown Denver at the time these four guards were massacred?"

King leaned into the mic, his disdain for Buckley becoming evident for the first time. "It was my misfortune," he said. "Yes, sir."

•   •   •   •

Walter Gerash reclaimed the podium for his redirect, asking his client why he hadn't immediately stored his backup floppy disks in the new safe deposit box once he determined they would fit.

King explained that he "hadn't completed the filling of the disks from the hard disk drive," a process he told jurors was laborious and time-consuming.

As for the incinerator room, he testified he would check in there because it was filled with used equipment including computer monitors and cabinets. Inexplicably, Gerash had him confirm, a second time, he knew exactly where the light switch was located.

After only 20 questions, the Bronx-born defense attorney was finished. He made no attempt to shore up King's ultra-weak testimony about the disposal of his gun, police belt, speed loaders, or ammo, his redirect failing utterly to ameliorate the damage Buckley had inflicted.

Yet when his client stepped down from the witness stand and resumed his seat at the defense table, he showed no outward indication he'd suffered as much as a pinprick.

True enough, Bill Buckley hadn't landed a knockout blow sufficient to end the fight once and for all. But he'd connected with numerous jabs and even a few sharp upper cuts that left the defendant reeling.

Whether he'd scored enough points to convince a unanimous jury of James King's guilt remained to be seen.

By any objective measure, however, the veteran prosecutor had achieved his objective of moving the needle back in the People's direction.

38

YODA, I AM

The defense evidence now complete, control shifted back to Bill Buckley and Lamar Sims to present their rebuttal case. Up first was Marjorie Priester, a victim advocate in the DA's Office, who told jurors she was seated in the gallery, two or three rows behind the defendant, during Kenetha Whisler's testimony at the preliminary hearing.

Though she wasn't able to hear what he said, Priester testified that she saw James King say something from his seat at the defense table. "I knew he was talking," she said, noting she observed the ex-cop's lips moving. While she was escorting Whisler from the courtroom following her testimony, the eyewitness told her that, from her vantage point on the witness stand, she'd actually heard the defendant's words.

During Robinson's brief cross, Priester elaborated, telling the defense lawyer King "leaned across the table. He put his arm on the table, and he was talking to somebody from your office. It was very brief, but it was very noticeable. He came right into my line of vision."

The People's second rebuttal witness, Randall Gordanier, was a criminal investigator also employed by the DA's Office. In early May, he'd accompanied Buckley and Sims to Roberto Trujillo's home to interview her about her recollection of Father's Day. He testified King's neighbor recounted going to her mother's house at least three separate times that day, first at around 9:00 a.m., next at about noon, and then at 1:30 or 2:00 p.m. Because she hadn't been wearing a watch, she told the trio she wasn't certain about any of the times.

As for her greeting, "Happy Father's Day, you old fart," Gordanier testified that Trujillo indicated she'd made that remark at around noon, not at 9:00 a.m.

Buckley brought Frank Kerber back to the stand to rebut the defense theory that Paul Yocum's ammo matched the bullets recovered from the deceased guards. The detective told the jury that seven of the 11 speed loaders seized during the searches of Yocum's apartment and his mother's house had been loaded with three different types of ammunition: (1) Remington-Peters semi-jacketed hollow-points, (2) Winchester-Western semi-jacketed hollow-points, and (3) silver-tip hollow-points.

Kerber testified that the shape of the base of the Remington-Peters and Winchester-Western bullets was inconsistent with the bullets recovered from the slain guards. The silver-tip bullets, he noted, didn't bear any similarity at all. He'd also inspected numerous additional bullet cartridges found during the searches that were either loose or stored in boxes—none of which matched the bullets extracted from the victims. During Robinson's brief cross, however, Kerber conceded that he inspected only small samples of Yocum's ammo, rather than each and every bullet.

Sims called Greg Fanselau as the People's next witness. From February to June of 1991, Fanselau had been employed as a records manager at United Bank. He testified that he spent hours in the records tunnel every day and that he often drank soda while working. The prosecutor had him inspect the 7-Up can and Styrofoam cup admitted into evidence at the beginning of the defense's case. Fanselau confirmed they were consistent with soda cans and cups he'd bring with him into the records tunnel.

Asked whether he always removed his beverage containers when his work was done, Fanselau testified that he didn't, and that, to his knowledge, the records tunnel was never cleaned.

Robinson used the former bank employee to hammer home a key defense theme. "On Sunday, June 16, 1991," he asked, "did you enter the records tunnel at 5:04 a.m. and work in it for four-and-a-half hours?"

Fanselau replied that he didn't, agreeing his department wasn't even open on Sundays. He also admitted that he couldn't say with any certainty whether the 7-Up can and Styrofoam cup sitting on the witness stand actually belonged to him.

For some reason, neither Sims nor Robinson bothered to ask the rebuttal witness whether he smoked cigarettes—despite cigarette butts having been found beside the 7-Up can and coffee cup—another confounding mystery the three-week trial would never solve.

••••

Not taking any chances jurors might actually believe that the gunman who'd terrorized David Barranco and his coworkers was Paul Yocum—rather than James King—Buckley called the Yoda-like, 51-year-old to the stand as the People's final witness.

As he stood to take his oath, clad in a light-blue sport coat, white shirt, blue tie, and khaki pants, jurors could see for themselves that the former guard with protruding ears, puckered lips, and Coke-bottle glasses didn't bear the slightest resemblance to the eyewitness descriptions of the robber—as wide-ranging as they were—or the composite sketch drawn by Agent George Noble.

Buckley's first questions were intended to drive that point home, with Yocum sharing that he stood only 5'8" and weighed just 140 pounds. Though the prosecutor didn't ask about the brain damage he'd suffered as a child, the way Yocum slurred his words left little doubt something about him wasn't quite right.

The longtime bank guard testified that he never owned a Colt-type firearm and that all of his revolvers were manufactured by Smith & Wesson. As for Father's Day, he denied being out and about that morning carrying a bag—as his neighbor, Jodine Lang, had testified—though he agreed he might have gone to the 7-Eleven to pick up a newspaper as was his custom on Sunday mornings.

"Did you go anywhere near the United Bank of Denver on the morning of Father's Day, June 16, 1991?" Buckley asked.

"No, I didn't," Yocum said, shaking his head.

"Did you kill any guards or rob the place on June 16, 1991?"

"No, I didn't," the former guard said in a soft voice.

"Were you the same Paul Yocum who was charged with a theft from the United Bank, sometime prior to that, and found not guilty?"

"Yes, I am," he lamented, nodding his head for emphasis. Five minutes into his examination, Buckley passed the witness.

Surprisingly, Robinson had just three minutes' worth of questioning for the man he and Gerash had been suggesting for weeks had been the mastermind behind the bank massacre—having already passed on the opportunity to call him as a defense witness.

"You were angry at Tom Tatalaski," Robinson declared, more a statement than a question.

"I was a little angry," Yocum acknowledged. "Yes."

"In part, because he and an eyewitness testified at your trial and testified against you?" Again, the floppy-eared witness agreed. He also admitted he resigned from the bank following the trial because he didn't want to work there anymore and that he'd tried to leave his apartment with evidence just as the police were arriving with a search warrant.

"As you know, one of the issues that has arisen in this case," Robinson asked, "is whether you were angry at the bank as a motive for committing the United Bank murders?"

"I'm not," Yocum said meekly with a slight headshake, his final words before Judge Spriggs excused him as a witness.

When Buckley rose to his feet to announce that the People had no further evidence—now after 5:00 p.m. on Friday, June 4—the bearded jurist had some news of his own to deliver.

When jurors returned on Monday morning, he told them, they needed to bring suitcases containing enough clothing and toiletries for a full week. Once deliberations commenced, they'd be sequestered overnight at the Warwick Hotel, their rooms stripped of TVs, clock radios, and telephones. On the plus side, he noted, they'd have unfettered access, when they weren't at the courthouse deliberating, to the hotel's antiquated rooftop swimming pool.

••••

The excitement and energy filling the courthouse reached a fever pitch the following Monday morning, spectator-hopefuls lining up long before the courtroom opened to the public, many of whom would fail to claim a seat.

Before jurors were ushered in, Robinson announced that a witness who'd been eluding a defense subpoena had finally shown up to testify—a gentleman named Kenneth Couch, who worked as a driver shuttling travelers to and from Stapleton Airport. He asked that the defense case be reopened to allow the additional testimony. Though Buckley objected, Judge Spriggs gave the defense the green light.

Couch shared with the jury that between 6:00 and 7:00 a.m. on Father's Day, he was driving his classic Ford van eastbound, heading in the general direction of United Bank, when he noticed a small, tan-colored car to his right—either a Toyota or a Honda Civic. The motorist, he said, "was driving rather erratically." As he was nearing Broadway, Couch peered through his passenger window to glimpse into the other vehicle's driver-side window.

The defense witness testified that the man behind the wheel was wearing a tweed fedora-style hat with a fluffy yellow feather and dark-colored sunglasses. Because the driver was darting left and right most erratically, he became worried he might be involved in an accident.

Both vehicles made a right turn onto Broadway, Couch recounted, with the tan car still to his right. As he approached Colfax, the other car pulled right in front of him as it turned left onto Colfax, forcing him to slam on his brakes. He too turned left on Colfax, keeping the other vehicle in his sight. He last saw it turning left on Lincoln, heading straight for the Cash Register Building.

Couch described the other driver as being somewhere between 40 and 45, with a "hawk nose" and dark hair flecked with gray, and wearing a tweed jacket. Having heard news about the homicides and robbery at United Bank, he called the DPD the very next day to report what he'd observed.

"The man you saw on Father's Day, between six thirty and seven o'clock," Robinson asked, "was that man Jim King?" When Couch answered in the negative, the defense lawyer yielded the podium.

During his cross, Buckley brought out that Couch had told the police that the other driver had a distinctive sunburn, no mustache, and kept changing lanes and looking around.

"And it was your impression, because he wasn't paying attention to his driving," Buckley asked, "that he was, quote unquote, looking for a hooker?"

The defense witness chuckled, smiling broadly. "Yes, that's correct. That's what I thought." He also agreed the man in the hat and sport coat hadn't been driving in a straight line, suggesting he didn't know where he was going—which implied he wasn't the same man who pulled off the elaborate heist a few hours later.

When Couch stepped down from the stand, Judge Spriggs swiveled in his chair to deliver instructions to the jury on the law they'd be required to follow once sent to the jury room to deliberate. When he finally looked up after reading the last of his instructions, he invited Lamar Sims to the podium to deliver his closing argument.

The prosecutors would have one final opportunity to convince the jury James King was the diabolical monster who executed Bill McCullom, Phil Mankoff, Scott McCarthy, and Todd Wilson in cold blood. Gerash and Robinson, for their part, would then do everything within their power to persuade jurors that ample doubt existed as to who'd committed the unspeakable crime. Whether King walked free, or met his maker in the execution chamber, literally hung in the balance.

39

PHOTO FINISH

Lamar Sims stood before the jury in a finely tailored double-breasted suit for the first of four closing arguments that would consume nearly eight solid hours. He began by trotting out the needle-pierced mannequin heads, naming each of the murdered guards in a solemn tone. The faux heads ended up in a tidy row at the front of the witness stand, their bone-white faces staring at jurors through the remainder of Sims' remarks—a tactic designed to inflame their emotions and garner their sympathy.

As he roamed the courtroom, the African American lawyer morphed into a gospel preacher—his rhythmic cadence mirroring that of an evangelical sermon—displaying fiery passion for the first time in the three-week trial. In a booming voice rivaling Gerash's, he asked, three separate times, "What manner of a man is this?" as he pointed and glared at the accused killer.

James King, he argued, was the type of man "who would slay four men in the prime of their lives on a Sunday morning." Though he claimed to be a family man, "the evidence tells you he is a coward and a killer" as well as "a psychopath who lies easily and convincingly."

Within ten minutes, the chief deputy DA turned to the subject that would dominate his hour-long summation: the tellers' eyewitness identifications. Wagging a finger at the defendant, he reminded the jury that "five good people" had come to court to tell them "what they saw him do and what they heard him say." Moreover, shown the composite drawing during his testimony, Mike McKown had offered his opinion, "That ain't nobody but Jim King."

As for the moles on the ex-cop's face the defense lawyers had droned on about incessantly, Sims told jurors to use their common sense. The band-aid on his cheek and hat over his forehead had covered most of the moles, which were merely flesh-colored bumps. Even having studied the defendant closely during his four hours of testimony, he said, "many of you probably didn't even notice … there was a mole on his cheek."

The Billy Dee Williams lookalike reminded jurors about the skirmish that had transpired during the preliminary hearing, when Gerash objected vehemently to his request that King stand up and speak. Kenetha Whisler, he asserted, "was the only one in the courtroom at the time who had reason to focus on the defendant."

"And she recognized that voice. It was *him*!" Sims shouted, pointing forcefully at King. When Gerash brought his client to within a few feet of Whisler, "think about what happened to her. Her body. Not what she said, but her body. She flinched. She recoiled. She shrank back in that chair because regardless of what she says, *her body knew*. Her body recognized that man."

He pivoted to King's mustache—something the mustachioed prosecutor knew a thing or two about—scoffing at the notion he'd shaved it off because it was irritating him. Hair is natural, Sims said, and doesn't irritate the skin. Shaving, on the other hand, does. "And if you shave a pimple, it hurts and it bleeds. If you shave a sore, it hurts. Shaving irritates. What he says makes no common sense."

He urged jurors to inspect King's most recent DMV photo and mugshot for any indication of pimples or sores under his nose. "You won't find it. Why? Because it didn't happen the way he said."

The deputy DA segued to King's alibi, scoffing at the notion he'd gone to play chess on Father's Day after not playing in-person games for years. Neither Ed Huntington nor Gary Hendry had seen any sign of him as they moved tables and chairs from one building to the other. And if a random visitor had been standing by the community center's front steps, he contended, Huntington or Hendry surely would have seen him.

The prosecutor belittled Dr. Greene's testimony, telling jurors the Harrison Ford overlay had been nothing more than a clever trick. "It was entertaining," he acknowledged, "but it was a trick." Why? Because the defendant's mustache was real, whereas the one on the movie star's face was part of a disguise. "Two different things," he insisted. Pointing to Nina McGinty in the gallery, he argued that the defense was using Dr. Greene to suggest the victimized tellers "couldn't see what they saw."

They were all "decent and reasonable people," Sims said, who had no "axe to grind against this defendant" or motive to lie. "It does a victim absolutely no good to accuse an innocent man, because that means the guilty person is still out there."

He asked jurors to consider the odds of all five tellers identifying the wrong man from the King lineup. With a black marker, he jotted down numbers on a flip chart, declaring as he finished that the chances of five people incorrectly picking the same person from six photos were one in 7,776. Dr. Greene's study, he argued, defied those odds. "It's like her taking this picture of Harrison Ford and taking it to five different people and them all saying, 'That's Telly Savalas.' It don't happen that way."

Nearing the end, Sims returned to the mantra, "You can't judge a book by its cover … We want our killers to look like the monsters that they are, but that ain't real life." Glowering at King through squinted eyes, he proclaimed, in a booming voice, "There is no one who *looks* like a killer until you learn that he is a killer. There is no one who *sounds* like a killer until you learn that he is a killer."

James King believed he was "better and smarter than everyone else," the prosecutor asserted, actually believing he'd become Chief of Police. Despite only five years working in the field, he considered himself an expert on police procedures, authoring a manual he expected others to purchase and read. "And he is a person who believes he can deceive the Denver Police Department, the Federal Bureau of Investigation, and the criminal justice system of which you are now a part."

• • • •

Walter Gerash lived for moments just like this. For him, delivering a closing argument on behalf of a criminal defendant was the highest calling—the Bronx native acutely aware he and his law partner were all that stood between the bloodthirsty prosecutors and his client's very existence.

Apropos for the occasion, thunder from a torrential rainstorm clapped loudly as he set his gaze on the jury. "This is a case of a rush to justice," he began, his words delivered in his thick New York accent. James King had been fully exonerated by all six tellers a mere four days after the crime, he insisted. The only reason he'd been charged was because of a "poisoned photo lineup." "What happened between June 20 and July 3, 4, and 5 that made these witnesses change their minds?" They'd been "pounded and cajoled to change their testimony to hurt Jim King."

Scowling at the prosecutors and Jon Priest, he reminded jurors his client had "protected our community … and never brutalized or hurt a soul in his 25 years of service, and yet he's charged with these unspeakable crimes. This is a case where a quiet family man of 30 years was rooted out of retirement, manacled and holed up *like a dog* for 11 months."

Fire and fury oozing from his pores, Gerash pounced on Sims' failure to utter a single word about the scientific evidence, pointing first to the shoeprints. The DPD had sent a pair of shoes to the FBI lab in D.C. "and the shoe didn't fit." The government had obtained permission to retrieve King's palm prints from his jail cell to compare with one lifted from the battery room's door jamb. Yet those prints didn't match either.

"The State has left no stone unturned on focusing in on Jim," he said. "By slander, by defamation, by contacting witnesses ten months later. They have used the power of the FBI and thank God … the FBI and the experts have exonerated Jim King."

Gerash argued that it made no sense, if his client knew the chess club had relocated from the Capitol Hill Community Center, why he'd have chosen that location as a fake alibi. It would have been just as simple for him to get his wife and kids to say he was at home. He told the jury to discount Huntington's and Hendry's testimony because they wouldn't have seen King while engrossed in their work.

"Innocent people don't create alibis," he asserted. Two of King's neighbors had confirmed his presence at home that morning. Roberta Trujillo had seen him at 9:00 a.m. and David Bell at 10:00 a.m., rendering it impossible for him to have been downtown from 9:14 to 9:56 a.m.

What about the new safety deposit box on June 17? Gerash had a retort for that too. "Would a person, if he's guilty, go to a safety deposit box and sign his name, rank, and serial number, and then go there several times thereafter?" He reminded jurors about James Jr.'s testimony that he'd advised his dad to store his floppy disks somewhere safe.

"They're taking innocent acts and elevating them as suspicious acts. That everything is curiously coincidental. The 'master planner' signs in five times after he changes his box," Gerash said, sarcasm dripping from his lips.

The circumstances and coincidences pointing to Paul Yocum, he argued, "are even greater than Mr. King." Yocum had been charged with a theft of the very same bank and had an arsenal of weapons and ammunition. He'd written in his diary, "God may show mercy, but I will not." Pointing at the prosecution table nearly exploding with umbrage, Gerash bellowed, "And this gentleman, the Racecar Driver Priest, he signed four affidavits that Yocum probably committed the bank robbery."

Surprisingly, it was the seasoned defense lawyer who brought out the abrupt about-face in David King's testimony, reminding jurors his initial statement was that his dad had told him he'd already trashed his Colt revolver—past tense—because it wasn't safe. Buckley's questions had confused him, Gerash asserted, by suggesting he'd testified that his father had told him he was merely planning to get rid of the gun—a clever trick, not a question designed to elicit the truth.

He reminded jurors of the DPD and FBI's herculean efforts to unearth incriminating evidence. "They dug in the ground, they used metal detectors, they dug up the backyard, they went into the attic—not only no loot, but no clothes, anything resembling what was used in this robbery. Nothing. They even went to Mount Olivet … where her parents and grandparents are buried. And they got underwater swimmers to go through the lake. They went through 170 banks."

Gerash insisted the killers were still "out there, and they'll be caught." Several latent prints had never been identified. "What are they waiting for?" he asked rhetorically.

The crime scene, he said, was a "slaughterhouse. There was blood all over." Forensic technicians could detect as little as one 250,000ths of a drop of blood. Yet when the shoes were tested, "there was no blood."

Who was it who'd called Agent Riley to the witness stand to reveal the results of his comparison between the McCullom bullets and the DPD ammo? "Why did we have to call Riley?" He paused for emphasis, leaned forward against the podium, and whispered, "Because they want to get King at any cost."

As for Kenetha Whisler's voice identification, "They didn't ask for his voice in court, did they?" Gerash mused, implying it had been the prosecutors whose gonads hadn't been large enough to perform an in-court experiment. Several of the tellers had told investigators the robber had a deep voice, he said. But King's—as jurors had surely noticed—was almost feminine.

"You are about to exercise your democratic duty. You cannot wake up a day after your verdict and say, 'I made a mistake.' Because this is a matter of life and death."

The bald-headed lawyer analogized the People's case to a house. "I submit this structure is a house of sand. The walls of shadowy suspicion. The halls are hunches. The foundations are imagination. The floors are speculation. And the roof is guesswork."

His voice roaring across the courtroom, he added, "A humble retired servant told the whole world where he was and what he did. They have twisted every part of his innocent comings and goings that only their police imagination can conjure."

"I submit this structure won't pass your inspection. This structure has been *pounded* by scientific evidence and there are gaping holes in the structure. The gaping holes are reasonable doubt."

"Jim King is innocent. He's not guilty." Gerash pointed over the jurors' heads. "Out there lurks the 5:04 person and the 9:32 person. He swiveled his head, glaring contemptuously at Jon Priest yet again. "Let them get to work with some DNA. Let them get to work and start checking those fingerprints. That's not our duty."

Priest and his fellow lawmen had made a big mistake, he insisted. "But when a mistake puts an innocent man on trial for his life, thank God we have this net" — the jury system. "Thank God we have this conscience of the community to protect the railroading power of the State."

He ended where he began. "On June 16, James King went out to finally resume his love of chess over the board. And on June 20, six victims cleared King … On July 3, 4, and 5, he was literally framed with the same photo."

Lowering his voice to just above a whisper, he beseeched the men and women in the jury box, "Will you bring an end to this torment?"

Walter Gerash lumbered back to the defense table after two-and-a-half hours behind the podium, physically and emotionally drained. He'd left everything he had on the courtroom floor, pouring his heart and soul into his argument, hoping against hope his words—his boundless passion—would be just enough to save his client's life.

•   •   •   •

Scott Robinson was the polar opposite of his senior partner in many ways beyond his height and youthful appearance. Unlike Gerash's theatrical performance—punctuated by derisive glowering and emotional outbursts—during his remarks, the Denver native's passion was more restrained, harnessing logic and common sense to persuade jurors, rather than hysterics and outrage.

"Reasonable doubt is everywhere in this case," he insisted. He reminded jurors of the ferocious kick to the sheetrock outside the guard supervisor's office that notched a hole in the wall, pointing to a photo to demonstrate how high the hole was off the floor. Such a kick, he argued, would have taken an agility and "youthful strength" his 55-year-old client never would have been able muster.

He held up the computer tape reflecting the Mosler security system's notations. "This small quiet record is what you have to take with you into the jury room. It tells us that this crime did not start with someone driving in from Pleasant View … and leaving a phony name at a phone at the loading dock. This tells you that this crime began much earlier that morning, at a time when Jim King was asleep."

At 5:04 a.m., Robinson said, while McCullom and Mankoff were the only guards on duty, someone had been allowed into the records tunnel. His implication was clear—that one of the two guards had deliberately let a person involved in the crime into the bank, either unwittingly or because they were in cahoots. "These men are dead," he added. "I'm not going to blacken their names." Yet throughout his argument, he came perilously close to doing just that as the slain guards' family members watched—aghast—from the front of the gallery.

Robinson reminded jurors that at 9:33 a.m., the tunnel alarm had been reset from the monitor room, "the single biggest unexplained fact in this entire case." All four guards were dead by then, yet "whoever was left alive in the monitor room had to step to the panel and re-alarm a room that the prosecutors tell you has nothing to do with this case."

"Why," he asked, "would *these people* care about what's been described as an innocuous tunnel, a storage tunnel? Why?"

The crime, he asserted, had been committed not only with insider information, but also with "insider cooperation. Again, I'm not implying a direct knowledge on the part of any of these guards that a robbery was planned, let alone a murder," though his continued reference to their possible role left those words ringing hollow. "But certainly someone had to leave that room open for a reason, just as the robber *and* the murderer, whoever *they* were, covered their tracks and re-alarmed the room."

"This crime was not committed by a cold, calculating person working alone," he declared. "This was committed by cold, calculating *people*."

Robinson drilled down on the eyewitness descriptions, in particular Nina McGinty's. She had a perfect profile view of the robber, he said. "So it makes sense that she would get the best look at the left side of the man's face ... She saw sideburns. Those sideburns are very important. Those sideburns stand between Jim King and death. Because Jim King has never had long silver sideburns to the bottom of his ear."

Like Gerash, he pushed back against Whisler's voice identification, noting most of the tellers had told investigators the robber had a deeper, low voice. "You heard Jim King testify for almost four hours. He is soft-spoken. He is calm. But he doesn't have a deep or low voice. He has a higher, kind of musical voice. Actually kind of a distinctive voice." Robinson neglected to mention, however, that he too had chickened out of confronting the tellers with his client's recorded voice.

As for Yocum, he suggested the floppy-eared former guard stood as a perfect example of how "anybody who ever worked at the bank could have been ensnarled in this web of suspicion." Yocum didn't have a good alibi, was seen downtown shortly before the crime, engaged in suspicious activities, attempted to leave his apartment with items the police tried to seize, and had a veritable armament at his home. Yet Robinson freely admitted the defense hadn't come close to proving Yocum's involvement in the massacre. "I hope I didn't disappoint you," he said. "I knew I couldn't."

He deftly rebutted Sims' attacks on Dr. Greene. "You were told that this was some sort of trick. It was not a trick." The Ford and Bush overlays established "the extreme ends of what the disguise does. Harrison Ford's disguise was so good that no one was able to identify him with the disguise. George Bush was much easier."

"What's important," he told the jury, "is that a disguise not just causes misidentification, but causes the witnesses in two-thirds of the situations to guess. It's the guessing."

The happy warrior turned to David Twist's "positive" identification. "Jim King's eyes are an integral part of his driver's license photo," he said. "That's the serious expression that David Twist may have been giving mention to when he saw this photograph the second time." Yet the robber's eyes had been hidden by dark sunglasses. "It couldn't be Jim King's eyes that caused these witnesses to identify him as the robber."

"We're not saying that these eyewitnesses are not telling the truth as they now see it," Robinson explained. "It's clear that they are sincere. What you may be doing is saving these people from making the worst mistake any of us could ever make, which is identifying the wrong man in a brutal set of murders."

He excoriated the prosecutors for asking jurors to play the role of amateur psychologists. "Why else would they bring to your attention Jim King's outline … about an autobiography entitled *A Life! What For?*" The implication "is that Jim King, out of feelings of worthlessness, committed these crimes to prove that he could do them."

"You're supposed to assume that because when a young man joins the police department, he'd like some day to become the police chief, that at 55 years of age, he is now a bitter and angry man," the defense lawyer said. "You had the opportunity to hear Jim King and to hear from his family. This is not an estranged man, a bitter man, who is angry at the bank or angry at the police … That sort of amateur psychology has no place in the jury deliberations and it has no place in a closing argument."

No evidence existed, he insisted, that his client was "the kind of cunning, calculated, cold-blooded killer that would commit these crimes, or be involved in any way whatsoever. You heard him. He's a quiet man. He's sometimes a painfully honest man." It was ironic "that a man who spoke so strongly about trying to protect people's lives, about keeping the guards armed, about improving security, now stands charged with a crime that may not have even been possible had the bank listened to him."

Flipping the script on Sims' mantra, Robinson agreed that "you can't judge a book by its cover, but once a person's life is 55 years in the making, I think you have a pretty good idea what's in the book."

"Last year on Father's Day, a terrible tragedy occurred," he said, striking a somber tone. "Four men, probably all innocent, were murdered for greed. Not for some amateur psychology. But for greed." Almost as horrible, he lamented, was "that a man like Jim King has to endure 11 months of accusations and not get a chance to speak until the end of his trial."

"It's an even greater tragedy," Robinson told the jury, "if you let the police close the book on this case and throw the book at Jim King, because out there, there are people who are watching knowing their secrets will be safe if Jim King is convicted. Don't let that tragedy happen."

• • • •

Although it had been a grueling day for everyone, already 30 minutes past their normal quitting time of five o'clock, Judge Spriggs felt it important for jurors to absorb all four arguments in the same day. Thus, though Buckley had hoped to deliver his rebuttal the following morning—after jurors had the benefit of a good night of slumber—he stepped up to the podium to look them in their weary eyes.

Of the four lawyers, the silver-haired prosecutor was the most clinical, laying out the evidence in methodical detail over the next two-and-a-half hours. He began by repudiating Gerash's contention that the ex-cop's arrest had been a "rush to justice," noting the defendant hadn't even become a suspect until 16 days after the crime—following hundreds of interviews by the DPD and FBI.

He derided the notion King had been identified because of a "photo-biased" lineup, reminding jurors the same eyewitnesses had also seen multiple images of Mike McKown and Paul Yocum and yet been certain neither was the gunman who'd robbed them.

As for Whisler's voice identification, Buckley argued the defense had omitted an important circumstance, that her victim advocate, Marge Priester, had taken the stand to corroborate her every word.

He also had an answer to all of the fuss Gerash and Robinson had made about the defendant's moles, holding up King's enlarged DMV photo—sans mustache—for jurors to examine. "I don't know if you can get much closer than this in a photograph," he said, pointing out that only one prominent mole was visible on King's cheek. "And what did he do? What did he do on Father's Day? He put a band-aid on that side of his face, to focus the attention on the band-aid, instead of on anything else."

The chief deputy DA doubled down on the significance of the DPD-issued ammo, seeking to rebut the contention that Agent Riley's analysis disproved a match with the McCullom bullets. Riley had merely testified that the metallurgical composition wasn't identical. But Frank Kerber had told jurors the McCullom slugs *were* consistent with the DPD ammo because both had an unusual concave base.

To Gerash's point that jurors couldn't wake up after a guilty verdict concluding they'd made a mistake, the converse, Buckley retorted, "is just as true. You can't wake up the day after a not-guilty verdict and say, 'I really felt he was guilty. I made a mistake.'"

Robinson, he said, had been "pretty smooth" claiming he wasn't implying McCullom or Mankoff had been part of a conspiracy with "this mystery man who they let in that morning. Get serious. That's exactly what he was implying." Buckley told jurors the one resource that likely would have explained the 5:04 a.m. alarm "was taken by the defendant when he ripped out the pages of the guard book that had been filled in. We can't look at them and use them to come in and salvage the reputation of these two dead guards."

All of the defense's alternative suspect evidence—Yocum, the man at Stapleton Airport trying to rent a car with cash, the motorist wearing a yellow-feathered hat—"all of it was a smokescreen," he told jurors. "Something meant to divert your attention from the true facts of this case and from the true guilty person, the defendant, James King."

"You saw Paul Yocum on the witness stand," Buckley said, unable to suppress a snicker. "He's 5'8", 140 pounds, and his ears"—he pulled the tops of his ears toward his nose—"stick out like this. The defendant's ears don't stick out like that. They're pretty close to the head." It was also "patently obvious," he said, that Yocum didn't possess the intelligence to have pulled off the elaborate heist.

Tossing out a Texas expression, he argued it was a "bunch of hogwash" that the DPD didn't look at anyone else. "Can you imagine how hard it was for the detectives in this case to focus on one of their own? A retired Denver police officer... Can you imagine how hard they wanted to find a reason to believe he *wasn't* involved? It doesn't make them proud. But nothing pointed away from him. Nothing. They had to do their jobs."

Buckley organized the remainder of his argument around four blowup charts filled with dense text, each focused on a separate theme: (1) King's insider knowledge of the bank complex, (2) evidence pointing to the involvement of an ex-police officer, (3) King's Colt Trooper, and (4) his inconsistent statements—nearly 100 discrete facts in all. Though his desire to be comprehensive was admirable, with the time approaching 6:30 p.m., nine hours into a marathon trial day, the massive info dump—a vast sea of minutiae—couldn't have come at a worse time, jurors' brains likely overloaded before the prosecutor got to his tenth fact.

Among the most convincing points he tried to impart was

that King hadn't made any calls to try to confirm the current location of the Denver Chess Club before—supposedly—driving to the community center on Father's Day. "Because it's not true. His alibi about chess, which dramatically fails, is obvious. He's caught in another fabrication."

Not mentioned once by Gerash or Robinson, he said, was that the slugs removed from Mankoff and McCarthy were +P+ bullets, only available to the police. "John Q. Public" couldn't purchase that ammo in a store. "This is the *signature*," the prosecutor declared, of an ex-cop.

He grew particularly animated as he discussed King's explanation for trashing his Colt Trooper. "He wants you to believe that when he was cleaning it he saw a crack in it and then continued to carry that *dangerous* gun for the next two months." Yet the whole point of his carrying the weapon was for protection. "It defies common sense for you to believe this story. Just totally outrageous"—especially considering the locker full of Smith & Wessons to which he could have helped himself at any time.

David King's testimony, he asserted, underscored that very point. "What kind of a father, knowing that his son wanted a memento of his police career, would not spend whatever was necessary to fix the gun so his son could have it, if this was not just a fabricated story to explain to you why he got rid of a gun he'd used in a murder. It makes no sense."

He reminded jurors of David's pregnant pauses and darting eyes as he struggled to answer difficult questions. "He comes up with this concocted story to try and go along with his father to say that his father was getting rid of this gun because it had something wrong with it."

Buckley implored jurors not to forget how the tellers had described the gunman's demeanor: "very calm, not impatient, not disoriented, and he knew what he wanted, and he seemed to be by himself, and he seemed to be familiar with his surroundings." Most people on trial for their life "would find it impossible to hide their stress, especially when they get on the witness stand and testify. But not this defendant. He was calm and cool and collected and prepared when he was on the witness stand in court, the same way he was calm, cool, collected, and prepared at the United Bank of Denver last Father's Day."

Though King had begun the trial cloaked with the presumption of innocence, Buckley argued, "that cloak has been removed, bit by bit, piece by piece, as the evidence has been fit together to expose the defendant for what he is and what he did last Father's Day. Jim King told you he was looking to play chess last Father's Day, and that's not true. I submit that he had a different, high-stakes competition of cunning and precise execution in his plans, a battle of wits with the bank and with law enforcement that he expected to win and *still* expects to win."

Nearing eight o'clock, the prosecutor ended his argument in a somber tone. "Those four guards were with us in the courtroom in spirit, and they're not forgotten. You know, if they could rise from the grave and point their fingers at the defendant, it wouldn't be enough for Mr. Gerash. He'd find some fault with that. But he has to attack and have you believe that these five hardworking, dedicated cash vault tellers—lucky to be alive—aren't telling the truth, are mistaken ... They've chased this man through the maze of the criminal justice system that we look to for justice ... And they've done all of that for one reason only. Because he's guilty."

His eyes swept across the jury box one final time. "Please use your common sense when you look at this evidence. And give the only just verdict based on this evidence. Tell him, 'We don't believe your stories. We find you guilty as charged of everything.' Thank you."

Buckley summoned his last ounce of energy to walk the few steps to the prosecution table. Though his lengthy argument had likely tried jurors' patience, he couldn't take a chance they'd neglect any of the hundreds of details he and Sims had worked so tirelessly to drill into their heads during the trial. Out in the gallery, three full rows of family members of Bill McCullom, Phil Mankoff, Scott McCarthy, and Todd Wilson were depending on them to deliver justice. If achieving that goal meant jurors being deluged with facts for hours on end, that was but a small price to pay.

As the bailiffs escorted the 14 exhausted jurors to the bus ready to shuttle them to their hotel, Judge Spriggs made a few remarks to those left behind. He congratulated the attorneys on a job "very well done," then looked the defendant square in the eyes. "Mr. King, I don't have any idea how this case is going to come out, but one way or the other, I hope you understand that your lawyers have absolutely knocked themselves out for you—they've done a marvelous job. And regardless of the outcome, you will be indebted to them for the rest of your days."

Precisely how many days James William King would be able to count those blessings—where he'd get to count them, too—was the very question 12 complete strangers were about to answer.

40

STUMPED

Joni Haack had never stepped foot in a courtroom before May 1992. Yet the 38-year-old was no stranger to the law, having worked as a legal secretary for a small personal-injury firm while studying to become a paralegal. In 1990, just shy of the credits needed to obtain her certificate—in the midst of an unpleasant divorce—Haack had an abrupt change of heart. She ended up becoming the office manager for Coldwell Banker, one of Denver's largest realtors, leaving the law in her rearview mirror. As it would turn out, however, her decision to scuttle a legal career wouldn't prevent Haack from playing a huge role in one of the biggest cases in Colorado history.

Her life had been a whirl of motion since she first reported for jury duty on May 11, impaneled to serve on James King's jury eight days later. During the trial, she'd race to the courthouse each morning, rush home to cook dinner and change clothes, and then head to her office, where she'd often work past midnight to clear whatever had piled up on her desk. That had actually been the easy part of her jury service. The hard part was just about to begin.

While the two alternates hunkered down at the hotel, Haack and the other 11 jurors boarded a blue prison bus for the short ride to the courthouse. When they arrived, the bailiffs escorted them to a new, more spacious jury room attached to Courtroom 11. Carts were wheeled in loaded with all of the exhibits admitted into evidence—all except the gun. The written jury instructions were placed on the table as were pens and pads for each juror. *Better late than never,* Haack thought.

Their first order of business was to select a foreperson. Based on the knowledge she'd acquired as a legal secretary and paralegal student, the others asked Haack to serve as their leader. Though she had no idea what she was getting herself into, she agreed.

As her first official act, Haack took a straw poll to determine whether a consensus might already exist. It didn't. She was one of seven who, at that initial stage at least, felt the evidence was sufficient to find King guilty of both first-degree murder and aggravated robbery, the only charges they were being asked to consider. The straw poll also yielded five jurors who were inclined to vote "not guilty." If they were going to reach a unanimous verdict, Joni Haack had her work cut out for her.

••••

By the time the marathon closing arguments finally ended on Monday evening, Bill Buckley and Lamar Sims felt confident they'd done enough to convince the jury of James King's guilt and send the case into a death-penalty phase. For their part, Walter Gerash and Scott Robinson were equally confident they'd blown enough holes in the prosecution case to obtain an acquittal and set their client free. Yet all four attorneys were experienced enough to know that, once the case was in the hands of 12 ordinary citizens, anything was possible—including a hung jury and a mistrial.

Though the defense lawyers were given permission to hole up at Gerash's Victorian law office while awaiting a verdict—the prosecutors at the DA's Office just across the street—all four were back in Courtroom 16 that Tuesday morning. Scott Robinson took to the podium to share with Judge Spriggs that new information had come to light that, in his view, required a halt in the jury deliberations—information about Dewey Baker.

The serial bank robber and California inmate, Robinson revealed, had written three letters the defense team had only just gotten to see—the first one dated May 13, a second on May 29, and a third on June 4. Baker's correspondence, he argued, went far beyond what the defense team had at its disposal earlier in the trial.

On May 13, the convicted felon had written defense counsel, "Your client, James King, is innocent. I know this because it is I who am responsible for the crimes he's charged with. I don't admit that lightly, and admit it only for my own peace of mind. I'm not trying to imprison innocent persons for my crimes." On May 29—the same day he'd spoken with Gerash's secretary—Baker had penned, "Alright, to the meat of the matter. Your client, James King, is innocent. I know this to be true because it is I who is guilty for that which he is charged."

And in his June 4 letter, Baker had declared, "That guy, Jim King, he wouldn't know how to rob a bank … I don't want to die. But I know it's got to happen sooner or later. And when it does, I don't want that poor guy's life on my mind."

Robinson sought permission to re-open the evidence to call Baker's Michigan-based girlfriend, Linda Johnson, to testify—just as he'd attempted during the trial. In the alternative, he asked Judge Spriggs to declare a mistrial.

What made his request so perplexing was that he and Gerash had all but conceded during their closing arguments that the murders and robbery had been an inside job—the complexity of the bank's layout and security system far beyond an outsider's ability to master. And that's precisely who Dewey Baker was—an outsider. Yet here they were, asking for a mistrial unless they could get evidence about him before the jury.

After nearly a solid month of one of the most publicized, complex murder trials in Colorado history, Dick Spriggs wasn't about to entertain such a motion. "I can't reopen the case for testimony because the jury has already been deliberating for a couple of hours," he advised the lawyers.

"I've examined the letters, and they clearly appear to contain statements that he's responsible for this, but that doesn't solve the problems we had before." Without any corroboration, he said, the three letters amounted to nothing more meaningful than "jailhouse chatter." Thus, there would be no additional evidence, and no mistrial.

For the prosecutors, defense lawyers, Jon Priest and his law enforcement colleagues, victims' loved ones, and James King's family members, the vigil for news from the jury could now begin in earnest.

••••

Having failed to reach a verdict on Tuesday—day one—the jury was deposited back at the Warwick Hotel, where they'd remain sequestered until completing their mission. The entire ninth floor was cordoned off for the 12 jurors, two alternates, and courtroom bailiffs assigned to watch over them, Frank Petee and Muriel Moon. Sheriff's deputies patrolled the hallway and elevator bay to make sure nobody from the press or general public came within their presence or earshot.

The circa-1967 hotel—which most locals considered a dive—sat just two blocks from the Cash Register Building, the iconic skyscraper a constant reminder of their task each time jurors boarded the bus to be taken to the courthouse or out to dinner. Though those seeking exercise were allowed to join Petee for a morning or evening stroll through downtown, the bailiff made sure to lead them in the opposite direction of what for the last six months had become known as Norwest Bank.

Beyond their walks and meals, the men and women making one of the most consequential decisions of their lives were completely cut off from the outside world. All phone calls were supervised and what little news they received came in the form of newspapers filled with giant holes. They couldn't even go to a public bathroom without Petee or Moon nipping at their heels.

With each passing day in the jury room, the "not-guilty" camp continued to pick off votes from those who'd been holding out for a conviction, much like in the movie *Twelve Angry Men*. The group pressing for an acquittal focused relentlessly on the bank tellers' shaky eyewitness identifications.

Thomas Brunn, a 45-year-old architect—initially a guilty vote—expressed his view that there was no way the tellers could have been as certain as they'd claimed during their testimony due to the robber's heavy disguise. Though he found King's story about discarding his Colt Trooper questionable at best, Brunn considered David Barranco's surprise testimony that he'd identified King from the blue photo binder the first time he saw his picture—but hadn't bothered to tell anyone—even more far-fetched.

The tellers' failure to identify King from the blue book on June 20—what Gerash referred to as their "exoneration" of his client—gnawed at other jurors as well. Equally troublesome for many was that none of the tellers, despite their intricate descriptions of the robber's face and attire, had mentioned anything at all about observing moles. Yet they could easily spot King's more prominent blemishes all the way from the jury box.

Those still clinging to their "guilty" votes pressed the others about all of the circumstances surrounding King the defense attorneys wanted them to believe were merely coincidences that had nothing to do with the crime: deciding to find an in-person chess game that very morning after not having played across-the-board chess in years, discarding his gun, police belt, speed loaders, and ammo, shaving his mustache, losing his driver's license, and acquiring a larger safety deposit box. How many coincidences did it take before logic dictated they weren't coincidences at all?

What made their deliberations so agonizing was that the majority of jurors believed in their guts King *had* committed the murders and robbery. Only someone who knew as much as he did about the bank's layout and security system, several of them opined, could have accomplished everything the killer had done in the time he'd done it—without getting caught. Moreover, the James King they'd gotten to know *was* a cold, calculating, antisocial misfit, aligning with how the tellers described the gunman's demeanor while he was robbing them. On an intuitive level, it made perfect sense the DPD had arrested the right man.

Every time their discussion veered off in an emotional direction, however, at least one of the jurors would circle back to the judge's written instructions. "The law states that our feelings cannot be part of this," said Michael Richards, a 23-year-old aircraft mechanic. "You've got to go on the evidence and the law."

Throughout it all, only one juror articulated an entrenched position that King had nothing whatsoever to do with the bank massacre. Richard Espinoza expressed his view that the bank tellers wanted *someone* to go to prison for the crime and that, when the DPD offered them a suspect, "they convinced themselves" after the fact that the ex-cop was the perpetrator.

Some jurors found King's testimony credible. Others didn't. Surprisingly, however, whether they believed he was telling the truth or lying wasn't at the center of their deliberations. Rather, the believability that mattered to them most was that of the only living victims of the heinous crime—the six cash vault tellers.

• • • •

During the first few days of deliberations, Joni Haack held firm to her belief that King was guilty as charged, trying her best to persuade those with a different view to change their minds. But nearly every time she recounted testimony that, to her, proved the defendant's guilt, someone in the group would indicate their memory about the same testimony was different. Because they hadn't been allowed to take notes, there was no way to determine whose recollection best matched the actual evidence—a conundrum that all by itself created more doubt.

They tried to make up for their lack of notes in another way, seeking permission to view the videotapes of the tellers' very first statements made the same day as the murders and robbery. But because the videos hadn't been admitted into evidence, Judge Spriggs told them to rely on their recollections of the testimony instead—despite those recollections diverging on key points.

Unlike the jurors in *Twelve Angry Men*, the King jurors didn't get in each other's faces and yell no matter how frustrated they grew over their lack of progress. But the tension did become overwhelming for a few. On several occasions, Valerie Taylor, a 28-year-old mental-health counselor, became so stressed out she climbed out the jury room window and sat on the ledge, her legs dangling off the side of the building, four stories high. When others begged her to come back inside, she wouldn't, claiming, "I just need to get away from you people."

Taylor was one of several jurors troubled by King's alibi. Exactly what time he was at home Father's Day morning was a mish-mash of inconsistencies, between the defendant's own testimony, his wife's, and his neighbors'. She wasn't even sure they were each testifying about the same day.

The question that continued to torment a cluster of jurors was the one both Gerash and Buckley had raised during their closings, though with different answers: was it worse to send an innocent person to prison—or the execution chamber—or to set a guilty person free?

"If we believe he did it," more than one of them asked the others, "how can we let him walk?" In response, others pointed to the instructions on proof beyond a reasonable doubt. If they had reasonable doubts, members of the "not-guilty" camp retorted, they were required to vote for an acquittal even if they believed King was the killer.

Jack Rushin, a 38-year-old, self-employed electrician, was so torn he sought out divine intervention—quite literally. He'd return to his hotel room after dinner, grab the Bible from the nightstand drawer, and toss it in the air so it would land on his bed in an open position. Rushin would then pick it up to see whether an insightful parable appeared on either of the open pages—one that would provide insight to guide his thinking. He repeated the experiment over and over again throughout the deliberations. Divine intervention, however, didn't pay him a visit.

While Rushin was tossing his Bible, other jurors up and down the ninth floor were tossing and turning in bed, experiencing nightmares about the bank massacre and their heavy responsibility. For several, the weight of the decision they were being asked to make was unbearable.

Though Michelle Ramirez, a 38-year-old administrative assistant, was among those who believed King was guilty, she was frustrated by the lack of evidence the prosecution team had introduced, and by the many directions to which that evidence pointed. Jurors who felt as she did formed their own camp: "not proven." As their deliberations progressed, more and more of them—including Brunn, Taylor, Haack, and Rushin—reluctantly found themselves in that camp.

Several jurors even came around to the view Robinson had expressed during his closing argument—that the crime could have involved more than one perpetrator. If the murderer and robber had been the same man, they asked, why didn't the gunman reek of gunpowder as he was robbing the cash vault?

By Saturday—day five—what in Haack's initial straw poll had been a majority in favor of King's conviction had flipped completely, with ten jurors now ready to vote for an acquittal. The two holdouts were Steven Divide, an unemployed actor—who mostly kept his views to himself—and 54-year-old Dorothy Stevenson, a food-service worker at United Airlines.

"They didn't prove his innocence," Stevenson told the others. "There are just too many coincidences. He is guilty." Though Haack and Rushin tried to help her understand that it was the prosecution's burden to prove the defendant's guilt, not the defense's burden to establish his innocence, the mother of seven held firm. The more the others pushed her, the more emotional she became, several times retreating to the corner to weep.

Rushin came at Stevenson hard, focusing on the prospect of a hung jury. "If we can't figure this out, why would we put anyone else through this?" he asked her. "Is that really what you want?"

Yet just as he was pressing Stevenson to switch her vote, the electrician still wasn't entirely convinced of his own. Though he'd been casting his vote with the "not-proven" camp, it wasn't because he didn't believe James King had killed the four guards and robbed the bank. He did. But he didn't feel the prosecution had proven so to the required legal standard. *What if we let him go free and he kills someone else?* He shuddered at the thought.

By that weekend, Haack found herself unable to relax enough to sleep. She ventured out onto the balcony of her hotel room and marveled at the lights twinkling across the skyline. She was failing in her efforts to coax and cajole her fellow jurors into reaching a unanimous verdict—the most important job she ever held.

• • • •

By Sunday, June 14—day six—a hung jury seemed increasingly likely. Prior to their lunch break, Haack had Frank Petee deliver a note to Judge Spriggs, which read: "1. What happens if we reach an impasse on a verdict? We feel we are at an impasse (which could be firm as a result of personalities). 2. At what point is a hung jury decided? 3. Is it possible to get a better definition of reasonable doubt (i.e., for lay purposes)?"

For the first time in days, Courtroom 16 sprang to life, the lawyers settling in at their respective counsel tables, journalists claiming the media seats, and relatives and spectators streaming into the gallery. Even James King was marched in from his courthouse holding cell—his "home" while the jury deliberated. As the room fell silent, the jury box slowly filled with the 12 extremely frustrated jurors.

Much to the jury's dismay, the judge had no magic wisdom to impart. "If you are hopelessly deadlocked and I declare a mistrial," he advised them, "the net result is that we go back to 'Go' and start all over again" with a new jury. The only definition of "reasonable doubt" he could offer, he said, was the same one he'd already given. He instructed them to return to the jury room and continue deliberating.

To the judge and attorneys, the futility of the situation had grown from a steady simmer nearly to a boiling point. After everything they'd poured into the trial, none of them had any desire for a do-over, most especially Gerash. He told report-ers he didn't think he'd be able to continue representing King since he wasn't getting paid. Plus, though the defense had en-joyed the element of surprise during this trial—the Harrison Ford overlay a prime example—that wouldn't be true at the next one. In all likelihood, the prosecution would fix their mis-takes and put on a better, more focused case.

Though Judge Spriggs told the lawyers he'd keep the de-liberations going until Christmas if that's what it took to re-solve the case, even he couldn't escape the harsh reality that the proceedings were teetering on the precipice of a mistrial.

••••

Tuesday, June 16, 1992, marked the one-year anniversary of the horrific massacre. Metro Denver was once again deluged with media coverage and painful images to commemorate the occasion. Though the jury was shielded from it all, the mile-stone injected a renewed sense of urgency for them to reach finality—on day eight—whatever that might look like.

Joni Haack scribbled another note to the judge, which made its way into the courtroom, where Spriggs, the lawyers, and the media assembled at 3:30 p.m. From its context, it was clear the note was intended to help flip a holdout juror from "guilty" to "not guilty."

"Twice one of the jurors has said she's not sure she un-derstands the difference between proving the defendant guilty beyond a reasonable doubt and proving he's innocent," the note began. "She doesn't understand that the prosecution must prove he's guilty beyond a reasonable doubt and that the defense *doesn't have to prove anything*. She continually says she's confused about that."

This time, the judge didn't ask the jury to return to the courtroom. After huddling with the lawyers, Spriggs scribbled his terse response at the bottom of the note. "Please refer to Instruction #1 and Instruction #6." Frank Petee carried the slip of paper down the hallway to Courtroom 11, where the 12 decision-makers awaited an answer.

After Haack read the judge's response aloud, she whipped out Instructions #1 and #6 and read them as well, emphasizing one particular sentence from the latter: "The burden of proof is on the *prosecution* to prove to the satisfaction of the jury *beyond a reasonable doubt* the existence of all of the elements necessary to constitute the crime charged." The same instruction stated that if the prosecution "failed to prove any one or more of the elements beyond a reasonable doubt, you will find the Defendant Not Guilty."

For Dorothy Stevenson, the lightbulb finally went off. She felt a heavy weight suddenly lifting off her shoulders, advising the group she was changing her vote. There were now 11 votes in favor of an acquittal and just one holdout remaining—Steven Divide, the quiet, unemployed actor. He told the others he still wasn't ready to let the person he felt certain had executed four defenseless security guards walk out of the courtroom a free man. Especially not on the anniversary of the crime. But he told the group he'd sleep on it.

At dinner that evening, at the Old Country restaurant in nearby Lakewood, management bestowed helium-filled balloons on each of the female jurors. As was their custom, the group selected one of their members as the "birthday" juror to receive a special cake. When they finished their dessert, the women removed their juror badges and attached them to the balloons, letting them rise to the rafters in mock celebration.

Was there reason to celebrate? Was their work nearly complete? And if so, would their decision actually represent justice under the law? For James King, his family, and the loved ones of Bill McCullom, Phil Mankoff, Scott McCarthy, and Todd Wilson, those answers—at long last—were about to be revealed.

41

THE ENVELOPE, PLEASE

Denver's TV stations began their broadcasts the following morning, June 17, predicting that the climax of the James King trial was imminent. A flood of locals began lining the hallway outside Courtroom 16 the moment the courthouse opened, hoping to be one of the 62 lucky enough to witness history as it unfolded. The would-be spectators whose lottery slips weren't pulled raced home to watch the proceedings on Court TV—alongside tens of thousands who'd been hooked on the legal soap opera since May 19.

At 11:05 a.m., Frank Petee responded to a knock on the jury room door. When he peeked inside, foreperson Joni Haack greeted him with a slight head nod. "We have a verdict," she said. The courtroom bailiff instructed her to hang onto the signed verdict form and await further instructions.

Nine consecutive days and 53 hours into their at-times heated discussions, Haack and her fellow jurors had set the record for the longest jury deliberation in Colorado history—a record not a single one of the 12 took any pride or delight in establishing.

By 12:30 p.m., the courtroom was filled to capacity, the defense lawyers at their table, Buckley, Sims, and Jon Priest at the prosecution table, and family members of the victims and of the defendant in their familiar places at the front of the gallery. Because the judge allowed local attorneys to occupy the seats typically reserved for the media, journalists eager to report on the verdict dotted the gallery, one seat allocated for each media outlet.

Though the tension and anticipation were palpable—the atmosphere even more electric than the trial's opening day—based on Haack's recent notes, the outcome appeared to be a foregone conclusion. Gerash and Robinson were extremely optimistic, fully expecting their client to be exonerated. By sharp contrast, the prosecution table was a morass of despair, the deputy DAs and lead detective dreading what they felt certain was about to happen. They couldn't bear to look behind them, where the loved ones of Bill McCullom, Phil Mankoff, Scott McCarthy, and Todd Wilson clung to hope for a miracle, though were prepared to hear the worst.

Flanked by a half-dozen sheriff's deputies, a bespectacled James King was marched into the courtroom in his camel-hair sport coat, flashing a hopeful grin as his eyes met his wife's. When Judge Spriggs assumed his perch on the bench just before one o'clock, the 12 jurors were ushered into the courtroom, taking their seats in the jury box one final time. His legs crossed and hands resting in his lap, the accused killer stared straight ahead, displaying not the slightest hint of emotion.

When the judge asked whether the jury had agreed upon a verdict, Joni Haack rose to her feet to announce they had. She handed the verdict form to Petee, who walked it over to the bench. After inspecting all nine pages, one for each of the charges—the first eight counts for murder in the first degree (two for each victim) and the final count for aggravated robbery—the judge read each of the jury's answers aloud, beginning with the two murder charges for the slaying of Todd Wilson.

"We the jury," Spriggs announced, "find the defendant, James William King *not guilty* of count number one, murder in the first degree, after deliberation, against Todd A. Wilson." As his words echoed across the courtroom, King sat impassively without moving a muscle, his stoic expression seemingly frozen in place. It didn't change an iota as he heard the words "not guilty" repeated eight more times, signaling a complete and total victory and the end of nearly a year in captivity.

When the jury confirmed their unanimous verdict with nods of all 12 heads, the judge asked sheriff's deputies to escort the defendant into his chambers. As he rose from his seat, King finally turned to face the men and women who'd just given him a new lease on life, mouthing the words "thank you" in appreciation before being whisked away.

The reaction from the front row on each side of the gallery couldn't have been more different. Nearest the defense table, tears slid down Carolyn King's cheeks as her three sons reached out to offer her comfort. "Now the whole world knows what I know," she said softly. The ex-cop's sister, Myra Church, sobbed openly, soaking up the moisture with a white handkerchief.

On the opposite side of the gallery, the relatives of the slain guards stared ahead with pained expressions—as if they'd been punched in the gut—the soul-crushing defeat beyond their capacity to understand or accept. The justice system, they believed, had failed them.

Before discharging the jury for good, Judge Spriggs thanked them for their tremendous public service, announcing that he'd authorized a parting lunch at the Warwick Hotel, lifting the prohibition on their consumption of alcohol as a further token of his appreciation. "But just remember, you gotta get home under your own steam," he added, "so don't overdo it."

All 12 jurors cast their eyes downward as they trudged out of the courtroom, deliberately not making eye contact with the lawyers, lead detective, or the victims' or King's family members. Though they were glad to be done and return to their own families, the verdict they'd just delivered—unanimous as it was—was nevertheless most unsettling.

When the door closed behind the last juror, Robinson rose to request his client's immediate release. The practical reality, however, was that the now-acquitted defendant needed to make one last visit to the county jail for processing before he was truly free.

"Mr. King will be discharged as quickly as the forces of democracy can accomplish the task," the judge announced. "That's the best I can give you." And with those final words, the courtroom slugfest that had dominated the local news—and cable TV airwaves all across America—finally came to an end.

••••

Bill Buckley swallowed hard before approaching the front row of the gallery, where tears now cascaded freely down the faces of the family members of each of the four victims. Phil Mankoff's widow, Ann, extended her arms, telling the lead prosecutor as she hugged him, "You guys really put your hearts into it." The disappointment etched into the face of her teenage daughter, Jennifer, was almost too much for Buckley to bear.

Nellie Wilson, Bill McCullom's mom, wasn't nearly as charitable as Ann Mankoff. "It seems these days that justice is something you can throw out the window," she told a reporter. "Justice won't be served, except before God." Tears pooling in her eyes, she added that she couldn't believe "the good State of Colorado didn't find him guilty, because I believe he was guilty." The jury, she said, had "let a murderer run loose."

Buckley racked his brain for what he'd done wrong. "You remember the ones you lose more than you remember your wins," he told the press. "It's the biggest case I've had. Obviously, I wished it had turned out differently." For his part, Lamar Sims expressed his "profound disappointment for the victims' families and the cash vault employees who have had to live through this during the past year."

A gaggle of nearly two dozen journalists and cameramen engulfed a triumphant Walter Gerash footsteps from the courtroom's entrance. "Our system is the quintessence of democracy," he proclaimed in a booming voice. "The power of the state to charge is the power to destroy! That's why we have the safety net of reasonable doubt. And thank God we do."

His always-smiling partner, Scott Robinson, told reporters he was happy for his client. "I think justice was done. I know a lot of people will think he was acquitted because of clever lawyers, but the reality is that the jury saw justice in the case."

When he was finally released from the county jail, reporters eager for a statement mobbed the newly freed ex-cop. As his wife waited patiently in the backseat of a Toyota station wagon, King said he knew he was innocent. "But until today I wasn't sure the system worked. Now I know one part of it works, because the jury found me innocent." He felt good, he added, "at least as good as you can feel when you've been abused by the system. I'd have felt a lot better today if they'd gotten the right man in the first place."

The one juror most certain the authorities *had* gotten the right man, Steven Divide—the final holdout—stood outside in the bright sunshine to read a statement that would later be shown on the evening news. He expressed solidarity with the victims' family members, saying, "I deeply regret that this difficult verdict will do nothing to relieve their grief and anguish."

Asked to provide his thoughts on the jury's decision, Detective Priest acknowledged his disappointment and frustration. "They obviously didn't think the ID witnesses were important … I can't fault the jury, because I'm sure they labored over it … If they were to believe he was guilty but it was not proven beyond a reasonable doubt, the law says they have to find him not guilty. That's just the system we have."

Foreperson Joni Haack told reporters that reaching a decision in the case "was probably the most difficult thing we did in our lives." Unlike Divide, she didn't express any regrets, stating that the prosecution "just didn't have the evidence to prove it beyond a reasonable doubt. We just couldn't convict him on it." The silver lining, she added, was that "even if we let a guilty man go free, he would still have to face God. And I would much rather let a guilty man go free than put an innocent man behind bars or to death."

Throughout it all, the one question that continued to nag at Haack—through each frustrating day of deliberations—was "why, with no statute of limitations on murder, they didn't put off the arrest until they had more evidence."

Walter Gerash would later make the same point. "If they really thought he was the one, they should have given him more rope"—to hang himself—"or a wiretap. Obviously, they should have waited. On the other hand, when you have four dead bodies, there's a hue and cry. People want someone to pay for what they've done."

The FBI's Bob Pence, offering his own 20-20 hindsight, echoed the defense attorney's sentiments. "When I look at the whole thing in retrospect, the only question would be, 'Should we have waited longer before making any arrests?' And when I ask that question," he told a journalist, "I come down on the side of the decision that was made, considering the violence involved and considering the probable cause information we had. I think you've got to consider the possibilities of flight or of repeated violence."

Or, as Priest bluntly put it, "You're damned if you do and damned if you don't."

42

DIAGNOSING THE MISFIRE

To be clear, the jury's verdict didn't signal a consensus that James King was an innocent man wrongfully charged for crimes he didn't commit. Not hardly. The nine days it took jurors to land on that decision is a testament to how deeply torn they were—a majority convinced he *was* the killer and robber. What emerged during their deliberations, however, was a begrudging recognition that the prosecution had failed to prove his guilt beyond a reasonable doubt. Or, viewed from another angle, that the defense had punched too many holes in the evidence to allow jurors to reach an unwavering conclusion that the retired cop was the man who killed the four guards and robbed the bank.

Considering how the evidence unfolded at trial, the outcome wasn't terribly surprising. Indeed, it would have been far more surprising had the jury convicted King despite the glaring problems with the prosecution's case. That said, an acquittal wasn't unavoidable. Conscious decisions made by the FBI and DPD in the way the case was investigated, and by the chief deputy DAs in how it was prosecuted, had a direct impact on why jurors were left to struggle so mightily over their decision.

For whatever reason, the FBI had assigned brand-new, inexperienced agents to interview key witnesses and suspects, including King himself. Their questions were rudimentary, failing to drill down on specific times, follow up on ambiguities, or to recognize inconsistencies. For instance, when King claimed he'd discarded his Colt Trooper because it had a cracked cylinder, they took him at his word, without subjecting his statement to rigorous scrutiny.

Both the FBI agents and their DPD colleagues arrived ill-equipped to probe what they were being told, such as why King would have driven to the Capitol Hill Community Center in search of a chess game when the chess club hadn't met there in years. Nobody bothered to ask whether he'd made any efforts to locate the club's current venue prior to Father's Day. The ex-cop also told the agents in his very first interview that he washed his car on Father's Day after returning from the cemetery. In view of the bloody massacre they were investigating, it is shocking that not a single follow-up question about that car wash was asked in any subsequent interview—or at trial.

Beyond the shaky field investigation was a basic failure of strategy that saddled Bill Buckley and Lamar Sims with an obstacle they'd never surmount: the photo binders of past and present guards. Whoever made the decision to assemble the red and blue books of grainy, black-and-white images—and then show them to the bank tellers—clearly hadn't thought through how the tellers' review of those books might ultimately play out in a courtroom.

What is most bewildering is why nobody at the helm of the investigation appreciated what Dr. Greene was able to establish with relative ease: that a well-placed hat, dark sunglasses, and mustache is a damn good disguise. In asking the tellers to review the photo books—flying George Noble in from Washington, D.C. to sketch a composite drawing—nobody paused long enough to realize they were engaging in an effort not only destined to fail, but to potentially derail a successful prosecution as well.

Instead of attempting to identify a robber whose disguise rendered a reliable identification impossible, those in charge of the investigation could have used an alternative, more reliable means of identification: James King's unique, high-pitched voice. Indeed, though the six tellers had gotten only brief glimpses of the robber's heavily disguised face, they'd heard his voice the entire time he was in the vault.

Once King was behind bars, it would have been logical to attempt an identification through a voice lineup. If Detective Priest and his FBI counterparts were so certain they'd nabbed the right man, why were they so afraid of doing so? Considering the lengths to which Buckley had gone to employ Kenetha Whisler's voice identification, why hadn't he taken the additional step of recording King's voice so all six tellers could take a stab at recognizing it from an audio six-pack? Wouldn't that have established overwhelming evidence of his guilt?

Even though Buckley and Sims appreciated from the outset how fraught with problems the eyewitness identifications were, they nevertheless constructed the People's entire case on their foundation. They signaled the critical importance of that very evidence by calling David Barranco as their first witness and having each teller except Chong Choe make an in-court identification. Time and again, they kept returning to the weakest component of their case as if they could somehow will it into becoming a strength.

That was particularly true of Lamar Sims' closing argument, in which he asked jurors to rely on the tellers' identifications because they were good people whose intentions were pure—and because, mathematically, they couldn't all be wrong. The prosecution's relentless focus on what the tellers had seen, quite naturally, led to their accounts being central to the jury's deliberations, all but assuring an acquittal.

At the same time, the prosecutors neglected what should have been a central feature of their case: motive. It wasn't enough to persuade jurors that the face behind the disguise was James King's, or that the bullets extracted from the deceased guards were consistent with police ammo. To convince jurors the defendant was a murderer, the prosecution team needed to help them understand *why* he committed the crime. Amazingly, at no point during the three-week trial did Buckley or Sims attempt to establish King's motive—consciously deciding not to introduce two pieces of evidence that could have elucidated his mindset.

The first was the Kings' acute financial distress, particularly after the ex-cop quit his job at United Bank, eliminating his only income apart from his measly $1,600/month pension. As of June 1991, the couple was still struggling to dig out of bankruptcy. Inexplicably, the only mention of that bankruptcy filing came during the *defense's* opening statement. For whatever reason, Buckley didn't believe jurors would find it compelling that the man standing trial for robbing a bank happened to be in desperate need of cash.

The second piece of evidence related to King's repeated efforts to improve security at the bank, efforts that were consistently rebuffed by his superiors. How frustrating must that have been for him? But they went even a step further, actually reprimanding him in February 1990 when he wouldn't allow a moving crew into secure areas of the bank. How angry had he become over being disciplined for trying to keep the bank safe? Angry enough to teach his superiors a lesson by showcasing the bloodbath their lax approach to security might cause?

Had Buckley and Sims devoted even a fraction of the energy they'd poured into the eyewitness accounts into developing King's motive—even with all of the warts in their case—that could have been enough to strengthen the hand of the seven jurors who initially voted in favor of guilt. But without a clear motive to help those jurors convince the others, it didn't take long for most of them to end up in the opposing camp.

•••

Despite all of those difficulties, the prosecutors might have convinced a unanimous jury of King's guilt by taking a drastically different approach to closing arguments.

Instead of having Sims make an initial argument focused primarily on the tellers' testimony, the prosecution team could have waived its first argument altogether, leaving the defense with nothing to rebut and no clue as to what they'd say once Gerash and Robinson uttered their last words. At that point,

Buckley could have presented a concise, laser-focused summation that deflected the defense's key points and relied exclusively on the most compelling evidence at his disposal. Imagine if his argument had sounded something like this:

"Ladies and gentlemen, you might find this surprising, but there's a lot Mr. Gerash and Mr. Robinson just said that we actually agree with. Dr. Greene *was* an excellent witness. Her research study proved something that makes perfect sense: that when a criminal uses a good disguise to conceal his identity, it's likely to prevent a reliable identification. For that reason, we are not going to ask you to rely on any of the eyewitness identifications made by the tellers.

"So forget about the photo lineup from which five of the tellers identified the defendant. You don't need to discuss that in the jury room at all. We agree it doesn't help us prove the defendant is the man who committed these horrific crimes.

"But I do want you to bear in mind what the tellers told you about the robber's demeanor, about how calm and collected he was. As you do, ask yourselves, was that what you saw of the defendant during this trial, a man who was calm and collected, not only these last several weeks, but during the four hours he was on the witness stand? That's the only part of the testimony you heard from the tellers I'm asking you to discuss in the jury room.

"The question at the heart of this case, ladies and gentlemen, is not whether you believe *them*, but whether you believe *him*." As he enunciated those words, Buckley would have swiveled to point stridently at the defendant. "That is the singular question you need to answer in the jury room to arrive at your verdict. And as you consider that question—whether you believe James King—I want you to focus on three stories that he's been telling FBI agents, police detectives, and now the 14 of you for a solid year.

"As I'm about to prove to you, all three of those stories are outright fabrications designed to conceal the truth of what actually happened last Father's Day—a cloak of deception the defendant has hidden under to protect himself from getting caught, hoping it would fool you into believing he had nothing to do with these despicable crimes.

"It is your sworn duty to the People of the State of Colorado to lift up that cloak, and to probe with logic, reason, and common sense whether the three stories he's telling you pass the test of believability." Now pointing to the gallery, Buckley would have added, "That's a solemn duty you owe not just to the People, but to the mothers, fathers, wives, brothers, sisters, children, aunts, and uncles of Bill McCullom, Phil Mankoff, Scott McCarthy, and Todd Wilson.

"This nightmare will never end for any of them. All they're asking for is justice. Do not consider your work in that jury room complete—as you analyze and pick apart what lies beneath the cloak the defendant has stitched together to protect himself—until you have made absolutely certain you are delivering justice for all of them.

"I'm about to go through each of the three stories the defendant has told you that collectively form his cloak of deception. As I discuss each one, ask yourselves, does it make common sense? Is it contrived? Is it just a little too convenient? Does it even fit with the rest of this man's life and everything you've come to learn about him? Is it abundantly clear that what he's telling you is nothing more than a web of lies?

"And here's what I need you to remember most of all. If he's not being truthful about a single one of these stories— indeed, if he's attempting to deceive you about anything at all—there's only one reason why. And that is, to get away with what he's done.

"An innocent man doesn't lie about what he's done, because the truth sets him free. A guilty man, on the other hand, *must lie* about what he's done, because the truth will send him to prison—or the execution chamber. You therefore know— by definition—that if the defendant is lying to you about *anything*, he's guilty as charged of killing those defenseless guards and of robbing the bank.

"So let's get to the three stories. Story Number One is his chess alibi. Story Number Two is his trashing of his Colt Trooper. Story Number Three is his safety deposit box. I'm not even going to discuss why he shaved his mustache, his claim that he lost his driver's license, or all of the inconsistencies in his own timeline, his wife's, or his neighbors'. You don't need to address a single one of those circumstances in order to find him guilty beyond a reasonable doubt. Just these three stories.

"Story Number One. His claim that he drove to the Capitol Hill Community Center a little after nine o'clock on Father's Day morning with the intention of meeting someone to play chess. Remember, he admitted he hadn't played chess at the community center since 1984 — *for seven years*. Does it make any sense to you that he would have gotten behind the wheel of his car, put the keys in the ignition, and pulled out of his driveway — on Father's Day of all days — believing for a second the community center was still the location of the chess club?

"Mr. Robinson actually anticipated that very problem during his opening. He told you that the defendant had tried calling the chess club a few days before Father's Day to find out where it met. That actually confirms his client had no idea where the chess club met. Why else would he have needed to make that call? But here's the kicker. The defendant sat on that witness stand for four solid hours and *never* said a single word about making any such phone call. The story would still be unbelievable even if he had. But he never did.

"The defendant told you he parked in the back and then walked toward the stairs leading down to the basement, intending to use the key in the lockbox on the wall — the one that was there for chess club members. Though he knew what the combination was — he told you it was Rook-King-Rook, R-K-R — he admitted that he fully expected it would have changed since he was last there seven years earlier.

"What that means — if you are the slightest bit tempted to believe any of this far-fetched nonsense — is that he drove to the community center knowing full well he wouldn't be able to access the key to get inside the building. *Whether the lockbox was there or not.* Then he tells you that seeing the lockbox missing was his signal that the chess club was gone and that his hope of playing chess that morning was dashed.

"Okay. Let's think this through. He knew he didn't have the right combination for the lockbox before he even pulled out of his driveway, but somehow believed he could still get into the building. Yet when he sees there's no lockbox, he throws up his hands, telling you that's when it sank in that he wasn't going to play chess after all. Picture him standing there, throwing up his hands in frustration. This man who so badly wanted to play chess he'd driven downtown on Father's Day morning to find a game, yet knowing all along he had no way of getting into the building.

"Is there any logic to this story whatsoever? But it gets even more fanciful, ladies and gentlemen. He told you that he then walked up to the front door and attempted, without success, to open it, but never descended the back stairs to the basement—where the chess club actually met—to see if that door would open. If he'd known before pulling out of his driveway he wouldn't be able to get into the building without somebody helping him from inside, is it logical that he never went down those rear steps, turned the doorknob, or knocked?

"Notice, ladies and gentlemen, I'm not even relying on the testimony of Mr. Huntington or Mr. Hendry. Whatever they saw that morning—or didn't see—has nothing to do with how you can conclude with complete confidence, from the defendant's own words, that he never went to the community center on Father's Day, because Story Number One turns into nonsense at every turn.

"And if you don't believe his story—each and every part of it—that means he isn't telling you the truth. Remember, there's only one reason for him to try to deceive you: because you're the last thing standing between him and the execution chamber.

"So we could stop right there. Because you can and should find him guilty beyond a reasonable doubt the moment you conclude he wasn't truthful about his chess alibi. If what he says he was doing at the time of the murders and robbery isn't what he was doing, we know with complete certainty what he was doing: mercilessly slaughtering four human beings and absconding with a bag full of cash.

"Story Number Two. His trashing of his Colt Trooper. Not in June 1991 after he used it to kill those four defenseless guards. Nope. Way back in August 1990, after he quit his job at United Bank. Again, I'm not asking you to rely on Tom Butler's testimony that cylinders in Colt Troopers don't just crack, they explode. Or even their expert, Ikey Starks', that he's never seen a Trooper with a cracked cylinder.

"Or for that matter, Mrs. King's testimony that she believed the defendant's revolver was in a metal box in the den all the way up until July 3, 1991. We're not asking you to focus on David King's gigantic flip-flop about the supposed conversation in the garage, telling you first his dad said he'd already trashed the gun, but then doing a 180, telling you his dad merely said he was *going to* get rid of it. Put all that aside. You don't need to rely on any of it. All you need to rely on are the words that came out of the defendant's own mouth.

"Here we have a 25-year veteran police officer who's written hundreds of pages about how to do the job safely. Prides himself on safety, both while on the police force and at the bank. And what is he asking you to believe? That he discovered a crack in his gun's cylinder after shooting at the firing range in June of 1990. That he knew how dangerous it was to have a gun with a cracked cylinder. But that he put it right back in his holster and carried it for another two months while working as a weekend guard. Even though he had unfettered access to a locker full of Smith & Wessons.

"Do you remember what he said when I confronted him, asking how he'd be able to protect himself and others with that dangerous gun? I wrote it down. He said, quote, 'If I ever had to use the gun, my life would be in danger and it wouldn't matter whether the person was shooting at me or I blew myself up. It wouldn't be much different.'

"That was his story, ladies and gentlemen. That a highly trained police officer is going to be shot to death by a bad guy whether his gun works or explodes in his face, so what's the point of carrying a gun that actually works? That was his explanation to you—and he made it with a straight face—of why he supposedly continued carrying a revolver he knew would explode if he pulled the trigger. Does that make any sense at all? Of course it doesn't. It's preposterous. And makes a mockery of the reason why police officers carry guns in the first place.

"Again, stop right there. Is there any doubt in your mind that this is a made-up story? Is there any doubt that the gun the defendant continued to carry was in perfect operating condition, not just from June to August of 1990, but also when he used it to shoot and kill Bill McCullom, Phil Mankoff, Scott McCarthy, and Todd Wilson on June 16, 1991? Don't you just know in your gut that that is when the defendant trashed his Colt Trooper—in order to conceal his involvement in the crime? Isn't that what logic and common sense are screaming at you to conclude?

"And that's not even all he said on this subject. Remember how he told you he had to be really careful about how he threw this dangerous weapon away—the one he carried during his last two months at the bank with a supposedly cracked cylinder? That he had to throw it away in pieces—the cylinder first and the remaining parts the following week—because it was *such a menace.* What about his police belt and speed loaders? 'Yeah, I threw those away too,' he told you. How about the bullets? Isn't it dangerous to toss live ammo in the trash? He had a pretty detailed explanation for that as well.

"Do you remember what he told you—again, all with a straight face? That he pulled the lead tips out of the 18 cartridges, emptied the gunpowder out of each and every one, and then threw the whole lot of them away. Can you picture him in the midst of that elaborate operation? Are *you* able to keep a straight face with that image in mind, of him carefully sprinkling the gunpowder out of all those cartridges? Can you think of any reason why he wouldn't have given the functioning speed loaders, or 18 perfectly good bullets, to one of his former colleagues—or returned them to the DPD?

"Do you believe his story about the cracked cylinder, trashing his gun, speed loaders, and bullets? Or are you convinced it's false—entirely made up? Again, ladies and gentlemen, if what I'm saying is convincing you that the defendant sat on that witness stand and *lied to you* about what he did with his gun, belt, accessories, and ammo, then you have no reasonable doubt that he is guilty as charged. Because he had no reason to lie to you about any of that if he had nothing to do with this crime.

"Story Number Three. The safety deposit box. The one he told Ms. Peralez at First Bank of Westland he needed 'right away' on Monday, June 17." At this point, Buckley would have pointed at the defense table. "They all know how incriminating that looks. The defendant walks into the bank the day after this robbery needing a bigger safe deposit box, and then comes back repeatedly in the days and weeks that follow with an expandable folder, each time heading straight for a private room where no one can see what he's doing. What's his explanation? What words came out of his mouth? That he needed a place to store his backup floppy disks for the police manual he was writing.

"Ladies and gentlemen, let's suspend reality for a moment and suppose that could somehow make a little bit of sense, that someone writing a book needs to go to the trouble of carrying backup disks to a safe deposit box at their bank—and use a private room to secretly place those disks in the box. Let's assume that makes more sense than storing the backups at his home, right next to his computer.

"What's the part of this story that makes no sense at all? That when the DPD had a locksmith break into that box on July 5, 1991, there wasn't a single floppy disk to be found. Do you remember how the defendant tried to explain away that rather inconvenient fact? By telling you it takes a long time to make the backup disks and he hadn't finished the process yet.

"But didn't he and his eldest son also tell you they'd been talking for *months* about backing up his book onto floppy disks? Didn't James Jr. agree that his dad stored hundreds of floppy disks in his den? Why were they there instead of in the larger safe deposit box if that was his reason for getting it? None of this makes any sense at all, does it?

"The absurdity of this story goes even one step further. Remember how Ms. Peralez told you that the defendant was carrying an expandable green folder each time he returned to her bank? And that he took both that folder and the larger box into a private room where nobody could see what he was doing? If there were innocent explanations for what was in that folder—for why he felt the need to use a private room—shouldn't you have heard it from his own mouth during his four hours on the witness stand?

"Guess what? His attorney never asked him what was in that folder—or why he kept using the private room. You will go back into that jury room not with a concocted, nonsensical story about the green folder and the private room—*but with no explanation at all.* Because unlike his chess alibi story and his Colt Trooper story, he couldn't even conjure up a story to try to fool you about what was in the folder and what he was doing in the private room.

"The explanation he's provided for why he needed a larger safety deposit box is yet another story that collapses of its own weight. Another stitch in the cloak of deception the defendant desperately needs you to buy into to make sure he isn't held accountable for what he did.

"You don't even need to believe that all three of these stories are after-the-fact explanations designed to help him elude detection for what he actually did on Father's Day. Take your pick. Is the chess alibi the most unbelievable? The cracked cylinder the most far-fetched? Or is it the floppy disks that were going to make it into that safe deposit box any day, had he not experienced the inconvenience of being arrested? Remember, you just need to conclude that *one* of them is false.

"Ladies and gentlemen, you now know everything you need to in order to conclude—beyond any reasonable doubt—that this defendant is the deranged sociopath who murdered Bill McCullom, Phil Mankoff, Scott McCarthy, and Todd Wilson last Father's Day, and who terrorized six bank tellers as he stole nearly $200,000 from the cash vault before vanishing into thin air. He's been hiding under a cloak of deception ever since. It is up to you to remove that cloak once and for all. To expose him for what you know him to be, and what all of the lies he's stitched together leave no doubt he is: a cold-blooded, savage killer.

"Use his own words, and the nonsensical stories he's tried

to deceive you with, to find him guilty on all counts. Hold the defendant responsible for the misery he's inflicted on four grieving families and the fear and anguish he's injected into our peaceful community. Only you have the power to right this horrible wrong. Only you have the power to mete out justice. You *are* the conscience of our community. We ask you to express that conscience through your verdict.

"This is the most important civic duty each of you will likely fulfill in your lifetimes. So please, summon every ounce of courage and fortitude you can muster and go back into that jury room and do your duty. And when you're done, when you've reached a unanimous verdict consistent with the evidence, with logic, and with common sense, come back into this courtroom with your heads held high, knowing that you've fulfilled your awesome responsibility to us all. The People of the State of Colorado will be forever in your debt. Thank you."

Had Bill Buckley delivered such a closing argument, would Joni Haack and her fellow jurors have returned a guilty verdict, sending James King off to a life in prison—or the execution chamber? Unfortunately for the victims' families—who were left to grieve all over again following his acquittal—we will never know.

43

THE REST OF THE STORY

Paula Woodward, the acclaimed investigative reporter for Channel 9NEWS—whose televised interview of Paul Yocum was largely responsible for the floppy-eared former guard receding as a viable suspect—had designs on another meaty interview subject: the man actually charged with the quadruple homicide and found "not guilty" by a jury of his peers. She reached out to the acquitted murder defendant a few months after the trial, asking if he'd speak with her "off the record." Though James King didn't agree at first, the crafty journalist eventually charmed her way inside his Golden, Colorado bungalow at the foothills of the Rockies.

Woodward's first visit to 665 Juniper Street occurred about six months following his acquittal. As she came through the front door—no cameraman in tow—she was surprised to see what a meager lifestyle he and his wife were leading. "I can't get a job now because I was tried as the United Bank killer," the ex-cop lamented, noting he and Carolyn were scraping by on his small police pension and her wages from Weight Watchers. He quickly established their rules of engagement, making clear he wouldn't agree to discuss any particulars regarding either the bank massacre or his trial and that not a single word of what he said could be released to the public.

Over the next two years, Woodward returned to 665 Juniper for pre-arranged visits nearly every other month, setting up camp in King's living room about a dozen times in all, typically for a half an hour to an hour. Though she never arrived with so much as a tape recorder, her interview subject did allow her to take notes. Once she finally established a modicum of rapport and trust, the broadcast journalist figured she had nothing to lose, approaching King's thoughts about the bank massacre with hypothetical questions.

"What kind of person would kill four unarmed people?" she asked one day, her attempt to get him talking. He said it had to have been a "terrible person, a cruel person." Unlike that type of individual, he said, he'd been a police officer nearly his entire adult life, always helping people. But his job had also given him a glimpse of the type of person capable of such a crime. "People who lie, cheat, steal, and hurt," he told her.

"Where would *you* hide the money?" she asked.

"I'd bury it in the mountains," he said. In the same breath, he pointed to his ramshackle surroundings. "You're not seeing that kind of money being spent around here. The most we've done is gone to Las Vegas a couple of times." The retired sergeant paused, before adding, "I can assure you the FBI went with us." He claimed that federal agents were watching him "all the time. I can't even go into my own backyard without feeling I'm being watched." He gestured to the nearby foothills. "They have a very clear view from there and know when I'm coming and going."

King had good reason for being paranoid. The FBI *did* periodically have him under surveillance, eager to bring federal charges against him for violating the slain guards' civil rights. As he surely knew from his few remaining contacts at the DPD, neither the feds nor police detectives were making any renewed effort to "solve" the case. As far as they were concerned, the jury had allowed the sole perpetrator—James King—to walk free.

That was also the sentiment of the broader community. The few times he ventured out in public, people gawked at him and shot him scornful glares, unable or unwilling to conceal their revulsion. Though he badly wanted to move to a place where nobody knew him, with their sons residing close by—David still living with them—Carolyn wouldn't consider it.

Woodward was struck by the shell of a human being King had become, sensing in him no more personality than that of a potted plant. He never smiled or laughed and talked only in generalities. She perceived nothing of substance going on in his life—no hobbies or interests.

Carolyn did all of their shopping and ran the family's errands. Her husband lived as a recluse, a pariah whenever he left home. Ironically, he even had iron bars installed behind every window, his cramped bungalow in many ways resembling the jail cell where he'd been held captive for a year.

••••

In the latter part of 1993, Woodward arrived for one of her pre-arranged visits as Carolyn was on her way out the door to run errands. It was the first time she and King were completely alone. The moment they sat down in the living room, the ex-cop launched into a soliloquy about the bank massacre—completely unprompted—the words flowing out of his mouth in a torrent.

"*I did not do this,*" he insisted, slamming his fist on the table, though without sufficient force to make a sound. "I wouldn't do that. I did not kill those people. And I did not rob the bank." Woodward found his performance completely out of character—contrived and unnatural—as if he'd been rehearsing it for days. Though King attempted to tinge his remarks with vehemence and umbrage à la Walter Gerash, he seemed more uncomfortable than annoyed.

Eight or nine minutes into his monologue, he finally ran out of words, gazing into Woodward's eyes to gauge her reaction. "Well?" he asked.

"What do you want me to say?" she asked back.

"Well, what do you think?"

"I think you believe what you're saying." She interpreted his full-throated denial as an invitation to lob additional hypothetical questions at him. "Why would someone not take the $2 million and only take $200,000?" she inquired. "That doesn't make sense to me. According to the tellers, the bag was big enough for a lot more. What do you think about that?"

King hemmed and hawed before telling her he didn't know. He also had little to say when she asked why "someone" would kill four unarmed men. "Do you think one of them recognized him?"

For a full minute, King stared back at her without saying a single word, his silence creating yet another uncomfortable moment. The journalist finally broke in with a question about his chess alibi. He repeated his testimony from trial, that he'd gone to the community center to play chess. She also broached the subject of the blueprints investigators had found in his home, but he clammed up, refusing to answer her question.

Though the TV journalist returned to 665 Juniper on several more occasions, she and King were never again alone—and never had any further discussion about the bank massacre. By late 1994, Woodward finally decided there wasn't anything left for them to talk about. She never saw King again. But she did keep her promise not to reveal anything he told her—at least not until his coffin was lowered into the earth.

• • • •

In an eerie twist of fate, the former murder defendant's middle son, Greg, would ultimately follow in his father's footsteps. In March 1999, the 34-year-old tattoo artist was himself hauled off to jail for a murder in nearby Westminster. But unlike his dad, Greg confessed to the investigating officers that he had indeed shot and killed his victim—though claimed he'd done so in self-defense.

He told the Westminster Police that while he was walking with his girlfriend at 1:00 a.m. on a Saturday morning, her estranged common-law husband—a 22-year-old named Robert Morvillo—jumped him from behind. Before he could get his bearings, the younger man had knocked him to the ground and was kicking him repeatedly in his head and torso. A bystander who saw what was happening came to Greg's rescue—pulling

Morvillo off of him before he caused any significant injury.

By his own account, the tattoo artist then rose to his feet and pulled out a gun, pumping several rounds into Morvillo's torso as he stood only five feet away. He was a good shot—just like his old man—his gunfire instantly killing his girlfriend's jealous ex. Greg told the police he fired at Morvillo because he was scared.

Though he was released on bail while the police investigated further, the possibility of another King murder trial loomed large. Word of Greg King's arrest eventually made its way to Jon Priest, who by then was the head of the DPD's homicide division. Priest told a reporter for the *Post* that he'd asked Greg what he knew about the United Bank massacre while his dad was in jail awaiting trial, "and never got the feeling that he knew anything one way or the other. But you just never know sometimes." Would Greg spill the beans on his father now that his own life was on the line?

"Investigation is a patience game," Priest added. "I'd like to keep my options open." He still considered the United Bank case "an ongoing investigation, and it will continue that way until we can bring closure to it."

The *Post* reporter also tracked down Scott Robinson to get his reaction to the news. "As much as I'd like to see the United Bank case finally solved," he said, "they aren't going to find the answer in Greg King. Jim King was in no way involved."

Whatever opportunity might have existed to garner information about the Father's Day massacre from James King's second-born child didn't last long. With no evidence to disprove his claim of self-defense, all charges against the 34-year-old were dropped just five weeks after his arrest. Jon Priest and his colleagues at the DPD and FBI would have to continue their pursuit of justice without any assistance from the "tattooed one."

• • • •

On June 15, 2001, the *Post* ran a lengthy retrospective to mark the tenth anniversary of the Mile High City's most infamous crime. Still reeling a decade later, several of the victims' family members spoke with a trio of staff writers working on the feature article.

Scott McCarthy's widow, Jenny—who'd remarried, gone to law school, and become a lawyer herself—told the reporters "it never, ever leaves. There's not a day in my life that I don't think about it." Her bitterness over the way the King trial played out was palpable. "I totally don't believe in the criminal justice system," she said. "I honestly think defense attorneys are crooks themselves."

John and Delia Wilson battled depression for years following their son Todd's murder and King's acquittal. They eventually stopped talking to each other. "Not only did we lose a son," John told the reporters, "we lost a friend—a friend in each other." With help, they were able to repair their marriage, finding refuge in their church, where they often prayed for answers. "We try to figure out why it happened—the everlasting question," John said. "We both believe that someday justice will be done, whether here or somewhere else."

Joni Haack shared with the *Post* team that her experience on the jury had drastically altered her perception of the legal system. She lamented "the fallibility of it" and how easily the process can be manipulated, stating she firmly believed King was the killer. "Unfortunately, given the jury instructions, we had to acquit. And that's something that's really hard to live with … I think they had a prosecutable case, but I think there were some mistakes made."

Another juror, Michelle Ramirez, said she thought King "could have done it," but the case had too many holes. "Had the prosecution been able to fill them, it would have been a different outcome." Not long after the trial, while she was in the concourse at Stapleton Airport awaiting a flight, a couple came walking up to her: James and Carolyn King. Ramirez told the reporters it was "one of those 'Twilight Zone' moments." Though they didn't speak, Carolyn smiled at her. "It was uncomfortable—like being married forever, getting divorced, then seeing your ex."

The *Post* writers also reached out to Bill Buckley, filling him in on Haack's and Ramirez's observations. "That's the worst thing that the prosecutor can hear," he said. "We thought you had the right guy, but you didn't prove it." He told the reporters he'd gone over in his mind "hundreds of times" what he could have done differently to be more persuasive, lamenting that his heart ached for the families who "have to spend the rest of their lives not having any closure."

••••

Carolyn King, a lifelong smoker, succumbed to emphysema in January 2009 at just 65 years of age. For 46 years, she stood by her husband through it all, the couple living in virtual seclusion the last 16-plus years of her life. By the time of her death, James King was in declining health himself, suffering from severe dementia.

On May 21, 2013, the 76-year-old retired cop and former murder defendant finally met his maker, nearly 21 years after Joni Haack and her fellow jurors set him free. He was still living with his son David at 665 Juniper, the mechanic's numerous cars filling their driveway as always.

James William King was laid to rest during a small ceremony at Mount Olivet Cemetery, right beside his wife—the same place both told the police they'd gone to pay their respects, just as the brutally murdered security guards were being discovered in the bowels of the United Bank of Denver.

Upon hearing the news of King's passing, Todd Wilson's dad summed up the sentiments of the victims' families in two words: "Good riddance."

To this day, the nearly $200,000 in stolen loot has never been accounted for. Perhaps the satchel full of cash is buried somewhere in the mountains.

EPILOGUE

Since 1992, much in the Mile High City has changed. The sky-scraper so central to this saga—the Cash Register Building—now bears the name Wells Fargo Center, the behemoth bank having acquired Norwest in 1998 for a cool $34 billion. The *Rocky Mountain News*, a Denver staple dating back to 1859, succumbed to the post-internet world, publishing its last issue in February 2009, less than two months shy of its 150th anniversary.

In addition to James and Carolyn King, several characters at the heart of this story have moved on to their final resting place. Mike McKown, the first suspect, passed away in 2018. Suspect number two, Paul Yocum, died of a massive heart attack just four months following King's acquittal. David Barranco, who returned to his native Arizona shortly after the trial, passed on in 2022 at the age of 55.

Judge Dick Spriggs left the bench in 1999 after wielding the gavel for 11 years, entering heaven's pearly gates as an 84-year-old in 2019. DA Norm Early, who relinquished his post to run for mayor a second time in 1993—again without success—died in 2022 at the age of 76. Walter Gerash, a genuine legend of the Colorado bar, was 96 when he passed away in 2023.

After working with Gerash for 19 years, Scott Robinson, now 75, hung out his own shingle in 1996. Ironically, though he was the only lawyer involved in the King case opposed to the proceedings being televised, Robinson became one of Denver's most prolific TV legal analysts. He's appeared frequently on each of the city's major networks, starting with the O.J. Simpson trial in 1995. He still has an active law practice, enjoying the courtroom every bit as much today as he did while quizzing David Barranco about the Harrison Ford exhibit.

Lamar Sims, 71, continues to prosecute accused criminals in neighboring Adams County, having called "the People" his only client for the last 43 years.

After a highly successful 24-year career as a prosecutor, Bill Buckley left the DA's Office for private practice in 1996, ultimately retiring in 2013. His mind remains razor sharp at 84, able to recollect each of the 55 murder cases he tried, all but two of which ended in convictions. Yet he still goes to bed each night haunted by the King case, "the one that got away." "I will go to my grave believing we had the right guy," he asserted in an interview for this book. To this day, he winces as he recalls the teary-eyed family members he had to face when the jury set James King free.

Jon Priest, now 70, received his sergeant stripes shortly after the King trial, attaining the rank of lieutenant in 1998. He retired in 2011 after a decorated 31-year career. Priest now works as an expert witness in crime-scene investigation and forensic analysis, having testified in courts all across the country. The former detective has also traveled the Centennial State many times over lecturing audiences about the biggest case on which he ever worked—the Father's Day massacre. As he told the *Denver Post* on the tenth anniversary of the crime, it's "the type of case that books and movies are written about." Prescient.

ACKNOWLEDGEMENTS

When I first became aware of this riveting story in November 2023 and commenced this project, I had no idea whether any of the central characters were even still alive. Fortunately, many were—all in their 70s and 80s—several of whom agreed to share with me their recollections and impressions.

I'm especially grateful to those who went the extra mile by reviewing portions of my manuscript as it was unfolding and who provided valuable insights and factchecking. On the law-enforcement side, thanks to the FBI's Bob Pence and DPD's Tom Haney for imparting what continues to stick with them all these years later. Prosecutors Bill Buckley and Craig Silverman were very generous with their time, not only in meeting with me during my visit to Denver, but also in fielding a plethora of questions over many months and helping me connect with others.

As for the defense, Scott Robinson, Dan Gerash (Walter's lawyer-son), and investigator Tony DiVirgilio offered numerous helpful observations from their own memory banks. I'm particularly grateful to Scott for inviting me into his home and providing me a treasure trove of materials, photos, and court exhibits he's hoarded since 1992. Always with good humor, he allowed me to pester him incessantly, chasing down answers to my endless questions, and reviewing drafts to help steer my writing to greater accuracy. I deeply appreciate the trust Scott placed in me to tell this story in an authentic way.

Despite the passage of more than three decades since he

last worked for United Bank of Denver, Jim Prado was able to educate me on intricate details of the facility's layout and security systems as well as the events and aftermath of Father's Day 1991. He was also kind enough to give me a live tour of the outdoor portions of the bank complex and review for accuracy each chapter that touched on bank-related issues. The finished product benefited significantly from Jim's considerable assistance.

Dr. Edie Greene enlightened me about the research study that proved one of the highlights of the trial—the Harrison Ford overlay too—and the role she played as an expert witness. Jurors Joni Haack and Jack Rushin shared their still-vivid recollections from the deliberations, verdict, and memories of being holed up at the Warwick Hotel for nine solid days. I couldn't have written Chapter 40 without their input, for which I'm most appreciative.

I'm especially indebted to Tom Costello—local 9NEWS reporter back then, NBC News national correspondent today—for loaning his name to the front cover and setting the table with his elegant foreword. And also to Paula Woodward—yet another 9NEWS alum—for allowing me to reveal details from her never-before-published interviews of James King. Tom and Paula were also kind enough to review lengthy drafts and provide extensive comments. Thanks as well to Brian Maass, still an investigative reporter for Denver's CBS4 after 41 years, whose recollections of events were most helpful. Getting to know these talented journalists was a truly special treat.

I owe a huge debt of gratitude to Myra Church, James King's 81-year-old sister, who not only helped me flesh out her older brother's biography, but also provided several images included in the photo insert. Though she had no idea how this book would turn out, she instilled her trust in me from our very first communications, never hesitating to answer my questions or provide information and materials.

I couldn't have written this book without obtaining the gavel-to gavel video footage of the King trial from Court TV, which I devoured over the course of several weeks and came back to time and again as I wrote about the trial. I also acknowledge my reliance on two books and a magazine article that provided important background and color: Walter L. Gerash and Phil Goodstein's *Murders in the Bank Vault* (1997), Kimberly Roessing-Anderson's *Frigid: A Very Cold Case* (2000), and Peter Carbonara's excellent piece, "A Case of First Impressions," which appeared in the September 1992 issue of *The American Lawyer*.

A special shoutout to the ace reporters and investigative journalists at the *Rocky* and *Denver Post*—some of whom have passed on—whose interviews, research, and crisp writing offered an easy-to-follow roadmap, and provided numerous quotes from which I borrowed liberally. Their superb work reminds us what journalism looked like in the good-old days, and was indispensable to me being able to weave this narrative together.

Though I was able to access the *Post*'s archive digitally, my review of the *Rocky*'s back issues on microfiche, and access to its photographs for the photo insert, was made possible by the talented staff of the Special Collections Unit of the Denver Public Library—which now owns and curates all things *Rocky*—who were very gracious with their time and assistance. So too was Marisa Kapsner, records supervisor at the Denver District Court and Jay Casillas in the Media Relations Unit of the DPD.

I am immensely grateful to two lawyer friends, Terry Cawley and Suzanna Geiser, who poured untold hours into scouring my drafts in order to offer helpful suggestions and corrections. The finished product benefited enormously from their efforts.

I work for an incredible law firm, Poyner Spruill LLP, that has supported my side hustle as a true crime writer since 2017. Special shoutouts to my managing partner, Dan Cahill, and my assistant, Sandy Chrisawn, who was the first person to read my drafts when they were still quite rough. Sandy continues to be my biggest cheerleader in both my law practice and my writing, and helps me look good—better than I deserve— every single day.

To the four women who have each played an instrumental role in my writing journey—Amanda Lamb, Anne Blythe, Kerry McQuisten, and C.J. Wynn—thank you for your friendship, guidance, and enthusiastic support. I am so blessed my path crossed with each of yours, for I would not be where I am today without you.

The encouragement and support I receive from my beautiful and talented wife—*my lewensmaat*—Alétia Ferreira, and (now adult) children Benjamin, Madeline, Enzo, Tucker, and Thomas, mean the world to me. I wouldn't be half the man I am today without them. My mother, Evelyn Epstein, gets a huge kick out of my sideline career, and I'm tickled it makes her so happy.

While laboring over this book, I crossed the twentieth anniversary of the loss of my Papa, Morris Goldstein, whose tutelage when I was a youngster is the primary reason I possess any writing skills at all. His pride in my accomplishments meant the world to me. How I wish he were still here to cheer me on. I miss him every day.

PHOTO GALLERY

Photo courtesy of Steven B. Epstein.

Formally 1 United Bank Center in June 1991, the 52-story Cash Register Building still stands out as the most iconic structure in Denver's skyline.

Photos courtesy of the Denver Public Library, Rocky Moutain News Collection.

Partners on the graveyard shift, Bill McCullom (above top) and Phil Mankoff (above lower).

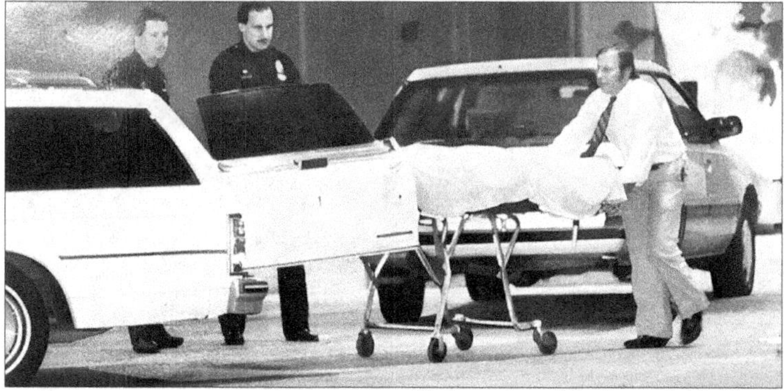

Photo courtesy of the Denver Public Library, Rocky Mountain News collection, Dennis Schroeder photographer.

Tragically, all four security guards left the bank complex in body bags.

Little could either have known at the August 1990 wedding of Scott Mc-Carthy (above right), he and his best man, Todd Wilson (above left), would be dead less than a year later.

Above left: Scott McCarthy's casket emerging from the Holy Trinity Lutheran Church following the best friends' joint funeral. Above right: Pall-bearers carrying Todd Wilson's casket to his final resting place at Crown Hill Cemetery.

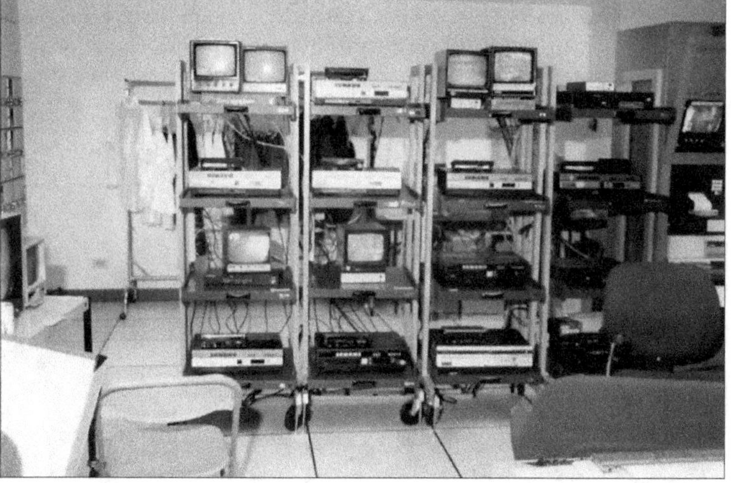

Top: The U-shaped security console in the guard monitor room, where Phil Mankoff fielded the call from the Bob Bardwell imposter at 9:14 a.m., and where Todd Wilson was shot and killed at 9:26 a.m.

Bottom: The area of the monitor room adjacent to the security console. The auxiliary battery room, where Mankoff and Scott McCarthy were killed, is to the left of the rolling carts of monitors/VCRs. One of the two had been seated in the folding chair when the killer entered. Notice the open cassette decks on the VCRs.

The guard supervisor's office, where a VCR had at one time been connected to a camera filming activity inside the monitor room, was accessed through the locked door on the right. Damage to the doorknob was caused by a bullet strike. To the left of the supervisor's office was a storage room the killer tried to access by kicking a hole in the drywall.

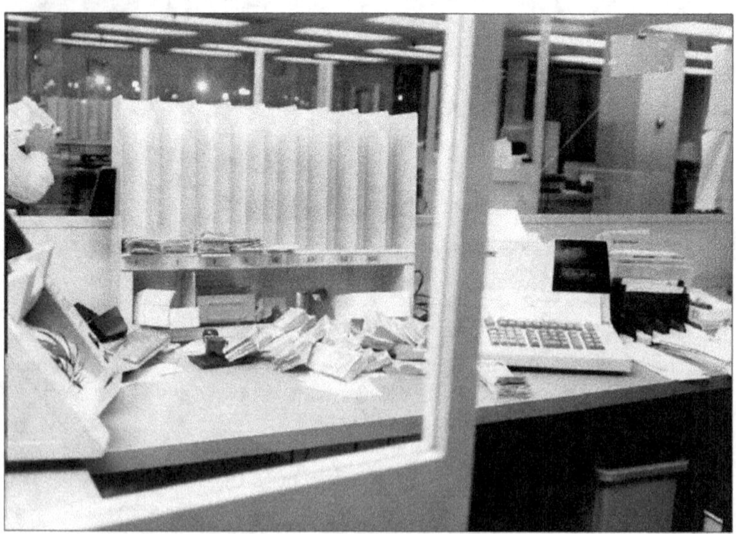

One of the teller booths in the cash vault following the robbery. Notice all of the cash the killer/thief left behind, both on the counter and in the columns above it.

 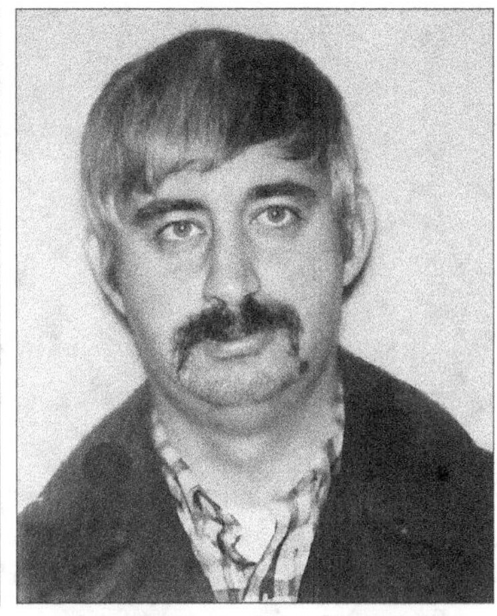

Left: The composite sketch drawn by FBI Agent George Noble with help from the cash vault tellers. Right: Suspect #1, Mike McKown, as he appeared in the first 6-pack. None of the tellers selected him.

Left: Detective Jon Priest was involved in virtually every aspect of the investigation, including the arrest of James W. King, and took the stand at trial nine separate times. Right: Suspect #2, Paul Yocum, on the phone with his attorney on June 24, 1991, the same day FBI agents first knocked on James King's front door.

From a baby-faced rookie in 1961 to a grizzled veteran, James W. King flew mostly under the radar during his 25-year police career.

In June 1985—six years before the massacre—James and Carolyn King downsized to this modest bungalow at 665 Juniper Street in Golden, at the foothills of the Rocky Mountains. They'd reside there until their respective deaths.

Photo courtesy of Myra Church.

From left to right: Greg, David, Carolyn, James W. King, and James Jr. Whereas David and James Jr. figured prominently at the trial, Greg (the "tattooed one") didn't claim a seat in the gallery until the very end.

Photos courtesy of Steven B. Epstein.

The Capitol Hill Community Center at the edge of Cheesman Park served as James King's alibi. Though he claimed he'd knocked on the front door (left), he testified that he never descended the rear steps to the basement door (right)—even though the Denver Chess Club had been located in the basement when he'd last played there.

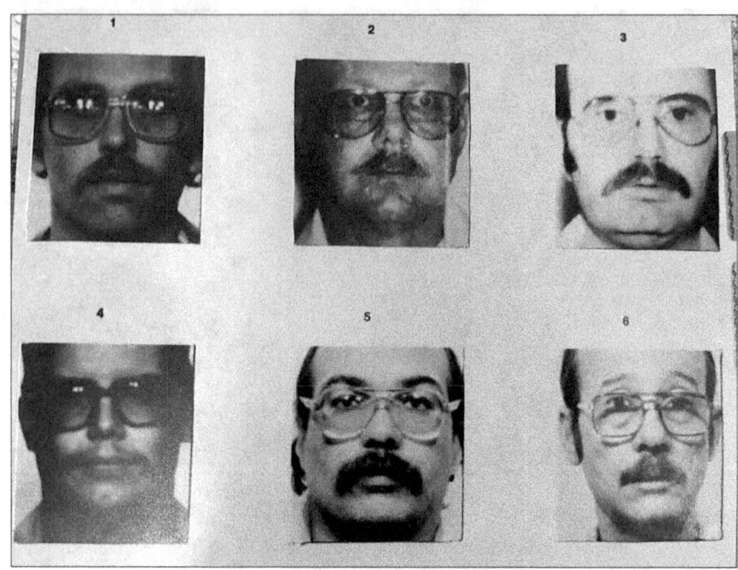

Photo courtesy of Scott Robinson.

Five of the six tellers selected King (#2) from the above 6-pack, starting with David Twist on July 3, 1991. Though his image was cropped tightly to simulate the features visible to the tellers during the robbery, it was the exact same DMV photo they had passed over on June 20.

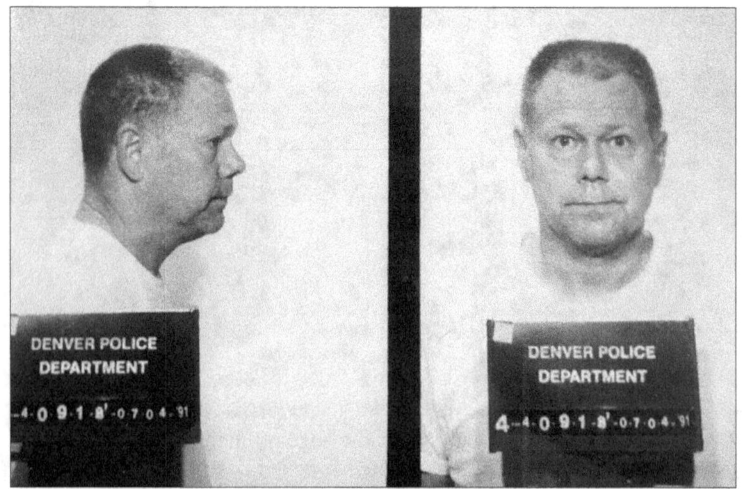

Photo courtesy of Dan Gerash.

The most notable change in James King's appearance between his June 24 FBI interview and July 4 arrest? No more mustache.

The venue for "The People of the State of Colorado v. James W. King," the Denver City & County Building.

Left: Though he'd never become the Mile High City's mayor, DA Norm Early loomed large over all aspects of the King case. Right: Judge Dick Spriggs ran a tight ship, often displaying impatience and a sharp tongue, but also lightening the mood with his whimsical quips.

Left photo courtesy of the Denver Public Library, Rocky Mountain News collection, Steve Groer photographer. Right photo reprinted from September 1992 American Lawyer with permission of ALM Global Properties, LLC.

Left: Chief Deputy DA Bill Buckley poured everything he had into his efforts to obtain justice for the victims' families. Right: Chief Deputy DA S. Lamar Sims musters passion—and a gospel preacher's cadence—during his closing argument.

Photo courtesy of Dan Gerash.

Though he took on many high-profile cases during his illustrious career, the James King case was unquestionably Walter Gerash's biggest.

Photo courtesy of Scott Robinson.

With his boyish good looks and buttery smooth delivery, Scott Robinson served as the perfect complement to Gerash's passionate—at times bombastic—displays.

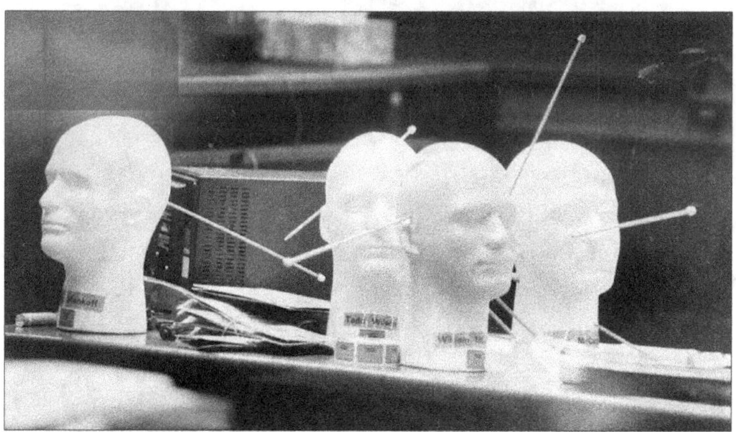

Photo courtesy of Dan Gerash.

Did the prosecutors go too far with this grisly display of the murdered guards? Though Judge Spriggs overruled Gerash's vehement objections, perhaps a tighter focus on King's alibi and his Colt Trooper would have served them better.

Photo courtesy of Scott Robinson.

The signature moment of the trial: catching the prosecutors flatfooted, Scott Robinson whips out the Harrison Ford overlay to stump cash vault manager David Barranco.

Photo courtesy of Dan Gerash.

Walter Gerash deep in thought as Judge Spriggs looks on from his perch on the bench.

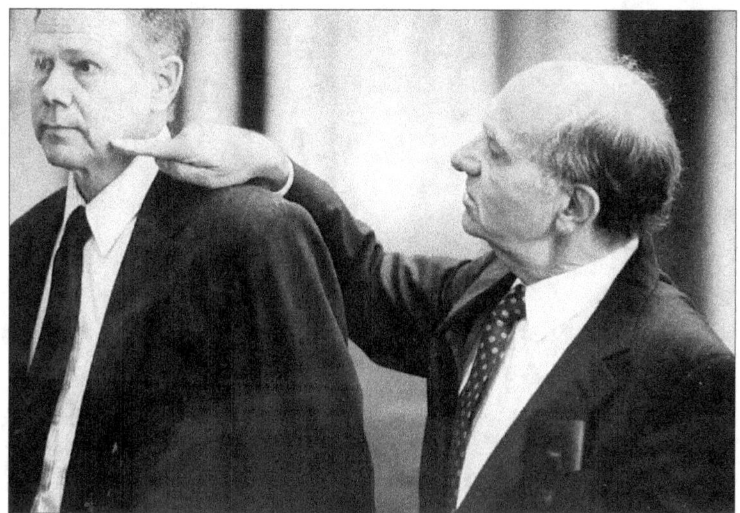

Photo courtesy of Dan Gerash.

The defense's relentless focus on James King's moles—his complexion differing from the tellers' recollections of the armed robber—helped create reasonable doubt in the jury room.

Photo courtesy of Scott Robinson.

Robinson effectively used prosecution witness Jim Prado to highlight several pieces of evidence that didn't fit the tidy picture of the crime painted by the deputy DAs.

Photo courtesy of the Denver Public Library, Rocky Mountain News collection.

The jury hung on James King's every word as he testified—in a calm, emotion-free monotone—in his own defense.

Photo courtesy of Dan Gerash.

Summoning his unique theatrical style, Walter Gerash, during his closing argument, implores the jury to set his client free.

Left photo courtesy of Joni Haack. Right photo courtesy of the Denver Public Library,
Rocky Mountain News collection, Thomas Kelsey photographer.

Left: Foreperson Joni Haack and eleven fellow Denverites set the record
for the longest jury deliberation in Colorado history. Right: Less than a year
after his arrest, James King, donning a Denver Chess Club T-shirt—Gerash's
idea—walks free.

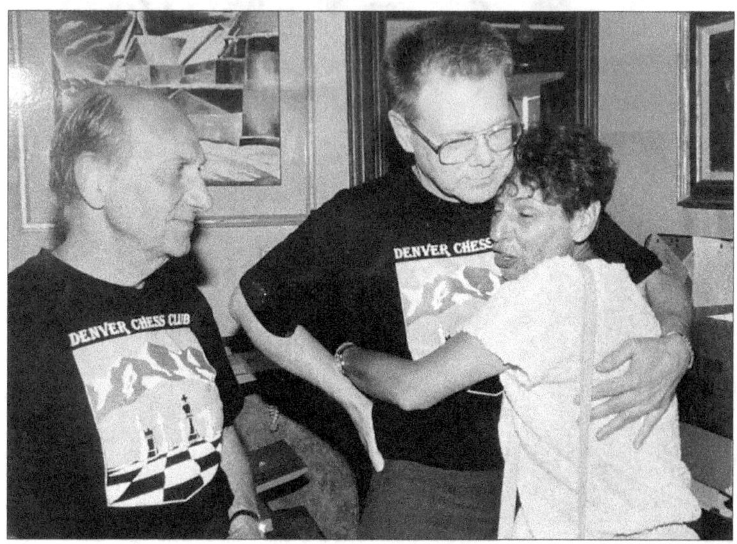

Photo courtesy of the Denver Public Library,
Rocky Mountain News collection, Steve Groer photographer.

Having stood by him since their home was turned upside down by investigators, Carolyn King enjoys a hug with her newly freed husband at the post-
verdict celebration at Gerash's law office.

In November 2009, not long after Carolyn's death from emphysema, James King—battling progressive dementia himself—poses for a picture with his son David.

More than 20 years after the jury found him not guilty of the quadruple homicide and armed robbery, James W. King finally met his maker, resting eternally at the Mount Olivet Cemetery beside his wife of 46 years.